IDEAS

that work with young children

v

Cover design: Caroline Taylor

Library of Congress Catalog Card Number: 72-86139
ISBN Catalog Number: 0-912674-68-7
NAEYC Number: 105

Printed in the United States of America.

Ideas That Work
With Young Children
Volume 2

**Leah Adams and
Betty Garlick,**
Editors

A 1979-80 *Comprehensive* Membership Benefit

The National Association for the Education of Young Children
Washington, DC

*Dedicated to all the young children
with whom we have worked,
with our thanks
for all we have learned from them.*

Contents

Introduction 1

Introduction

Editing this volume of articles was a pleasurable task, but one that presented a triple challenge. First, the challenge of following in the footsteps of one of early childhood education's most eminent professionals, Katherine Read Baker, who first conceived the idea of compiling practical articles from *Young Children*, the journal of the National Association for the Education of Young Children, in a volume entitled *Ideas That Work with Young Children*. And what an excellent idea it was! Not all people working with young children have access to the collected issues of the journal, and those of us who have them often fail to refer to them once they have been read initially. A volume of selected articles, sectioned by topic and indexed, becomes a handy resource for teachers and teacher educators.

Ideas That Work with Young Children, edited by Katherine Read Baker, was published by NAEYC in 1972. Two years later Jan McCarthy and Charles R. May edited another collection of articles called *Providing the Best for Young Children*, creating a companion volume for Baker's book. (Both of these volumes are now out of print.)

Therein came our second challenge—to create a new volume that would, in turn, follow *Providing the Best for Young Children*. We have picked up where McCarthy and May left off, drawing from articles published in *Young Children* beginning with the November 1974 issue and continuing through the July 1979 issue.

The third challenge proved to be the most difficult of all. Those issues of *Young Children* contain an abundance of excellent articles filled with valuable ideas. Selecting a limited number was difficult. While the chosen articles provide practical suggestions on a wide range of topics, this book is not all-inclusive, and we assume the reader will use this volume along with other NAEYC resources such as those listed on page 238.

Our sincere thanks go to the editorial staff of *Young Children* for their help and encouragement with this publication. We feel we have succeeded in compiling a volume that will prove useful to those who care for children. **These ideas work.**

Leah Adams
Betty Garlick
July 1979

I. Ideas for Program Planning

Teaching and parenting are clearly related. Working with young children necessarily includes working with, and supporting the efforts of, their parents. It seems appropriate to open this book with an article on parenting and teaching by one of the strongest advocates for children and their families, the late Ira Gordon. Gordon's five "P's," four "R's," and "old reliable TLC," based on both research and common sense, tell us where to begin in planning and implementing programs.

Few educators would argue against the premise that enhancing the child's self-concept is an important, if not the most important, goal of early childhood. Washington describes a program called SUCCESS that addresses this challenge and suggests a humanistic approach for parent-teacher collaboration to achieve a more positive self-concept in the child.

Good programs for young children are also based on knowledge about how children learn. Principles derived from Piaget's theory are suggested by Bingham-Newman and Saunders as a framework for teachers to develop a creative curriculum for children.

The final chapter, by McLoughlin and Kershman, of this first section identifies a variety of new resources available to aid in curriculum development for handicapped children who are mainstreamed.

Thus we get under way in planning programs by looking at the relationships between how children learn and their need for social and emotional growth.

Ira J. Gordon

Parenting, Teaching, and Child Development

The processes of parenting and teaching have much in common. Based on what we know about child development, we can specify good teaching and help prepare people for more effective parenthood.

What we do as teachers and parents, as adults, makes a difference in what happens to children. The common view now is that development equals learning, not that the development and learning are parallel and do not meet, but it wasn't many years ago that parents were told there was very little connection between development and learning. If you were a parent, you were supposed to buy Gesell (1941), which was the standard "bible" and had a maturational orientation. If you had a two-year-old, you turned to the right page in Gesell and checked out your child. If he or she were behaving like a two-year-old, you sighed with relief; if the child was behaving like a one-year-old, you locked the child in the back room. But you did not do anything about it.

Today, our view is that the parent is a primary teacher of the child. What we do, both as parents and teachers, makes a considerable difference, not only in children's learning of facts but in their total development, self-concept, intellectual development, in all areas of their life. How do parents as the primary teachers teach their children? They teach essentially the way teachers teach. They provide a learning environment, model behavior, and engage in direct instruction with the child. These three means are common to parents and teachers.

An old custom that originates in the Rabbinic oral tradition is the use of the alphabet as a way of remembering the order of things. The following discussion of those three will be handled by an alphabetical device. There are five "P's," four "R's," and the old reliable "TLC."

This article was adapted from a speech presented in April 1975 at the Midwest Association for the Education of Young Children, Madison, Wisconsin.

The Five "P's"

The first "P" is the **provision of the learning environment.** We have now a body of literature from a variety of places, not simply in the United States but from around the world, concerning the relationship between the learning environment in the home and the achievement of the child in school. The findings transcend nationality and social class. There seem to be conditions that occur throughout the western world; the following examples, however, come from recent United States research. Elardo, Bradley, and Caldwell (1975) observed in a number of homes in Arkansas when children were six months old, and tested these children on the Stanford-Binet at age three. They reported that there were many ways in which what they saw in the home at three months could be related to the performance of the children at three years of age. The two main factors, in terms of the provision of the learning environment, are (1) opportunities for variety of stimulation and (2) the organization of the environment, the arrangement and order in the home.

In a study in Illinois by Wachs, Uzgiris, and Hunt (1971), homes of children below the age of one were observed. The parents' competence was measured by the Uzgiris-Hunt scales, based on Piaget. They indicated one very positive and one very negative characteristic on this first "P." The positive characteristic was simply the presence in the home and the availability of magazines to the child at nine months of age. You know nine-month-old children really do not read these magazines, but just having them around and being able to feel them, touch them, taste them, smell them seemed to make a difference with these nine-month-olds. The negative factor was noise: Higher levels of noise in a home seemed to specifically affect, in a negative way, the development of the child.

In some of our own work (Gordon and Guinagh 1974), we have gathered information on homes of a number of primarily low-income families in Florida. We gathered information, beginning at three months of age, again at three years of age, and we now can relate this to child performance at age six after a year of kindergarten. In this respect it is different from the other studies, since we can see how long home effects last, and how they affect performance when the child has already been exposed to school. The most important provision of learning experience is out-of-home experience—the planning and use by the family of the environment outside the home for learning. That environment can be broadly defined. The experience can be a car ride, a trip to the supermarket, zoo, library, or museum. It does not have to be cultural, as in terms of the Metropolitan Opera. It can be planning for and using many of the natural kinds of experiences that could go on in any family. For the boys in our study, the presence of reading

Ira J. Gordon, Ed.D., was Kenan Professor and Dean, School of Education, University of North Carolina at Chapel Hill. He died on September 7, 1978.

material in the home at age six related positively to Stanford-Binet scores *within* the experimental group. If the parent made an issue out of reading itself, this had a positive effect on the girls. There are similar findings in North Carolina (Landsberger 1973).

If we look at day care centers, we can find some similar provisions of learning environment as important criteria in child development. The work especially of Prescott, Jones, and Kritchevsky (1972) in California indicates that significant variables are the organization of space, staff, and time, and whether they are integrated.

> Kritchevsky concluded that the poor use of space led to tired and irritable teachers and obviously such tired and irritable teachers can do little about creating an affectionate relationship with children. What do they agree are good spatial arrangements? (1) Sub areas for different activities not lined up in a row, (2) opportunities for activities for the single child (a swing for example), as well as (3) arrangements for privacy [not everything is a great big open space], (4) division of space by the type of activity and the noise level (quiet—noisy, clean—dirty), (5) mixtures of manmade and natural materials (a whole is to dig), (6) one which allows the child to explore in safety, (7) that allows the child to try new things but also to continue to play with old, and (8) an uncluttered environment, but one with much diversity. [How do you keep it both uncluttered and diverse?] (Gordon 1975, p. 148)

One of our problems in some of our parent education work, with both the parent educators and with mothers, is the check off system. You know, the children played with the toy, now on to the next, without recognizing that they need to do what Murphy called "mess and manipulate" (Murphy 1958). They need to go back to the old, familiar, and dog-eared object and enjoy it all over again, and perhaps enjoy it in some new way. There needs to be space in which children can play with new things, but also to go back to the old familiar.

Staffing guidelines, as part of the learning environment, are not so much just the adult-child ratio as the use of staff.

> Infants and young children need continuity of care. This means that the same adult should be with the same children for long enough periods of time so that a bond can develop. Just to have a 1 to 5 ratio in a center with 30 or so children does not guarantee this. (Gordon 1975, p. 148)

We have some kindergartens that have the appropriate ratio 1 to 10, but there are 120 children in a huge room and 12 adults roaming around. Although a ratio is important, assignment and organization will determine if there is the provision of an adequate learning environment.

> Time is a third factor. Children's own energy needs, own rhythms, own sleep needs are highly individual. Centers even more so than homes often override these needs by imposing standard time. It is difficult to organize around individual rhythms, and it is possible for children to learn the schedule. The point here is the awareness of individuality within a scheduled day. Every child does not need the same amount of sleep. If space is arranged properly, some can take longer naps, while others engage

in noisy play. Some take longer to eat, and need more help than others. With adequate space arrangements, and staff, it should be possible for them to have this time and help while another toddler is finished and goes off to play. (Gordon 1975, p. 148)

All these are combined—space, staff, time—in the first "P."

The second "P" is **predictability.** There are varied studies that show the need of young children, if not indeed of all of us, for some sense of order and system. Children need to know what is happening. They need to know that behavior allowed today will not lead to punishment tomorrow; behavior approved by mom is also approved by dad. They need the comfort that parents do not operate from whim, but from some sense of consistency, both within the individual parent and between the parents.

We see this also in schools. Kounin (1970) observed Detroit classrooms to find out why it was that in some classrooms the child who had been labeled disturbed was really climbing the walls, and when the bell rang and periods changed, the child moved into the next classroom and could not be located apart from anybody else. As Kounin checked into this, he uncovered two elements that relate to predictability. One of them is transition. How smoothly do you, as either a parent or a teacher, move a child from one activity to another? I know that one of my own faults as a college teacher is making bad transitions. I will start on a new topic, and then remember that there was something more to say about the old, and shift back to it. That may be fine for 21-year-olds; they can handle it, but young children cannot. They need to know what the arrangements

are and are influenced by the smoothness with which the things flow. The second element Kounin called thrusting—interruption of the child's on-going activities because it suits adult needs at the moment. Who among us has not been guilty of this?

An example is the typical three reading group situation, groups B and C are busy while the teacher is with group A. Right in the middle of A's activity, the teacher looks at the clock and says, "11:00: Group B come up." Everything goes to pot. We do a lot of thrusting, because we have time schedules that do not match the learning experiences and the timing of children. They need to know when to shift, but it can be handled in rather simple ways.

You can use what Soar has called gentle control (Soar 1974, p. 7). He defines this as suggesting changes in behavior or giving feedback on pupil behavior in fairly gentle and noncoercive ways. You could say, "We have 5 minutes to wrap that up." This does not mean their 5 minutes matches your 5 minutes, but it does mean that they have some signal to begin to taper off, and move on to something else. It sounds like common sense; unfortunately, it is not very common.

Predictability relates to the amount of control. It's one thing to say that children need order and system. It is another to find that magic line between too much and too little. Soar has observed in classrooms all over the United States, from kindergarten through third grade, and up to fifth and sixth grade. Not only has he come up with this notion of gentle control, but he has also examined the whole point about how you can tell the differences in amount of control in classrooms.

> One of the major ways in which classrooms differ from each other, is in the extent to which the activities in the classroom emanate from the teacher rather than from the pupil. [The same thing applies to parent-child.] At one extreme the teacher sets the problem, directs the activities in which pupils are engaged, monitors and reinforces the work of pupils and evaluates the results of their efforts. Pupils have little choice about what they do, how they do it, or the basis on which they will be evaluated. They have little or no wiggle room. At the other end of the scale, pupils have a high degree of freedom to choose the activity on which they will work, with whom, how long, and decision as to which it was useful may be theirs, if the question occurs at all. The teacher is available as a resource, may set the outer limits to the behavior which is permitted, but even these are likely to be broad. Of course, these are extremes of a dimension along which classrooms scale, with most classrooms somewhere in-between. . . . In four sets of data the finding has emerged that when classrooms were rank ordered, from those in which the pupils have least freedom, to those in which pupils have most freedom, gains increased. But this was only true up to a point, and beyond that point as pupil freedom increased, gain no longer increased but began to decrease. That is, there is an optimum point, a balance, between

teacher control, and pupil freedom at which the greatest pupil subject matter growth occurred. (Soar 1974, p. 6)

It is fine to discover this fact, but the problem is that it does not help us to find out, in our classrooms and homes, where that "magic" line is. Baumrind (1970) describes the parent who is authoritative, as distinct from the authoritarian parent. The authoritative parent sets limits, has standards, and conveys them with reasoning and explanation. This is another aspect of predictability. Children need to know not only what is expected, but why it is expected.

In studying teacher-pupil relations and parent-child situations we found three other "P's." These come primarily out of our infant work (Gordon and Jester 1972). We videotaped 128 families every 6 weeks beginning when the baby was 13 weeks old until he or she was 49 weeks old. We measured the youngsters on the Bayley scale at age one. The first of these three "P's" is a very positive "P"; it is called **ping-pong** because it looks like a ping-pong game. I do something, you do something, I do something, you do something. It can be related to reinforcement concepts, but also to concepts described by White (1972) and Escalona and Corman (1973, 1974). For example, Escalona and Corman observe for sustained reciprocal social interaction. Our shorthand is ping-pong. There is a new study by Kaye

---

Children need to know not only what is expected, but why it is expected.

(1975) in which ping-pong is begun and controlled by the children through their gazing techniques. They get busy in something, the mothers watch; when they gaze away, mothers know it is time to get back into the act again. White and Watts (1973) indicate that ping-pong is often initiated by the child, and is not necessarily a very long volley. Odd moments in natural situations are optimum times for parent-infant ping-pong.

The second positive variable is **persistence**. The child gets interested in an activity and is permitted and encouraged to continue it. The parent or teacher needs to learn when to step aside and leave the child alone. I saw two examples of this recently. One was in a day care center in Haarlem, The Netherlands, where they were trying to involve parents. Parents were asked to model on the teachers. At the time I observed, the children, who were all four years old, were doing jigsaw puzzles. Everytime a child got stuck on a puzzle, five adults would descend. If the child needed help, surely not that much help was needed! The adults did not know how to get themselves out of it again, and it turned into a dependency relationship in which they were cuing the child, practically handing the child the right piece to fit in.

---

*The parent or teacher
needs to learn when
to step aside and
leave the child alone.*

The other situation was in the United States. The project is based on the notion that if mothers watch their children being tested, they will learn good child stimulation techniques and apply these at home. However, if you have watched a Bayley test being given, you know that as soon as the child performs, the item is scored and the child goes on to the next task. So it may be that parents were seeing a disruption of persistence rather than the encouragement of persistence. We need to know how to start a child and back out when too much is too much.

We also uncovered a pattern that was a poor teaching pattern—the label is **professor.** This behavior is talking followed by talking followed by talking, without paying any attention whatsoever to whether anybody is tuned in, responding, or attending.

These three patterns, *ping-pong, persistence*, and *professor* are observable not only in the first year of life but also in the preschool, the primary grades, and all the way through formal education.

Ping-pong is a successful form of social as well as learning interaction and professor is not, yet we persist in professing to young children. One of the reasons people have made that error in infant work may be that we kept telling them how important language was. We kept saying you have to surround the child with a language envelope. And they did. They stuck them inside the envelope and sealed it up.

Since it is painful and I do not wish to profess, let us turn to the four "R's" and leave the five "P's." These four "R's" bear no resemblance to the traditional three R's at all.

The Four "R's"

The first of these is **responsiveness** to the child's initiative and the child's needs. Many parents have been told by some learning theorists that when children cry, the most effective technique is to ignore the inappropriate behavior. We now have some very good studies in Baltimore by Ainsworth and Bell (1974) that demonstrate that when the mother is responsive to the child's crying between three months and six months of age, this leads to a lessening of crying between six months and nine months. Responsiveness to the six- to nine-month-old leads to a reduction in crying from nine to twelve months. My hypothesis is that this occurs because the child knows his or her needs are being attended to and moves on to superior and other ways of communicating. The child leaves the most primitive way because it is not needed anymore. There is a close relationship between responsiveness and ping-pong.

We also need to learn to be far more responsive to children's rhythms, to their built-in biological clocks. This applies not only in day care centers, but also we need to make arrangements even in schools and certainly at home. Husbands and wives do not necessarily have the same rhythm. One may be a morning person and the other an evening person. They learn, somehow, to find noontime. Likewise, we need to observe the child's rhythm and to find when we can communicate most effectively, rather than insisting that simply because this is an industrial world and the child may eventually have to live too by the clock, that he or she must live by the clock at age two.

There is another technique that indicates responsiveness, which has its origins in some elementary science work by Rowe (1973). She calls the variable "wait time." She counts the amount of time between when a teacher asks a question and how long,

if the child does not answer it, before the teacher either asks the next child or asks another question. The average, believe it or not, in elementary science classrooms, is one second! What is even more devastating is that the brighter the child, the longer the wait time; the slower the child, the shorter the wait time. This is probably just the opposite of what it ought to be. Further, Rowe found that if she trains teachers to hold off for three seconds, the tenor of that whole classroom shifts in terms of the level of responses, the type of questions the children ask, and the level of questions the teachers ask. They move away from the single right word answer type question to more elaborated response and open-ended questions. We need to learn to give children time before we make our demands. Both at home and in school we need to learn to be more patient.

The other kind of responsiveness is the "deliver us from temptation" responsiveness. It is related to the organization of the environment, and is based on understanding what a child is like. I visited one of our home learning centers during 3 o'clock snacktime. There were six two-year-olds, and the staff had decided that each child was entitled to one cookie. However, the plate had more cookies than there were children, and they left the cookies out after each child had one. Then they wondered why the children were doing everything to get more cookies, not understanding that the simplest procedure was to avoid the temptation. We do a lot of this. We take toys out and say, "Do not play with them." My son went to a kindergarten that was fully equipped but he was not allowed to touch anything because the materials could get dirty. We need to match our expectations to the children, not the other way around.

The next "R's" are **reasoning** and **rationality,** which represents giving the child the "because." Miller (1971) analyzed a number of studies in England. He found that those children who did well in English schools came from homes which he could identify as allowing for and encouraging independent thinking and freedom of discussion.

---

*We need to match
our expectations
to the children,
not the other way around.*

Reasoning and rationality also represent accompanying our control with explanation. This is something that Baumrind (1970) pointed out in her work. Soar (1974) found that there are three kinds of control going on in the classroom, and most teachers do not differentiate among them: One is the control of the behavior, the second is the control of thought, and the third is the control of subject matter. He found that if behavior is tightly controlled in a classroom, the chances are very good that the teacher also controls the thought processes and the choice of subject matter. If one is free, all are likely to be free, but he suggests that the effects of freedom of behavior may be different from those of freedom of thought. For example, in looking at classrooms reflecting both the Becker-Engelman and British Infant School Follow Through programs, there was a positive relationship between free but orderly teacher-pupil interaction (in which children were free to think but there was both wait

time and ping-pong) and children's gains in creativity. However, if children were simply physically free to roam around the room, this was negatively related to gains not only in creativity but also in regular academic skills.

The last "R" is **reading.**

In our longitudinal study (Gordon and Guinagh 1974), we found sex differences between home environment and Stanford-Binet scores at age six. Provision of reading materials seemed to be important for boys and reading press seemed to be important for girls. The work of Wachs et al. (1971), Elardo et al. (1975), and the earlier work of Bloom's students (Dave 1963, Wolf 1964) all indicate that the modeling behavior of the home is a critical element in reading for young children. If parents do not read, if children do not see parents reading, then this is a poor beginning when they come into school. Moreover when parents read to their children this seems to be positive, but we are learning to go beyond the symptoms or beyond the simple overt behavior and look a little further. One can read to children in a way that would make them never want to read again, or one can read to them in a way that would make them climb back into one's lap and ask for more.

In keeping with what we are learning about language development, reading to the child needs to be the responsive, highly personalized dialogue encouraging reading. There also should be a good deal of repetition. People do not automatically know how to read to a child. When a teacher of preschoolers says to parents, "I would like you to read to your children," that is a very inadequate message.

Guinagh and Jester (1972) studied parent reading skills in Appalachia and in rural and urban areas. They gave a book to a mother of a two-year-old. It was a delightful book emphasizing sounds. They found that rarely did the mothers do anything with the possibilities of the sounds. Some mothers would simply point to the picture and say, "Cat, say cat." Some, from the same income group, maybe even a next-door neighbor, would say, "Do you remember when that cat came by, and what kind of sound does a cat make?" Such a mother would have a nice dialogue going between her and the child.

We need to work harder not on the formal teaching of reading but on the real beginnings which are the interpersonal, social, warm experiences wrapped around reading. We want responsive reading. There are as many different ways to do that as there are different children. I would like to present to you one of my few orthodoxies: When in the face of orthodoxy, run as far as you can the other way. So if somebody tries to sell you the perfect reading package, run.

So much for those "R's." Let us come to "TLC" (tender loving care).

TLC

It does not help the child if you have provided for a stimulating material environment, played some barren form of ping-pong, reasoned with your child, responded in certain kinds of ways, set up rules and so forth, if all this was done without **warmth**. We have known this for a long time. But there are a lot of people in the last ten years who have tried to separate affect and cognition, who have tried to talk about stimulation as though you are stimulating a portion of the brain and paying no attention to the heart and the gut. There is considerable evidence to suggest that they are wrong.

We can easily identify, even within the first few weeks of the child's life, parents who can be placed on scales from warm to hostile, from involved to noninvolved. Schaefer (1969) pointed out that the hostile, noninvolved mother could not only be found, but also was not very effective as a mother in enabling children to grow. Ainsworth and Bell's (1974) study of advantaged parents indicated that 43 percent of them, almost half of them, were not responsive to the cues the children were giving them.

We need to work harder not on the formal teaching of reading but on the real beginnings which are the interpersonal, social, warm experiences wrapped around reading.

Responsiveness in a warm fashion does a variety of things for children. It influences more than personality development; it has definite effects on intellectual development as well. In one of our infant studies (Gordon 1974), we found that while ping-pong was good for both boys and girls, what seemed to be more predictive for boys was the affective behavior of the type that Escalona and Corman (1974) measured. Parent and child gazing lovingly into each other's eyes, observed as early as 13 and 19 weeks of age, predicted the child's greater language development and general intellectual development at age one.

11

*Affection should be
shown when you feel it
and the child feels it
and when it is natural.
Children know
the difference.*

Erikson (1963) taught us the importance of building basic trust; Bowlby (1969) taught us about attachment. Burlingham and Freud (1944) indicated that children need three important things in these early years: a close transaction in an affectional way, a stimulating environment, and consistency of care. The one they place first is the affectional relationship. Children need to know that we care deeply for them. It takes a hug, a pat, a smile. It is not scheduled behavior. You do not pull out your schedule and say, "What's the baseline? Joe gets three pats today and Anne gets two." Affection should be shown when you feel it and the child feels it and when it is natural. Children know the difference.

Conclusion

I have tried to indicate from a variety of research and viewpoints, with my obvious biases, that we do indeed know a good deal about effective parenting, teaching, and child development for young children. Although we still have much to learn, we are past simply sloganizing that the parent is a teacher. We can specify good teaching and we can prepare people for parenthood, as well as helping present parents. Further, the good learning environment needs to be matched to the child. This is what Hunt (1961) called the problem of the match. What we know about good parenting applies equally well to good teaching. The processes are common. They reflect respect for the individual, understanding of children's needs, and a faith that what we do indeed does count. It really is more than rhetoric to say that the future is in your hands. 🔾

References

Ainsworth, M., and Bell, S. "Mother-Infant Interaction and the Development of Competence." In *The Growth of Competence*, edited by K. Connolly and J. Bruner, pp. 97-118. London: Academic Press, 1974.

Baumrind, D. "Socialization and Instrumental Competence in Young Children." *Young Children* 26 (1970): 104-119.

Bowlby, J. *Attachment and Loss, Vol. 1: Attachment*. London: Hogarth Press, 1969.

Burlingham, D., and Freud, A. *Infants Without Families*. London: George Allen and Unwin, 1944.

Dave, R. H. "The Identification and Measurement of Environmental Process Variables That Are Related to Education Achievement." Doctoral dissertation, University of Chicago, 1963.

Elardo, R.; Bradley, R.; and Caldwell, B. "The Relation of Infant's Home Environments to Mental Test Performance from Six to Thirty-six Months: A Longitudinal Analysis." *Child Development* 46, no. 11 (1975): 71-76.

Erikson, E. *Childhood and Society*. Second Edition. New York: W. W. Norton, 1963.

Escalona, S. K. "Basic Modes of Social Interaction: Their Emergence and Patterning During the First Two Years of Life." *Merrill-Palmer Quarterly* 19 (1973): 205-232.

Escalona, S., and Corman, H. "Early Life Experience and the Development of Competence." *International Review of Psycho-Analysis*, 1974, pp. 151-168.

Gesell, A. *The First Five Years of Life*. New York: Harper, 1941.

Gordon, I. J. "An Investigation into the Social Roots of Competence." Final Report to NIMH on Project No. 1 R01 MH 22724. Gainesville, Fla.: University of Florida, Institute for Development of Human Resources, October 1974.

Gordon, I. J. *The Infant Experience*. Columbus, Ohio: Charles E. Merrill Co., 1975.

Gordon, I. J., and Guinagh, B. "A Home Learning Center Approach to Early Stimulation." Final Report on Project No. R01 MH 16037-04. Gainesville, Fla.: University of Florida, Institute for Development of Human Resources, November 1974.

Gordon, I. J., and Jester, R. E. "Instructional Strategies in Infant Stimulation." *Catalog of Selected Documents in Psychology* 2 (1972): 122 (Journal Supplemental Abstract Service).

Guinagh, B. J., and Jester, R. E. "How Parents Read to Children." *Theory Into Practice* 11, no. 3 (June 1972).

Hunt, J. McV. *Intelligence and Experience*. New York: Ronald, 1961.

Kaye, K. "Gaze Direction as the Infant's Way of Controlling His Mother's Teaching Behavior." Symposium paper presented at the Biennial Meeting of the Society for Research in Child Development, April 1975, Denver, Colorado.

Kounin, J. *Discipline and Group Management in Classrooms*. New York: Holt, Rinehart & Winston, 1970.

Landsberger, B. Home Environment and School Performance: "The North Carolina Experience." *Children Today* 2 (1973): 10-14.

Miller, G. W. *Educational Opportunity and the Home*. London, England: Longman, 1971.

Murphy, G. *Human Potentialities*. New York: Basic Books, 1958.

Prescott, E.; Jones, E.; and Kritchevsky, S. *Day Care as a Child Rearing Environment*. Washington, D.C.: National Association for the Education of Young Children, 1972.

Rowe, M. B. *Teaching Science as Continuous Inquiry*. New York: McGraw-Hill, 1973.

Schaefer, E. "Home Tutoring, Maternal Behavior, and Infant Intellectual Development." Symposium paper presented at the American Psychological Association Annual Convention, September 1969, Washington, D.C.

Soar, R. S. "Program Evaluation and Validation in PBTE." Paper presented at a conference titled "Assessment PBTE: The Search for Evidence," sponsored by Bureau for Educationally Handicapped, October 1974, Glenmount, New York.

Wachs, T.; Uzgiris, J.; and Hunt, J. McV. "Cognitive Development in Infants of Different Age Levels and from Different Environmental Backgrounds: An Explanatory Investigation." *Merrill-Palmer Quarterly* 17 (1971): 283-318.

White, B. L. "Fundamental Early Environmental Influences on the Development of Competency." In *Third Symposium on Learning: Cognitive Learning*, edited by M. Meyer. Bellingham, Wash.: Western Washington State College, 1972.

White, B. L.; Watts, J. C.; et al. *Experience and Environment*. Englewood Cliffs, N.J.: Prentice-Hall, 1973.

Wolf, R. "The Identification and Measurement of Environmental Process Variables Related to Intelligence." Doctoral dissertation, University of Chicago, 1964.

13

Kenneth R. Washington

SUCCESS: A Parent Effectiveness Approach for Developing Urban Children's Self-Concepts

A Black child was asked to list some things that he was good at. His answer was "I don't know—nothing." A Black teenager was asked by her teacher why she was always putting herself down. The teenager looked at the teacher blankly and said, "Because I never seem to do things well."

Both the child and the teenager represent the result of years of emphasis on deficit- and fault-finding. Neither of these children had a positive concept of self and so were unable to view themselves as successful and competent individuals. "I can't" had replaced "I can."

Numerous research studies (Clark and Clark 1958; Pettigrew 1964; and Brown 1966) document the difficulty Black children have in developing a positive view of self. Findings from these studies suggest that the early years can be an especially traumatic period for Black children who, in addition to experiencing the normal problems of early childhood, must also face the difficult task of trying to survive in a hostile world pervaded with racism. Assessing one's sense of self-worth is for this group of children an experience often filled with anxiety and emotional frustration.

Many of the current writings on self-concept state that the feelings a child develops about himself or herself are formed primarily during the early years (Felker 1974). Further, it is maintained that self-concept is largely determined by interactions between the child and the most "significant others" in the child's world—parents. Indeed, it can be argued that whether a child exhibits an attitude of "I-canness" or "I-willness" upon entering school depends to a large extent on the ability of parents (especially mothers) to facilitate the development of a positive self-definition during the early formative years.

SUCCESS is a systematic program designed to help urban parents improve their effectiveness as educators and builders of self-esteem (Washington 1974, 1975). The program can be especially useful to early childhood educators who are in search of humanistic techniques which foster teacher/parent collaboration. It is an approach that places special emphasis on the teacher's role in helping parents to assist their children in developing more positive self-concepts. In short, SUCCESS is a self-esteem building technique that encourages teachers and parents to work together in a joint effort to change the "I can't" syndrome into a lifelong pattern of increased self-confidence and self-worth.

HOW SUCCESS WORKS

The SUCCESS program is based on two fundamental notions: (1) success (achievement of predefined goals) plays a major role in determining a child's self-concept and future goal-setting behavior (Klausmeier and Ripple 1971); and (2) systematic parental attention and positive reinforcement are basic to helping each child feel successful and valuable as a person (Becker 1971). The experiences embodied in the program are designed to help each urban child answer the key question, "Who am I?"

The SUCCESS program consists of three action phases. Initially, it is important for teacher trainers (or program administrators) to schedule parent orientation workshops for purposes of introducing the program and getting parents committed to the program and its goals. The major emphasis during these workshops is on helping parents realize that they are primary contributors to their children's sense of worth. Various humanistic small group exercises help parents see the importance of meeting the affective needs of young children by first looking at their own affective needs (Washington 1974).

After the orientation workshops, parents are involved in small workshops of 10 to 15 participants that help them become skilled in the techniques of the program by role playing. Parents teach the program to each other by alternating the role of parent and child. Teachers facilitate this process by demonstrating, monitoring, and providing feedback. The action phases described below constitute the major components of the SUCCESS program.

Action Phase I: Rapport Building

The teacher trainer begins by explaining to parents that initially it is important to concentrate on establishing a climate that encourages children to openly share and give of self. Next, some rapport building activities are suggested which parents can use to get children interested and involved. One such activity is storytelling. Parents begin by informing their children that a special time will be set aside each week for conversation and storytelling. Some examples of information that can be shared are "When I was a child two activities I enjoyed doing most were. . . . Can you name two activities that you really enjoy doing and explain why?" or "When I was a child, I liked myself best when. . . . Can you tell mommy what you like best about yourself?"

Typically, the responses of parents and children are similar. Swimming, telling jokes well, sports, bicycling, getting a good report card, making parents happy, and playing with a special friend are examples of responses that are frequently given. Parent responses must be sincere, genuine, and arouse the interest of children. It is important that parents understand that the success of this activity depends on their effectiveness as models. As noted by Bandura (1961), early learning is greatly facilitated by parents who model what they wish to teach. For children who are reluctant to talk about themselves, a mirror can be used to elicit information. (Tell me

Kenneth R. Washington, Ph.D., is Associate Professor of Education in the School of Education at the University of Massachusetts in Amherst. His areas of experience include early childhood education, leadership and administration, urban education, research, and teacher training.

something about the handsome/beautiful face you see in the mirror.)

These rapport building activities encourage a sharing of personal experiences that help children realize that parents too were once children. In addition to creating an open climate of trust and acceptance that enables children to relax, these exercises also help parents gain a general impression of the child's feelings about self.

Action Phase II: Mutual Goal Setting

Once parents have a good grasp of the rapport building activities, the stage is set for introduction of the next phase in the SUCCESS program—mutual goal setting. Parents learn how setting and accomplishing goals contribute to a child's sense of personal accomplishment and growth in

self-esteem. They are then given an explanation of the mutual goal setting method and are involved in several practice exercises. The first step involves the parent sharing several goals that he or she would like to achieve with the child. Solicitation of the child's help in making a decision is an important aspect of this activity. Some examples of parent goals are: Knit a sweater for the child, prepare a special meal, paint a picture, read a story to the child at least once each week, put together a family album.

After parents have set their goals, they move to the second step—encouraging the child to set a goal. Here, the parent must be patient and offer suggestions to the child who finds it difficult to name a goal. Goal identification by children can be facilitated by asking them to respond to the question, "What are some things you would like to learn to do well?" Examples of goals that urban children might list are: Help set the table, be nice to a friend, learn a new word each week, learn their address and telephone number, get to school on time, learn a new dance, dress without any assistance, hit a baseball three times out of ten, keep the play area neat.

During the training session, it is crucial to emphasize the importance of setting reasonable and realistic goals. Role playing that encourages participants to alternate the roles of child and parent is one technique to help parents see the need for initially assisting children to set easily obtainable, short-term goals. Then gradually the emphasis can shift to the setting of long-term goals (Klausmeier, Jeter, Quilling, and Frayer 1973). For example, getting all "A's" in school next term is the classic case of setting a bad goal. On the other hand, studying spelling for five minutes each night is an example of a good goal that involves the development of small working dimensions in step-by-step increments. This type of goal offers parents the chance to be with the child and offer praise for five minutes rather than criticize the absence of everything.

Step three of the mutual goal setting procedure is concerned with the monitoring process. The need for a mutual monitoring and support system is discussed and again parents are asked to participate in several practice sessions. Emphasis is placed on how monitoring and providing frequent reinforcement for any progress can help parents and children accomplish their goals. Children tend to especially like the ideas of monitoring the progress of their parents and reminding them of the goals they have set when they temporarily lose sight.

Special weekly conferences provide both parents and children with the opportunity to get support and positive feedback. The mutually agreed upon goals set by parents and children can be recorded in a special "I Am Somebody Book" (younger children can use scribble to write their goals). An excellent idea for the book's cover is a snapshot of the child or parent with the caption "Here Is a Beautiful/Handsome Picture of Me." This goal-setting approach focuses on enhancing the child's feeling of belonging and competence. It also helps parents better understand their role as feedback agent, evaluator, and model (Felker 1974). Perhaps, the greatest value is its emphasis on building a pattern of success that ultimately leads to an increased willingness to try new activities.

Action Phase III: Success Sharing

The success sharing phase concentrates on helping children feel good about their goal achievements. Training given during this phase describes how the accomplishment of goals helps children get in touch with the positive self, and is designed to encourage parents and children to share their feelings about successes (accomplishment of goals) immediately after they occur.

The first step involves parents sharing a success (telling how they feel about the success) with the child, and subsequently the child shares a success with the parents. Again, during training sessions, parents are encouraged to play parent/child roles. Washington (1974) noted that discussing personal successes tends to elicit good feelings and make children more aware of their overall ability to do well. This activity gradually builds the child's sense of pride and confidence. It also increases the frequency of statments such as "I want to try it!" or "I know it!" or "Let me do it!" or "Look, I did it!"

When individuals share and discuss their successes, they also reveal information that can be used to identify personality strengths (Washington 1974). The second step in the success sharing process—strength identification—focuses on getting parents to identify children's positive attributes. As children talk about their successes, parents are asked to listen carefully to identify the various strengths that

Betsy B. MacMillan

helped the child achieve the success. Once a child's strengths have been identified and recorded, parents tell the child what strengths they have found. A good idea for displaying successes and strengths is to write them on a piece of paper and attach it to the refrigerator.

Through this experience, children become more aware of their personality strengths and their uniqueness as individuals. Success sharing is an important step in the self-esteem building process because it cultivates within each child a strong sense of power or "I-canness," i.e., children come to believe that their efforts can make a difference (strong sense of fate control).

EVALUATION AND IMPLICATIONS

I have used the SUCCESS program effectively with several groups of urban early childhood teachers and parents. Both teachers and parents were involved in training sessions where the techniques of the SUCCESS program were taught. During these sessions much stress was placed on the role played by parents in helping children establish a success-oriented pattern of growth. Parents learned how to set realistic goals for themselves and how to help their children with this task. Participants were shown how to structure special conferences during which mutually agreed upon goals could be set and accomplishment of goals highlighted. The overall evaluation of the SUCCESS program showed positive self-concept gains for most of the participating urban children. Further, and perhaps most importantly, teachers and parents had become more aware of their role in helping each child develop a positive self-concept (Washington 1975).

The need for self-esteem building techniques, like the SUCCESS program, which place emphasis on teacher/parent collaboration is long overdue. The importance of a parent-centered approach to self-concept development is underscored by the research of Bronfenbrenner (1974) who suggests that early intervention is most effective and has more staying power when

18

". . . its target is not the child as an individual but the mother-child dyad as an interactive system" (p. 26). Indeed, one could argue that much of what a child feels toward self is determined by the quality of interactions that occur within the mother/father-child dyadic system. When feedback is positive and supportive, the child feels good about self and is motivated to set self-improvement goals that will bring additional praise.

Clearly, SUCCESS is an approach that urban parents can use to provide their children with a sustained reinforcement history with respect to self-worth. It is one strategy that seeks to program children for success. Klausmeier and Ripple (1971) point out that experiencing success and the expectation of additional success tends to have a positive effect on an individual's motivation, achievement, and future goal setting behavior.

Felker (1974) identified several important points to bear in mind when setting goals. First, children, like adults, have to be actively involved in the goal setting process. Second, goals should relate to past performance by being one step above a previous goal. Third, the goals must be attainable within a reasonable period of time. The key to mastering the SUCCESS approach is not to expect too much too soon. If it has taken seven years to produce a seven-year-old with no self-confidence, it certainly will take a long time to change that pattern. Patience and frequent reinforcement of any progress made by the child are absolute musts.

To summarize, urban parents need to understand that whether their children succeed or fail will, to a great extent, depend upon their effectiveness as "parent educators"; the area that deserves greatest attention is that of affective development. SUCCESS is one humanistic technique that can be used to facilitate positive affective growth. It is an approach that highlights the importance of providing early and frequent success experiences for urban children. The challenge facing urban parents and teachers is to come to grips with the tremendous responsibilities resting on their shoulders. Unlocking that vast reservoir of human potential existing within each child has to become a priority for inner-city parents and educators. If parents and teachers fail children in this very critical area of development, then ultimately they fail themselves.

References

Bandura, A., and Huston, A. C. "Identification as a Process of Incidental Learning." *Journal of Abnormal and Social Psychology* 63 (1961): 311-318.

Becker, W. C. *Parents Are Teachers*. Champaign, Ill.: Research Press, 1971.

Bronfenbrenner, U. "A Report and Longitudinal Evaluations of Preschool Programs" (620-148/2160 1-3). Washington, D.C.: U.S. Government Printing Office, 1974.

Brown, B. R. "The Assessment of Self-Concept among Four-Year-Old Negro and White Children: A Comparative Study Using the Brown IDS Self-Concept Referents Test." Paper presented at the Eastern Psychological Association Meeting, April 1966, New York.

Clark, K. B., and Clark, M. K. "Racial Identification and Preference in Negro Children." In *Readings in Social Psychology*, edited by E. Maccoby, T. Newcomb, and E. Hartley, pp. 602-612. New York: Holt, Rinehart and Winston, 1958.

Felker, D. W. *Building Positive Self-Concepts*. Minneapolis, Minn.: Burgess Publishing Co., 1974.

Klausmeier, H. J., and Ripple, R. E. *Learning and Human Abilities*. New York: Harper & Row, 1971.

Klausmeier, H. J.; Jeter, J. T.; Quilling, M. R.; and Frayer, D. A. *Individually Guided Motivation*. Madison, Wis.: Wisconsin Research and Development Center for Cognitive Learning, 1973.

Pettigrew, T. F. *A Profile of the Negro American*. Princeton, N.J.: Van Nostrand, 1964.

Washington, K. R. "The Effects of Systematic Reinforcement and a Self-Awareness Program on the Self-Concept of Black Pre-School Children." Research paper, University of Massachusetts, Amherst, 1975.

Washington, K. R. "Self-Concept Development: An Affective Educational Experience for Inner-City Teachers." *Young Children* 29, no. 5 (July 1974): 305-310.

Ann M. Bingham-Newman and Ruth A. Saunders

Take a New Look at Your Classroom with Piaget as a Guide

Often the search for solutions to the problems facing educators today reminds one of Pooh's hunt for the Woozle in *Winnie-the-Pooh*.[1] Recall that delightful episode in which Pooh and Piglet follow a set of footprints with increasing alarm as they notice new sets of tracks added to the first. Pooh's original problem of identifying who made the footprints almost immediately becomes the overwhelming problem of finding the mysterious Woozle (or Woozles). In hastily designating the unknown footprint-maker as a Woozle, Pooh overlooked valuable observational data. Only when Christopher Robin, from his perch in the big oak tree, points out that Pooh and Piglet have been going in circles does Pooh take a new look at the situation. He realizes that he has indeed been going round and round the thicket and, as a matter of fact, his own feet fit the prints perfectly.

Has the same thing happened in education as we become so enmeshed in our tracks (the problems in applying various methods) that we forget our original concern—the children whose thinking and learning abilities have led us to devise those methods? If so, Piaget's theory can be our Christopher Robin in leading us to look again at some of our assumptions. Let's go back to the classroom with Piaget as our guide for a new way to look at children and their intellectual development.

Like Freud's analysis of the emotions and Gesell's description of physical development, Piaget's work stands as a massive and carefully documented analysis of one aspect of human development. For nearly sixty years he has observed and interviewed children, seeking to understand the origins of logical thought. Perhaps his most important conclusion for teachers is that

---

[1] The inspiration for the use of the "Woozle episode" came from a similar use of this episode made by J. F. Wohlwill in an article entitled "Piaget's System as a Source of Empirical Research," published in *Merrill-Palmer Quarterly* 9 (1963): 253-262.

logic *develops*. Young children cannot use the reasoning we depend on in the adult world. Logical thought develops slowly and with certain recognizable steps in every normally developing child. The implications of this for education, though not elaborated on by Piaget, are tremendous. Young children are unaware, not only of specific facts but of the very tools of rational thought adults depend on for useful application of those facts. Adults cannot assume that their logic will convince children of a truth if only the terms are simple enough.

Because Piaget's theory represents an attempt to understand logical reasoning and is not a theory of education, the implications drawn from it have been varied. They range from revisions of specific subject areas such as science and math in many British infant schools to the creation of whole programs based on the theory, such as the preschool program of Kamii and Devries in Chicago or that implemented by the authors at the University of Wisconsin. The application of Piaget's theory to education is very difficult because it consists neither of prescribed materials nor techniques, but rather it describes how children think. What the theory does give to teachers is a framework from which to be creative.

Principles of Development

Several principles from Piaget's theory provide a basis for classroom atmosphere, curriculum development, and teacher role:

1. Learning is an active process;

2. There is a fixed sequence in development with individual variations in pace;

3. Language, alone, is not the answer—one cannot assume that because a child can say a word, the concept has been learned, or that simply teaching the word will teach the concept;

4. Intellectual development is fostered by social interaction with peers and adults.

First of all, Piaget states clearly that learning is an active process, both physically and mentally. Thought is the internalization of action. This indicates that children should be able to actively explore and manipulate materials in their environment. By so doing, the child is constructing his or her own knowledge. Therefore, teachers must create an environment in which children will be active and initiate their own activities. This environment includes not only the materials and equipment but also the teacher-child

Ann M. Bingham-Newman, Ph.D., is Coordinator of the Interdisciplinary Child Development Program, California State University, Los Angeles. Formerly, she was Coordinator of the University of Wisconsin Early Childhood Center and Child Development Lecturer at the University of Wisconsin. Her areas of experience include Piagetian theory, observational methods, values clarification, infancy, and parent education.

Ruth A. Saunders, Doctoral Candidate, is Project Specialist for the Wisconsin Research and Development Center for Cognitive Learning at the University of Wisconsin, Madison. Previously, she has directed and taught day care, Head Start, and nursery school. She is currently working on a project for developing, implementing, and evaluating a Piagetian-based preschool program.

and child-child relationships. Interest centers where children may choose from a variety of activities, with or without teacher inolvement, can encourage active problem solving and valuable interchange with peers.

The second principle, that there is an invariant sequence to development and that individuals go through this sequence at their own pace, means that teachers can have a fairly clear picutre of a child's present reasoning capacities and what can be anticipated in the near future. Knowledge of the stages of development in a child's thinking helps teachers to plan with appropriate expectations. We can be aware of the limitations at a particular stage and of the new possibilities offered when the next stage is reached. It must be emphasized, however, that all children are not at the same place at the same time.

Children think about the world very differently than adults do—they make different interpretations and draw different conclusions. This is because each successive stage in the development of thinking or intelligence is characterized by the emergence of new ways of thought. A young child looking at a figure similar to Figure I might come to a very different conclusion than an adult would when asked, "Do both of these rows have the same number of circles?"

Figure I

A.　○　○　○　○　○

B.　　○○○○○

A child between four and seven years of age might say *A* has more. The preoperational child tends to focus on one attribute only—either the length of the row or the amount of space it takes up. Or this child might say *B* has more because the circles are so close together. Even if the child counted the circles and could say there were five in each row, before age six or seven, he or she would still probably say one or the other has more.

The third principle is that language training alone does not lead to intellectual development. Language helps to focus on concepts and to retrieve them or sort them out, but it does not in and of itself build concepts. We all have known the child who could say the word *five* but didn't know what *fiveness* was.

The final principle is that intellectual growth is fostered by social interaction with peers and adults as well as interactions with the physical environment. It is precisely this social interaction which enables the young child to begin to take into account different perspectives. The fact that children usually are only capable of seeing, understanding, and feeling things from their own individual viewpoints is what Piaget terms *egocentrism*. Consider, for example, the child standing up when other children are sitting. He or she is unable to understand why someone in back can't see. After all, it may be explained, "I can see perfectly well." Or reread some of the Winnie-the-Pooh stories by A. A. Milne. They are filled with examples of egocentric thinking. Egocentrism decreases with age as new types of thought appear, but it never completely disappears. Did you ever sit at a red light saying, "1, 2, 3—change!"?

By hearing different ideas, by having their ideas challenged, children begin to evaluate and reexamine their own ideas. Knowledge is gradually reshaped and reconstructed—going from one wrong answer to another and gradually coming closer to an adult view of reality. Remember the many times you have thought a child's answers to questions were absurd. Far from being absurd, the child has answered correctly the question as it was perceived. The cause of the "error" is that the child did not ask himself or herself the same question that you asked.

When asked if one set of beads is in the same order as another, for example, the question may be reinterpreted to mean whether one set has a bead to match each of those in the other set, regardless of order. It takes skill and patience to be accepting of those seemingly absurd answers so that the child's confidence is built up instead of destroyed. Many opportunities for guiding the child toward reality will occur on other days. Children's answers, though, can provide excellent information about their thinking, that is, where they are and where we can help them go. By accepting children's egocentric answers, we also encourage them to be intellectually honest rather than to be looking, listening, or waiting for us to give the right answer. As teachers, we must listen *to* an answer, not *for* an answer. Be on the lookout for the unexpected answer and use it advantageously as another starting point.

Children between four and eight years of age are in transition from what Piaget calls the *preoperational* stage to the *concrete operational* stage. They can use mental symbols to think about things which are not present; they can use language to represent objects; but they are perceptually oriented—their thinking is still dependent on how things appear. Piaget calls this thinking *intuitive*. That is, they believe things are as they appear to be rather than

considering them from the adult's logical perspective. For these children, if it appears bigger, it is bigger. Even if their thinking tells them the correct answer to a problem, they become uncertain if what they see looks otherwise, and they will usually rely on the way it looks rather than on their thinking.

In other words, not until the age of six or seven does a child exhibit what Piaget speaks of as *conservation*—that is, understanding that some properties or attributes remain invariant despite perceptual changes. A friend has related to us a memory of her feelings before she developed the concept of conservation. She remembered her fear of going down into a deep canyon after having seen other people down at the bottom and noticing how tiny they had become. Not absolutely convinced that size was an invariant property, she didn't want to risk becoming any smaller than she already was. Like other children, she ignored one variable (distance) and focused only on apparent size. Until the major breakthrough of conservation, children's answers to questions and their solutions to problems are constantly shifting as their perceptions take precedence over their thought.

The Teacher's Role

What does all of this mean for our role as teachers? In her application of Piagetian theory to an early childhood classroom, Kamii (1972) has identified three kinds of knowledge which children acquire. Each type of knowledge is learned differently by the child and involves a correspondingly different teacher role. This division, of course, is arbitrary—it is impossible for one kind of knowledge to exist without the other two. As a guide for work with children, however, the distinction is an extremely useful tool. The three kinds of knowledge are:

I. Social Knowledge—acquired through feedback from people.

II. Physical Knowledge—acquired through feedback from objects.

III. Logico-Mathematical Knowledge—acquired through relationships which the child must invent or reconstruct, e.g., relationships between and among objects, people, and events.

JOHN KIRK

Social Knowledge

The first of these includes the cultural use of language, social conventions, and social expectations. This kind of knowledge can be communicated directly to children, and the right answer reinforced. For instance, we can tell a child to ask for something instead of simply taking it, that a particular color is called red, or that a certain object is called a table. Social knowledge, then, is acquired directly through feedback from people. This type of knowledge should not be confused with what we typically think of as "social development."

Physical Knowledge

Physical knowledge includes a knowledge of properties or attributes of objects (such as hardness, flexibility) and of physical phenomena (such as causality and gravity). Physical knowledge can be effectively learned

through feedback from objects and the effects of one's own actions on the objects. Children learn by dropping, folding, squeezing, stretching, smelling. In other words, they must be actively involved in doing things to objects and observing the results. As they learn that an object reacts in different ways in accordance with their actions upon it, they build a repertoire of actions which can be used in solving problems. In this repertoire will be many actions, and the reverse of each. In addition, children are accumulating a data bank of facts about what objects can do. Eventually this information can be used to accurately anticipate and predict outcomes.

The teacher's role in the area of physical knowledge is to encourage the child to become actively involved with objects—to find out what can be done with them, what can be done to them, and what kinds of questions can be

24

asked about them. The teacher attempts to stimulate the child's curiosity and to encourage exploration of materials. For instance, one might ask, "What would happen if you didn't put the ice cube tray back in the freezer? How can you find out?" or "What can we do to this clay—squeeze it, tear it, . . .?" or "I wonder if this marble will stay at the top of this incline you're building. Hm, I wonder why it did that?" The teacher has to create an environment, present materials, suggest activities, and assess what is going on inside the child's mind from moment to moment. An on-the-spot curriculum developer, the teacher can interact with the child according to the kind of knowledge involved and the level of the child's thinking. Without intruding or interrupting, the teacher can respond to the child in a way which encourages the extension of the child's ideas. This extension of the child's own activity will be the most meaningful learning situation.

Logico-Mathematical Knowledge

The third kind of knowledge is called logico-mathematical knowledge. This consists of an understanding of relationships between and among objects, people, or events. This knowledge comes as a result of the child's own actions and thoughts about those actions, and must be constructed by the child.

Social knowledge involves names for things and social conventions—the kinds of information that come from people. When the question or problem involves physical knowledge of attributes and actions, the answer can be found in the physical environment. When the question is in the area of logico-mathematical knowledge, however, only the child's thinking can construct the answer. The child makes use of knowledge of actions, attributes, and properties in formulating logical relationships such as "more," "same," "some," etc. A solid foundation of physical knowledge based on the child's active involvement with the environment is vital to the construction of logico-mathematical knowledge.

Let's use some of the things a child knows about clay as an example. Felicia's *social knowledge* includes knowing a variety of related words (such as *clay, pound, roll, sticky*) and knowing what she is and is not allowed to do with it (such as that she must not throw it at other children). Her *physical knowledge* of clay probably includes an awareness of a wide variety of properties of clay (such as that it dries and gets hard when left out in the air or that it gets soft when water is added) as

CHARLES L. BENN

well as a rather extensive list of what she can do with the clay. For example, a ball of clay can be made into a flat pancake and the pancake can be made back into a ball.

The child's understanding that there is the *same amount* of clay in the pancake as there was in the ball which was flattened involves *logico-mathematical knowledge*.

She draws this conclusion after much experience in acting on the clay (flattening a ball of clay), reversing her action (remaking the ball), and observing that the re-formed ball always has the same amount as the original one. Eventually, she no longer interprets that somehow the pancake has more clay "because it's wider" or less clay "because it's so thin," or that whenever it is reshaped into the ball it "magically" reverts to its original amount. She begins to coordinate the increase in width of the pancake with the decrease in thickness and constructs for herself a notion of compensatory effects.

Teachers can help children formulate questions by interacting with them or by changing the environment so that previous interpretations are challenged. For instance, when children have been sorting red and white objects, the teacher might introduce some objects which are half red and half white; or if children are classifying liquids and solids, the teacher could introduce some Silly Putty. In addition, teachers can select materials that make the children become conscious of a problem and look for the solution themselves.

Teachers must be particularly careful to refrain from telling or reinforcing the "right" answer. The "pasting on" of logico-mathematical knowledge often tends to confuse children, who can't understand why they are wrong and you are right. They merely become unsure of their own powers of reasoning. Unlike social or physical knowledge where a correct answer can be accepted as fact by the child, logico-mathematical knowledge involves inference. You can correct a child who consistently calls you by the wrong name; you can demonstrate how easily glass breaks or water spills; but how do you explain why it's true that if all spiders have eight legs, and *A* is a spider, then *A* has eight legs?

As another example, recall for a moment the two rows of circles in Figure I. A child may have the social knowledge of counting to five and the physical knowledge of how the cirlces can be spread out or moved together, yet fails to understand why there are just as many circles in row *A* as in row *B*. We may patiently explain that one row just looks like more, but in the logic of the preoperational child "if it *looks* like more, then it *is* more." It takes time for the child to construct the concept of numerical equivalence.

Another reason for avoiding a heavy emphasis on the right answer in logico-mathematical knowledge is that one "right" answer doesn't necessarily mean the child's way of reasoning has changed. Remember, young children are in a period of transition, of constantly shifting answers. What they answer correctly at one time (whether by chance, because of specific perceptual factors, or because of a glimmer of our adult way of thought) they may well answer differently the next time.

Gradually children move closer and closer to our logical, adult thought—or, as Piaget calls it, to an operational approach to the world. *Operations* are flexible, reversible thought processes which enable the child to understand that a person can be a doctor and a mommy at the same time or that the amount of water is the same no matter what the shape of the container into which it is poured.

Types of Logico-Mathematical Knowledge

The time between kindergarten and fourth grade is the time the child establishes operational intelligence. It is this kind of reasoning ability which enables children to master content. The education of young children, therefore, must concern itself with the child's ability to reason *before* the typical concern with content. This is where we have much to learn from Piaget's work. With this in mind, we can look at logical knowledge in more detail.

This type of knowledge is of primary interest for Piaget. In order to handle its many aspects, he breaks it into five distinct (but still overlapping and interactive) areas. These include three areas of strictly *logical thought (classification, seriation,* and *number)* and two areas of what he calls *infra-logical thought* (these being *space* and *time*).

Classification, Seriation, and Number

Classification is the grouping of objects according to similarities or differences, i.e., color, shape, size, or function. The important aspect here is that children be able to choose a criterion and use it consistently. Very young children tend to sort inconsistently, starting perhaps with one color, forgetting it in the middle of sorting, and then finishing the sort using a different criterion. Gradually, children begin to form hierarchies of classes

and to see that one object may belong to two classes at once—that it can be both red and round; or both a daddy and a teacher.

A second area, *seriation,* includes the ability to order objects, people, or events according to relative differences (e.g., biggest to smallest, most fun to least fun, or loudest to softest). Here, again, children become aware that an object can be two things at once—it can be bigger than one object and at the same time smaller than another.

For a little practical experience in dealing with classification and seriation, take out a handful of change. (1) Group everything into two piles. What criteria did you use? Possible criteria include the kind of metal, the date, the place it was minted, the amount (less than a dime or more than a dime), size, or how well worn they are. Are there

SALLY GALE

others you think of? Is one way of sorting better than another? What if you were a coin collector or were melting them down for the metal or looking for sizes which would fit in your piggy bank? Would you still do it the same way? (2) Now mix them up again and seriate them—order them according to a relative difference. How did you do it? A variety of ways can work and are equally valid—depending on your thoughts and your needs. The same is true for children in their activities. They often come up with unusual criteria which teachers have not thought of but which are equally valid.

So classification and seriation are legitimate areas of reasoning ability, but what does that have to do with the real world? We are constantly using our ability in these two areas to organize and cope with our world. Just for a moment, think of your closet, your kitchen cupboards, or your workbench. You have probably classified and seriated most of the objects in these places. Big nails are separated from small ones; screws are separated from nails; screwdrivers are seriated by size. How about kitchen cupboards—are all the big plates stacked together, then the next size plate, and then the saucers? How complicated our everyday chores would be without an easy system for finding what we need.

As Piaget views it, ability in the areas of classification and seriation are vital for an understanding of number relationships. Counting is one of the first number ideas taught to children, but the numbers themselves have little meaning for them—and the relationships between the numbers are even more difficult. The child must come to know that each number contains the number preceding it (that five contains four, for example). Before understanding this, the child must know that number is not an attribute of the objects themselves but an abstraction applied to objects. For example, a young child often will refuse to be counted as number seven in a group of children, insisting instead that he or she is four years old. Conservation of number must be acquired in a manner similar to conserving amount in the example with the clay.

What kinds of experiences can you provide for children which will help them construct an understanding of number? Instead of counting two groups of objects, children could be encouraged to put the objects into pairs, one from each group, to check for equivalency. This type of task will be repeated over a period of time with many different kinds of materials before the concept of equivalency is understood. Materials in units (e.g., Cuisenaire rods, unifix cubes, unit blocks, or Dienes blocks) which can be ordered, grouped, arranged, and disarranged provide experiences in seriation and classification. Again, encouragement of peer interaction and peer teaching provides challenges to young children's thinking.

Space and Time

Spatial understanding is another concern in Piagetian theory. This involves concepts of linear order, distance, part-whole relationships, right and left orientation symmetry, and spatial judgment. Realizing that there are several ways of perceiving the same spatial arrangement depending on one's vantage point is one such spatial concept.

Young children may often have difficulty copying a sequence of more than four objects, as they might attempt in bead stringing. The problem here is similar to that of the unconscious shifting of criteria in classification. A child may start out copying the order from left to right and in the middle reverse to copying the order from right to left without realizing a reversal in direction has been made. A sequence of beads such as red, blue, orange, green, yellow may be copied as red, blue, green, orange, yellow.

A related spatial orientation problem exists when children have difficulty distinguishing b from d. Activities which invite children to move consistently in one direction either up to down, right to left, left to right, or northwest to southwest will give them experiences in spatial orientation which may apply to reading skills. Practice in making judgments about distance and whether one object will fit

DONNA J. HARRIS

inside another contribute to a child's understanding of measurement as well as being useful for everyday living. Imagine the spatial problem-solving when learning to drive a car, or when packing a trunk for a trip.

Concepts of time involve much more than telling time by the clock. They involve both the sequence of events and the estimation of time intervals. Recalling story sequences and the order of activities in a cooking project or scientific experiment help young children better understand time relationships. Time intervals could be measured or estimated in minutes, in number of claps, by distance walked, by the number of verses which can be sung, or by amount of work achieved.

Summary

It is evident that these understandings of space and time, as well as of classification, seriation, and number all overlap and seldom operate in isolation. In fact, most activites can involve all of these. This is another good aspect of a Piagetian curriculum—no need to buy expensive kits, or new materials, or make drastic changes in the classroom. Instead, activities with children can be viewed in terms of the three basic kinds of knowledge and the five areas of logical thought. This knowledge may be separated for ease in explanation and study, but in Piaget's view, development proceeds simultaneously in all the arbitrarily separated parts. Growth in classification, for example, is accompanied by and enhanced by growth in any or all of the other areas.

With Piaget as a guide, take a look at your classroom and the activities you have planned. With an understanding of the development of young children's thinking the principal goal of education can be pursued, which in Piaget's view

is to create men who are capable of doing new things, not simply of repeating what other generations have done, men who are creative, inventive, and discoverers. The second goal of education is to form minds which can be critical, can verify, and not accept everything they are offered. The great danger today is of slogans, collective opinions and ready-made trends of thought. We have to be able to resist individually, to criticize, to distinguish between what is proven and what is not. So we need pupils who are active, who learn early to find out by themselves, partly by their own spontaneous activity and partly through material we set up for them; who learn early to tell what is verifiable and what is simply the first idea to come to them.[2] 🔽

---

[2] Ripple, R. E., and Rockcastle, V. N., eds. *Piaget Rediscovered: Report of the Conference on Cognitive Studies and Curriculum Development.* Ithaca, N.Y.: Cornell University School of Education, 1964, p. 5.

References

Almy, M.; Chittenden, E.; and Miller, P. *Young Children's Thinking.* New York: Teachers College Press, 1966.

Athey, I., and Rubadeau, D., eds. *Educational Implications of Piaget's Theory.* Waltham, Mass.: Ginn-Blaisdell, 1970.

Copeland, R. W. *How Children Learn Mathematics — Teaching Implications of Piaget's Research.* New York: Macmillan Co., 1970.

Evans, E. D. *Contemporary Influences in Early Childhood Education.* New York: Holt, Rinehart and Winston, 1971.

Furth, H. G. *Piaget and Knowledge.* Englewood Cliffs, N.J.: Prentice-Hall, 1969.

Furth, H. G. *Piaget for Teachers.* Englewood Cliffs, N.J.: Prentice-Hall, 1970.

Ginsburg, H., and Opper, S. *Piaget's Theory of Intellectual Development.* Englewood Cliffs, N.J.: Prentice-Hall, 1969.

Hess, R. D., and Croft, D. J. *Activities Handbook for Teachers of Young Children.* Boston: Houghton Mifflin Co., 1972.

Kamii, C. "An Application of Piaget's Theory to the Conceptualization of a Preschool Curriculum." In *The Preschool in Action,* edited by R. K. Parker, pp. 91-133. Boston: Allyn & Bacon, 1972.

Kamii, C. "One Intelligence Indivisible." *Young Children* 30, no. 4 (May 1975): 228-238.

Lavatelli, C. S. *Piaget's Theory Applied to an Early Childhood Curriculum.* Boston: American Science and Engineering, 1970.

Piaget, J. *The Child's Conception of Number.* New York: W. W. Norton & Co., 1952.

Piaget, J. *Play, Dreams, and Imitation in Childhood.* New York: Humanities Press, 1952.

Piaget, J. *Six Psychological Studies.* New York: Vintage Books, 1968.

Piaget, J., and Inhelder, B. *The Child's Conception of Space.* New York: W. W. Norton & Co., 1956.

Piaget, J., and Inhelder, B. *The Early Growth of Logic in the Child.* New York: W. W. Norton & Co., 1964.

Picard, A. J. "Piaget's Theory of Development with Implications for Teaching Elementary School Mathematics." *School Science and Mathematics* 69 (1969): 287-298.

Pulaski, M.A.S. *Understanding Piaget.* New York: Harper and Row, 1971.

Schwebel, M., and Raph, J. *Piaget in the Classroom.* New York: Basic Books, 1973.

Sharp, E. *Thinking Is Child's Play.* New York: Avon Books, 1969.

James A. McLoughlin and
Susan M. Kershman

Mainstreaming in Early Childhood
Strategies and Resources

Mainstreaming encourages the inclusion of the handicapped into regular education placements to the maximum extent advisable for the individual child.

Mainstreaming is a belief which involves an educational placement procedure and process for exceptional children, based on the conviction that each such child should be educated in the least restrictive environment in which his educational and related needs can be satisfactorily provided. This concept recognizes that exceptional children have a wide range of special educational needs, varying greatly in intensity and duration; that there is a recognized continuum of educational settings which may, at a given time, be appropriate for an individual child's needs; that to the maximum extent appropriate, exceptional children should be educated with non-exceptional children; and that special classes, separate schooling, or other removal of an exceptional child from education with non-exceptional children should occur only when the intensity of the child's special education and related needs is such that they cannot be satisfied in an environment including non-exceptional children, even with the provision of supplementary aids and services (Council for Exceptional Children 1976, p. 3).

Mainstreaming thus does not mean that every handicapped child can best be served in a regular early childhood program (Howard 1977). There are many ways to serve the handicapped (Deno 1970). Although initially the handicapped child who is mainstreamed has increased

visibility, the purpose behind the philosophy is to enhance the broadbased acceptance of individual differences. Ultimately, exceptional children's weaknesses will become less visible as their strengths and similarities with normal children are shifted into focus.

Staff Training and Preparation for Mainstreaming

How can we best prepare our staff? Administrative support is vital for any program's success. Christopherson (1972) has described the role and activities of the program administrator who supports mainstreaming. Appropriate inservice training is also essential for successful mainstreaming. Consultants from local school systems, universities, and state departments of education can help plan and implement staff training. Two projects offering consultant services are the

James A. McLoughlin, Ph.D., is Assistant Professor, Department of Special Education, University of Kentucky, Lexington, Kentucky.

Susan M. Kershman, Ph.D., is Coordinator, Early Childhood Education of the Handicapped, Department of Special Education, University of Kentucky, Lexington, Kentucky.

Regional Resource Centers in Special Education and the Technical Assistance Development Systems; your state department of education can refer you to the nearest such service.

Suggested materials for training are listed in Table 1. During and after training, continuous staff supervision and feedback are needed to ensure that programs are being implemented in ways most appropriate for children.

Table 1. Suggested Training Materials

Early Childhood Education for Exceptional Children, ed. J. B. Jordan, A. H. Hayden, M. B. Karnes, and M. M. Wood. Reston, Va.: Council for Exceptional Children, 1977.
Principal Training Program. Austin, Tex.: Region XIII Education Service Center, 1975.
P.L. 94-142—The Education For All Handicapped Children Act. Reston, Va.: Council for Exceptional Children, 1976. (Multimedia kit)
Selected Readings in Early Education of Handicapped Children, ed. D. L. Braddock. Handicapped Children in Head Start series. Reston, Va.: Council for Exceptional Children, Head Start Information Project, 1974.
Training of Nonprofessionals in Early Childhood Education Centers, by A. Rister. Reston, Va.: Council for Exceptional Children, Head Start Information Project, 1974.
Teacher Training Program. Austin, Tex.: Region XIII Education Service Center, 1976.
Teaching Exceptional Children in All America's Schools, by M. C. Reynolds and J. W. Birch. Reston, Va.: Council for Exceptional Children, 1977.

What are the essential topics for inservice training? The following six critical areas should be discussed in inservice training:

- identifying handicapping conditions;

- recognizing individual learning styles;

- adapting activities and materials;

- using special assessment devices and methods;

- involving parents; and

- communicating with fellow teachers and support personnel.

Early Identification

How do we identify the handicapped child? According to the regulations of P.L. 94-142 each state department of education is responsible for a Child Find Project. The primary emphasis in most states is locating and identifying handicapped children of school age. The degree to which Child Find activities must incorporate young children is determined by the mandatory school age in that particular state. However, screening is most effective when it can identify children with problems early so the problems do not become cumulative.

Child Find activities include making initial contact with the target population and increasing public awareness of services (Cross and Goin 1977). Your local state department of education or school district can provide you with information about Child Find activities in your area. In states where early childhood education is not widely available, Head Start personnel have often made significant contributions to the identification of young handicapped children.

Literature informing parents about recent legislation, their legal rights, and strategies to work with their children is available from state departments, Head Start, and organizations such as Closer Look, the Association for Children with Learning Disabilities, and the National Association for Retarded Citizens. See Table 2 for the names and addresses of these and other organizations.

Within any community there are many resources that can help identify and locate handicapped children. Neonatal intensive care units, local hospital departments, and physicians can identify handicapped children at an early age. Other sources are the state departments of social welfare, human resources, and public health. Television and newspapers can also be recruited to publicize the effort.

A screening program to identify handicapped children can then be implemented.

Table 2. Sources of Information

Alexander Graham Bell Association for the Deaf
3417 Volta Place, N.W.
Washington, DC 20007

American Association of Workers for the Blind
1511 K Street, N.W.
Washington, DC 20005

American Association on Mental Deficiency
5101 Wisconsin Avenue, N.W.
Washington, DC 20016

American Association of Psychiatric
  Services for Children
1701 18th Street, N.W.
Washington, DC 20009

American Council for the Blind
1211 Connecticut Avenue, N.W.
Washington, DC 20006

American Foundation for the Blind
15 West 16th Street
New York, NY 10011

American Humane Association
Children's Division
P.O. Box 1266
Denver, CO 80201

American Physical Therapy Association
1156 15th Street, N.W.
Suite 500
Washington, DC 20005

American Printing House for the Blind
1839 Frankfort Avenue
Louisville, KY 40206

American Speech and Hearing Association
9030 Old Georgetown Road
Washington, DC 20014

Association for Children with
  Learning Disabilities (National)
4156 Library Road
Pittsburgh, PA 15234

Association for Education of the
  Visually Handicapped
919 Walnut Street
San Francisco, CA 94121

Child Welfare League of America
67 Irving Place
New York, NY 10003

Clearinghouse on Programs and Research
  in Child Abuse and Neglect
Herner & Company
2100 M Street, N.W., Suite 316
Washington, DC 20037

Closer Look
Box 1492
Washington, DC 20013

Conference of Executives of American
  Schools for the Deaf
5034 Wisconsin Avenue, N.W.
Washington, DC 20016

Convention of American Instructors
  of the Deaf, Inc.
5034 Wisconsin Avenue, N.W.
Suite 11
Washington, DC 20016

Council for Exceptional Children
(ERIC Clearinghouse on Handicapped
  and Gifted Children)
1920 Association Drive
Reston, VA 22091

Council of Administrators of Special Education
1920 Association Drive
Reston, VA 22091

Council on Social Work Education
345 East 46th Street
New York, NY 10017

Epilepsy Foundation of America
1828 L Street, N.W.
Washington, DC 20036

International League of Societies for
  the Mentally Retarded
12 Rue Forestiere
Brussels 5, Belgium

Library of Congress
Division for the Blind and Physically Handicapped
1291 Taylor Street, N.W.
Washington, DC 20542

National Association for Retarded Citizens
2709 Avenue E East
P.O. Box 6109
Arlington, TX 76011

National Association for the Visually Handicapped
3201 Balboa Street
San Francisco, CA 94121

National Association of the Deaf
814 Thayer Avenue
Silver Spring, MD 20910

National Association of the Deaf-Blind
2703 Forest Oak Circle
Norman, OK 73071

National Association of Hearing
and Speech Action
814 Thayer Avenue
Silver Spring, MD 20910

National Association of Private
Residential Facilities for the Mentally Retarded
6269 Leesburg Pike
Falls Church, VA 22044

National Association of Social Workers
1425 H Street, N.W.
Washington, DC 20005

National Center for Child Abuse
and Neglect
Office of Child Development
P.O. Box 1182
Washington, DC 20013

National Center for the Prevention and
Treatment of Child Abuse and Neglect
1205 Oneida
Denver, CO 80220

National Deaf-Blind Program
Bureau of Education for the Handicapped
Room 4046 Donohoe Building
400 Maryland Avenue, S.W.
Washington, DC 20202

National Easter Seal Society for
Crippled Children and Adults
2023 West Ogden Avenue
Chicago, IL 60612

National Epilepsy League, Inc.
6 North Michigan Avenue
Chicago, IL 60602

National Federation for the Blind
Suite 212, Dupont Circle Building
1346 Connecticut Avenue, N.W.
Washington, DC 20036

National Foundation—March of Dimes
(Birth Defects)
1275 Mamaroneck Avenue
White Plains, NY 10605

National Headquarters for Mental
Health Association
1800 North Kent Street
Rosslyn, VA 22209

National Institute of Mental Health
5454 Wisconsin Avenue
Chevy Chase, MD 20015

National Paraplegia Foundation
333 North Michigan Avenue
Chicago, IL 60601

National Quadraplegia Foundation
333 North Michigan Avenue
Chicago, IL 60601

National Rehabilitation Association
1522 K Street, N.W., Suite 1120
Washington, DC 20005

National Society for Autistic Children
169 Tampa Avenue
Albany, NY 12208

National Society for the
Prevention of Blindness, Inc.
79 Madison Avenue
New York, NY 10016

The Orton Society, Inc.
8415 Bellona Lane
Towson, MD 21204

Parents Anonymous
2930 West Imperial Highway
Suite 332
Inglewood, CA 90303

The President's Committee on Mental Retardation
Department of Health, Education, and Welfare
Room 2614
Washington, DC 20201

Spina Bifida Association of America
343 South Dearborn Street
Room 319
Chicago, IL 60604

United Cerebral Palsy Association
66 East 34th Street
New York, NY 10016

U.S. Department of Health, Education, and Welfare
Parklawn Building
5600 Fishers Lane
Rockville, MD 20852

U.S. Senate
Subcommittee on Children and Youth
443 Old Senate Office Building
Washington, DC 20510

Classroom observations, teacher ratings of child performance, parent interviews, and administration of screening devices to children, and other similar evaluations can be conducted. Two excellent overviews for resources and procedures are "Identification, Screening and Assessment" (Hayden and Edgar 1977) and *Developmental Screening in Early Childhood: A Guide* (Meisels 1978).

What areas need to be included in a screening project? The critical areas for screening are motor development, verbal comprehension and expression, auditory and visual acuity and perception, cognitive development, adaptive behavior, and self-help skills. The screening instruments should be quick, efficient, inexpensive, and both developmental and behavioral in orientation. Screening should lead toward a more in-depth study of individual children whose test results indicate a possible problem. Examples of tests that you may wish to consider are listed in Table 3. Hayden and Edgar (1977) summarize and describe a wide variety of available screening tools. One caution: tests should be carefully selected to ensure that the results will be accurate for the population being screened.

Who can help in the screening? A professional consultant is recommended to design the screening plan, but trained volunteers, college students, and others can help administer screening interviews, questionnaires, and rating scales. Hirshoren and Umansky (1977) have developed a list of states in which there are teacher certification and known teacher preparation programs in early childhood education for exceptional children. You may need to contact consultants in special education, pediatrics, psychology, ophthalmology, audiology, and speech and language. Meier (1976) and Rojcewicz and Aaronson (1976) are major resources for a discussion of screening.

Ultimately, exceptional children's weaknesses will become less visible as their strengths and similarities with normal children are shifted into focus.

William Lupardo

Table 3. Screening and Assessment Instruments for Young Children

Skill Areas	Screening & Assessment Instruments
Motor Development	Bruininks—Oseretsky Test of Motor Proficiency (Bruininks 1977)
	Developmental Test Visual-Motor Integration (Berry & Buktenica 1967)
	Southern California Perceptual Motor Tests (Ayres 1969)
Verbal Comprehension and Expression	Receptive-Expressive Emergent Language Scale (Bzoch & League 1971)
	Illinois Test of Psycholinguistic Abilities (Kirk, McCarthy, & Kirk 1968)
	Goldman-Fristoe Test of Articulation (Goldman & Fristoe 1969)
	Verbal Language Development Scale (Mecham 1958)
	Test of Language Development (Newcomer & Hammill 1977)
Vision: Acuity/Perception	Home Eye Test for Preschoolers (National Society for the Prevention of Blindness 1975)
	Frostig Developmental Test of Visual Perception (Frostig, Lefever, and Whittlesey 1964)
Auditory: Acuity/Perception	Wepman Auditory Discrimination Test (Wepman 1958)
	Goldman-Fristoe-Woodcock Test of Auditory Discrimination (Goldman, Fristoe, & Woodcock 1970)
	Audiological examination
Cognitive	Boehm Test of Basic Concepts (Boehm 1971)
	Basic Concept Inventory (Engelmann 1967)
	Basic School Skill Inventory (Goodman & Hammill 1975)
	Leiter International Performance Scale (Leiter 1948)
Adaptive/Self-Help	Bayley Scales of Infant Development (Bayley 1969)
	Vineland Social Maturity Scale (Doll 1965)
	AAMD Adaptive Behavior Rating Scale (Nihira, Foster, Shellhaas, and Leland 1969)
Comprehensive	Denver Developmental Screening Test (Frankenburg, Dodds, & Fandal 1970)
	Learning Accomplishment Profile (Sanford 1975)
	Performance Objectives for Preschool Children (Schirmer 1974)

Assessment

Why are assessments necessary? More detailed assessments may be necessary following screening to verify and define possible problem areas. The main goal of assessment is to identify learning styles and levels of development of the individual child. Knowledge of the child's strengths in learning can then be used to set goals and directions for the child's educational program and to support individualized instruction.

What is involved in an assessment? Some techniques used in screening, such as interviews and classroom observations, may again be used in an assessment, but more intensively. Specialized assessments may be performed by ophthalmologists, audiologists, pediatricians, psychologists, and others as needed. The educational assessment, according to Harbin (1977), should involve observation, norm-referenced tests, criterion-referenced tests, and Piagetian evaluation devices. Systematic observations of the child in the school and at home are revolutionizing assessment techniques (Cartwright and Cartwright 1974; Medinnus 1976). Norm-referenced or standardized tests compare the performance of one child to that of a normative group; criterion-referenced tests compare a child's skill in a specific area (e.g., gross motor ability) to a performance criterion. There are many commercial tests available at the early childhood level for a variety of purposes (see Table 3). Comprehensive references on this subject have been developed by Meier (1976), Cross and Goin (1977), and the Coordinating Office for Regional Resource Centers (1976). An example of a standardized test is the *Meeting Street School Screening Test* (Hainsworth and Siqueland 1969). Examples of criterion-referenced developmental scales are the *Lexington Developmental Scale* (Irwin, Ward, Deen, and Greis 1973) and the *Learning Accomplishment Profile* (Sanford 1975).

How can I justify all this effort for one group of children? The results from accurate assessment scales and inventories can be one important factor in determining the structure and direction of a program. They can be used to the benefit of *all* children, without dominating the flavor of a program or discouraging flexibility or creativity. Assessments are necessary to formulate individual educational plans (IEPs) mandated by P.L. 94-142 for all handicapped children. These IEPs must contai: a summary of the present levels of a child's performance, yearly goals, short-term objectives for each yearly goal, a list of the specific educational and support services needed to meet each objective, evaluation criteria for each objective, and procedures for reevaluating the IEP (Hayden and Edgar 1978).

Who can assist in the testing? Consultants are of course necessary, but many instruments can be administered and scored accurately after a brief training session. Volunteers, aides, and others can help. Wiegerink and Parrish (1976) have described parent-implemented programs. The interpretation of the information gathered is enhanced by the experience and training of the staff. Local colleges and clinics often have interns who can offer great support.

What does one look for in assessment? The early childhood educator specifically looks for strengths and weaknesses in the child's performance and development, indications of learning style, and any skills deficits. Results can be equally applicable and effective in program planning for normal and handicapped children. Through careful observation of the child's approach to solving problems, the teacher can identify appropriate teaching strategies and activities for children.

Methods and Materials

What are the critical curriculum areas? The major areas in which young disabled children may need individual attention are motor development, verbal comprehension and expression, auditory and visual acuity and perception, cognitive development, adaptive behavior, and self-help skills. Obviously they are the same areas used in screening and assessment and, not coincidentally, are areas in which the normally developing child may also need assistance and/or instruction. For a discussion and description of early childhood curriculums, see Wood and Hurley (1977), Safford (1978), and Shearer and Shearer (1976).

Does a particular handicapping condition call for a specific modification in the content of a program? Depending upon the child's disability, one may emphasize certain areas of instruction:

- for the physically handicapped—handling, positioning, and movement (including feeding);

- for the visually handicapped—maximum use of residual vision/vision stimulation, listening skills, and social skills;

- for the hearing impaired—maximum use of residual hearing/auditory training, communication techniques, and specific speech and language instruction.

Structure, training for generalization, and practice are needed by all handicapped children.

What materials are available for preschool handicapped children? Materials must be chosen on the basis of knowledge of the child's needs and learning style (see Table 4). Materials should be developmentally appropriate, safe, useful, durable, appealing to children, and priced reasonably. One excellent comprehensive listing of materials for exceptional preschoolers has been developed by Thorum, Sterns, Harms, Van Vliet, and Martinez (1976). Table 5 presents a selected list of guides to consult in selecting appropriate materials.

What can be done when a child has difficulty with a learning task? Useful procedures for evaluating a child's performance are task analysis and component analysis. Task analysis describes exactly what steps (components) are needed in the skilled performance of a certain task. A second level of analysis, component analysis, describes the prerequisites, or simpler behaviors necessary to perform specific problem components. Task and component analyses have been used considerably in the development of curriculums for young children (Resnick, Wang, and Kaplan 1970).

What factors can enhance the learning achievements of a handicapped child? The degree to which the child's parents are involved in the program increases the chances for its success. The teacher's ingenuity in adapting materials and designing alternate forms of activities for children can enhance children's growth and development. Sensitivity to complications created by a language or other problem can inspire alternative modes of instruction. Learning environments should be free from architectural barriers, extreme visual and auditory distractions, and other hindrances. Finally, learning tasks selected especially for the child's needs are a key factor in the success of a program.

Is the regular early childhood program the best place for every handicapped child? Not necessarily, although constant evaluation must take place to ensure that children are placed in the least restrictive environment possible. Placement should be determined only after assessment and determination of the educational goals for the child and the program. The choice of the most appropriate arrangement is dependent on many factors. Exemplary program models for exceptional children are described in *The Preschool in Action* (Day and Parker 1977).

How can parents be involved? Calvert (1971) has described the rationale for parent participation. In general, the more the parent participates in the child's program,

Table 4. Teaching Materials and/or Idea Books for Young Children

Skill Areas	Materials and/or Books
Motor Development	*Move, Grow, Learn* (Frostig & Maslow 1969)
	Dubnoff School Program (Dubnoff & Chambers 1968)
	Beginning to Learn: Fine Motor Skills (Thurstone & Lillie 1970)
Verbal Comprehension and Expression	Engel (1972)
	Karnes (1968)
	Distar Language I (Englemann, Osborn, & Englemann 1969)
	Peabody Language Development Kit: Level P (Dunn, Horton, & Smith 1968)
	MWM Program for Developing Language Abilities (Minskoff, Wiseman, & Minskoff 1973)
Vision: Acuity/Perception	*Frostig Remediation Program* (Frostig, Horne, & Maslow 1973)
	Ruth Cheves Program I: Visual-Motor Perception (Cheves 1969)
Auditory: Acuity/Perception	Zigmond & Cicci (1968)
	Sound, Order, Sense (Semel 1968)
	What's Its Name (Utley 1968)
	GOAL: Language Development (Karnes 1972)
	Play It by Ear (Lowell & Stoner 1963)
Cognitive	*GOAL: Mathematical Concepts* (Karnes 1973)
	Inquisitive Games: Discovering How to Learn (Sprigle 1969)
	Peabody Language Development Kit (Dunn & Smith 1965)
Adaptive/Self-Help	DUSO (Dinkmeyer 1972)
	Beginning with the Handicapped (Hart 1974)
	Project "ME" (Schaeffer 1972)
Comprehensive	Thorum, Sterns, Harms, Van Vliet, and Martinez (1976)
	Portage Guide to Early Education (Bluma, Shearer, Frohman, and Hilliard 1976)
	Project Memphis (Quick, Little, & Campbell 1974)
	Curriculum Cards for Preschool Children (Schirmer 1976)

the greater the long-range impact of early intervention (Bronfenbrenner 1975). Parents have successfully fulfilled many roles in early childhood programs for the handicapped, including those of assessor of skills and teacher (Shearer and Shearer 1977). However, primary emphasis should be given to the development of a fulfilling parent-child relationship. Lillie and Trohanis (1976) describe numerous models for parent participation, including school-based and home-based strategies.

Table 5. Guides in the Selection of Equipment and Materials for Early Childhood Programs

Directory of Selected Instructional Materials, by C. Van Etten. Reston, Va.: Council for Exceptional Children, Head Start Information Project, 1974.

Early Childhood Facilities, by A. M. Baas. Educational Facilities Review series No. 9. Washington, D.C.: National Center for Educational Research and Development (DHEW/OE), 1972. ERIC Document No. ED 070 138.

Innovative, Inexpensive, Instructional Materials. Lexington, Ky.: Lexington Child Development Centers of United Cerebral Palsy of the Bluegrass, 1974.

A Priceless Playground for Exceptional Children, by P. G. Adkins. El Paso, Tex.: Early Learning Center for Exceptional Children, 1973.

Suggested Equipment and Supplies for Infant-Toddler Centers, by A. Mazyck. Greensboro, N.C.: North Carolina University, 1969. ERIC Document No. ED 062 012.

Toys for Early Development of the Young Blind Child: A Guide for Parents, by the Illinois State Office of the Superintendent of Public Information. Washington, D.C.: U.S. Department of Health, Education, and Welfare, Office of Education, 1971, ERIC Document No. ED 065 201.

Why should we gather evaluation information? Evaluations of child progress, teacher performance, and program effectiveness supply the bases for making decisions. Child progress records are a major criterion to determine the effectiveness of teaching strategies. Parents appreciate indications of child progress and are usually more supportive of both the child and the program when specific information is available to them. Administrators require measures of the effectiveness of a specific component of a program in order to determine its future. Funding agencies routinely require program accountability. Moore (1977) discusses forms and issues in program evaluation.

What is involved in program evaluation? Evaluations may be formative (a measure of ongoing progress) and/or summative (a product or outcome score that summarizes whether the performances of participants met stated program objectives). Information may be measured in many ways, such as formal tests, questionnaires, graphs of progress, and so forth. Moore (1977) and Caldwell (1977) describe procedures and issues in program evaluation.

How can we measure the effects of mainstreaming? The frequency and quality of social interactions of children can be measured. Attitudinal surveys of teachers and parents, peer ratings by the children, and measures of skill progress can be extremely useful and informative. Reynolds and Birch (1977), Brackett and Henniges (1976), Devoney, Guralnick, and Rubin (1974), and Guralnick (1978) describe sample strategies for studying the effects of mainstreaming in early childhood.

Conclusion

Programming for young handicapped children is a major commitment that entails efforts in staff inservice training and preparation, identification of handicapped children, educational and other in-depth assessment of learning styles and levels of development, specific instructional methods and procedures, and child and program evaluation. There are no set formulas for the successful integration of young handicapped and nonhandicapped children. Administrators, teachers, and parents must cooperatively set mainstreaming as a priority.

References

Adkins, P. G. *Structured Experiences for Developmental Learning.* El Paso, Tex.: Learning Resource Press, 1972.

Ayres, B. *Southern California Perceptual Motor Tests.* Los Angeles: Western Psychological Services, 1969.

Bayley, N. *Bayley Scales of Infant Development.* New York: Psychological Corporation, 1969.

Berry, K. E., and Buktenica, N. A. *Developmental Test of Visual-Motor Integration.* Chicago: Follett, 1967.

Bluma, S.; Shearer, M.; Frohman, A.; and Hilliard, J. *Portage Guide to Early Education, No. 12.* rev. ed. Portage, Wisc.: Cooperative Educational Service Agency, 1976.

Boehm, A. E. *Boehm Test of Basic Concepts.* New York: Psychological Corporation, 1971.

Brackett, D., and Henniges, M. "Communicative Interaction of Preschool Hearing Impaired Children in an Integrated Setting." *Volta Review,* 78, no. 6 (1976): 276-285.

Bronfenbrenner, U. "Is Early Intervention Effective?" In *Exceptional Infant, Vol. 3: Assessment and Intervention,* ed. B. Friedlander, G. M. Sterritt, and G. E. Kirk. New York: Brunner/Mazel, 1975.

Bruininks, R. H. *Bruininks–Oseretsky Test of Motor Proficiency.* Circle Pines, Minn.: American Guidance Service, 1977.

Bzoch, K., and League, R. *Receptive-Expressive Emergent Language Scale.* Gainesville, Fla.: Tree-of-Life, 1971.

Caldwell, B. M. "Evaluating Program Effectiveness." In *Infant Education: A Guide for Helping Handicapped Children in the First Three Years,* ed. B. M. Caldwell and D. J. Stedman with K. W. Goin. New York: Walker and Co., 1977.

Calvert, D. R. "Dimensions of Family Involvement in Early Childhood Education." *Exceptional Children* 37 (1971): 655-659.

Cartwright, C. A., and Cartwright, G. P. *Developing Observation Skills.* New York: McGraw-Hill, 1974.

Council for Exceptional Children. "Delegate Assembly Issues Mainstreaming Challenge." *CEC Update* 7, no. 4 (Summer 1976): 3.

Cheves, R. *Ruth Cheves Program I: Visual-Motor Perception.* Boston: Teaching Resources, 1969.

Christopherson, J. "The Special Child in the Regular Preschool: Some Administrative Notes." *Childhood Education* 49, no. 3 (1972); 138-140.

Coordinating Office for Regional Resource Centers (CORRC). *Preschool Test Matrix: Individual Test Descriptions.* Lexington, Ky.: University of Kentucky, 1976.

Cross, L., and Goin, K., eds. *Identifying Handicapped Children. A Guide to Casefinding, Screening, Diagnosis, Assessment and Evaluation.* New York: Walker and Co., 1977.

Day, M. C., and Parker, R. K. *The Preschool in Action: Exploring Early Childhood Programs.* Boston: Allyn and Bacon, 1977.

Deno, E. "Special Education as Developmental Capital." *Exceptional Children* 37 (1970): 229-237.

Devoney, C.; Guralnick, M.; and Rubin, H. "Integrating Handicapped and Nonhandicapped Preschool Children: Effects on Social Play." *Childhood Education* 50, no. 6 (1974): 360-364.

Dinkmeyer, D. *Developing Understanding of Self and Others (DUSO).* Circle Pines, Minn.: American Guidance Service, 1972.

Doll, E. *The Vineland Social Maturity Scale.* Circle Pines, Minn.: American Guidance Service, 1965.

Dubnoff, B., and Chambers, I. *Dubnoff School Program I: Perceptual-Motor Exercises, Level III.* Boston: Teaching Resources, 1968.

Dunn, L.; Horton, R.; and Smith, J. *Peabody Language Development Kit: Level P.* Circle Pines, Minn.: American Guidance Service, 1968.

Dunn, L., and Smith, J., eds. *Peabody Language Development Kit: Level Number I.* Circle Pines, Minn.: American Guidance Service, 1965.

Engel, R. *Language Motivating Experiences for Young Children.* Sherman Oaks, Calif.: Rose Engel, 1972.

Engelmann, S. *Basic Concept Inventory.* Chicago: Follett, 1967.

Engelmann, S.; Osborn, J.; and Englemann, F. *DISTAR Language I.* Chicago: Science Research Associates, 1969.

Frankenburg, W.; Dodds, J.; and Fandal, A. *Denver Developmental Screening Test.* Denver: Ladoca Project and Publishing Foundation, 1970.

Frostig, M.; Lefever, D.; and Whittlesey, J. *Frostig Developmental Test of Visual Perception.* Palo Alto, Calif.: Consulting Psychologists Corp., 1964.

Frostig, M.; Horne, D.; and Maslow, P. *The Frostig Remediation Program.* Chicago: Follett, 1973.

Frostig, M., and Maslow, P. *Move-Grow-Learn.* Chicago: Follett, 1969.

Goldman, R., and Fristoe, M. *Goldman-Fristoe Test of Articulation.* Circle Pines, Minn.: American Guidance Service, 1969.

Goldman, R.; Fristoe, M.; and Woodcock, R. *The Goldman-Fristoe-Woodcock Test of Auditory Discrimination.* Circle Pines, Minn.: American Guidance Service, 1970.

Goodman, L., and Hammill, D. *Basic School Skills Inventory.* Chicago: Follett, 1975.

Guralnick, M. J., ed. *Early Intervention and the Integration of Handicapped and Nonhandicapped Children*. Baltimore: University Park Press, 1978.

Haase, R. W. *Designing the Child Development Center*. Washington, D.C.: Project Head Start, Office of Child Development, 1969.

Hainsworth, P., and Siqueland, E. M. *Meeting Street School Screening Test*. East Providence, R.I.: Crippled Children and Adults of Rhode Island, 1969.

Harbin, G. "Educational Assessment." In *Identifying Handicapped Children*, ed. L. Cross and K. Goin. New York: Walker and Co., 1977.

Hart, V. *Beginning with the Handicapped*. Springfield, Ill.: Charles C. Thomas, 1974.

Hayden, A. H., and Edgar, E. B. "Developing Individualized Education Programs for Young Handicapped Children." *Teaching Exceptional Children* 10 (1978): 67-73.

Hayden, A. H., and Edgar, E. B. "Identification, Screening and Assessment." In *Early Childhood Education for Exceptional Children*, ed. J. Jordan, A. Hayden, M. Karnes, and M. Wood. Reston, Va.: Council for Exceptional Children, 1977.

Hirshoren, A., and Umansky, W. "Certification of Teachers of Preschool Handicapped Children." *Exceptional Children* 44 (1977): 191-193.

Howard, A. E. "Viewpoint. Putting Humpty Dumpty Together Again? Mainstreaming in Early Childhood." *Young Children* 33, no. 1 (November 1977): 14-15.

Irwin, J.; Ward, M. N.; Deen, C.; and Greis, A. *The Lexington Developmental Scale*. Lexington, Ky.: Child Development Centers of United Cerebral Palsy of the Bluegrass, 1973.

Karnes, M. *Helping Young Children Develop Language Skills*. Reston, Va.: Council for Exceptional Children, 1968.

Karnes, M. *GOAL: Language Development*. East Long Meadow, Mass.: Milton Bradley Co., 1972.

Karnes, M. *GOAL: Mathematical Concepts*. East Long Meadow, Mass.: Milton Bradley Co., 1973.

Kirk, S.; McCarthy, J.; and Kirk, W. *Illinois Test of Psycholinguistic Abilities*. rev. ed. Urbana, Ill.: University of Illinois Press, 1968.

Leiter, R. G. *Leiter International Performance Scale*. Los Angeles: Western Psychological Services, 1948.

Lillie, D. L.; and Trohanis, P. L.; with Goin, K. W., eds. *Teaching Parents to Teach*. New York: Walker and Co., 1976.

Lowell, E. L., and Stoner, M. *Play It by Ear: Auditory Training Games*. Los Angeles: John Tracy Clinic, 1963.

Mecham, M. J. *Verbal Language Development Scale*. Circle Pines, Minn.: American Guidance Service, 1958.

Medinnus, G. R. *Child Study and Observation Guide*. New York: John Wiley and Sons, 1976.

Meier, J. "Screening, Assessment and Intervention for Young Children at Developmental Risk." In *Intervention Strategies for High Risk Infants and Young Children*, ed. T. D. Tjossem. Baltimore, Md.: University Park Press, 1976.

Meisels, S. J. *Developmental Screening in Early Childhood: A Guide*. Washington, D.C.: National Association for the Education of Young Children, 1978.

Minskoff, E.; Wiseman, D.; and Minskoff, G. *The MWM Program for Developing Language Abilities*. Ridgefield, N.J.: Educational Performance Associates, 1973.

Moore, N. G. "Program Evaluation." In *Identifying Handicapped Children*, ed. L. Cross and K. Goin. New York: Walker and Co., 1977.

National Society for the Prevention of Blindness. *Home Eye Test for Preschoolers*. New York: National Society for the Prevention of Blindness, 1975.

Newcomer, P., and Hammill, D. *Test of Language Development*. Austin, Tx.: Empiric Press, 1977.

Nihira, K.; Foster, R.; Shellhaas, M.; and Leland, H. *AAMD Adaptive Behavior Scales*. Washington, D.C.: American Association on Mental Deficiency, 1969.

Platts, M. E. *LAUNCH: A Handbook of Early Learning Techniques for the Preschool and Kindergarten Teacher*. Stevensville, Mich.: Educational Service, 1972.

Quick, A.; Little, T.; and Campbell, A. *Project Memphis: Enhancing Developmental Progress in Preschool Exceptional Children*. Belmont, Calif.: Lear Siegler, Fearon Publishers, 1974.

Resnick, L. B.; Wang, M. C.; and Kaplan, J. *Behavioral Analysis in Curriculum Design: A Hierarchically Sequenced Introductory Mathematics Curriculum*. Monograph 2. Pittsburgh: Learning Research and Development Center, University of Pittsburgh, 1970.

Reynolds, M., and Birch, J. *Teaching Exceptional Children in All America's Schools*. Reston, Va.: Council for Exceptional Children, 1977.

Rojcewicz, S. J., and Aaronson, M. "Mental Health and the Medicaid Screening Program." In *Intervention Strategies for High Risk Infants and Young Children*, ed. T. D. Tjossem. Baltimore: University Park Press, 1976.

Safford, P. L. *Teaching Young Children with Special Needs.* St. Louis: C. V. Mosby Co., 1978.

Sanford, A. *Learning Accomplishment Profile.* Winston-Salem, N.C.: Kaplan School Supply, 1975.

Schaeffer, F. *Project "Me".* Glendale, Calif.: Bowmar, 1972.

Schirmer, G. *Performance Objectives for Preschool Children.* Sioux Falls, S.D.: Adapt Press, 1974.

Schirmer, G., ed. *Curriculum Cards for Preschool Children.* Sioux Falls, S.D.: Adapt Press, 1976.

Semel, E. *Sound, Order, Sense.* Boston: Teaching Resources, 1968.

Shearer, D. E., and Shearer, M. S. "The Portage Project: A Model for Early Childhood Intervention." In *Intervention Strategies for High Risk Infants and Young Children,* ed. T. D. Tjossem. Baltimore: University Park Press, 1976.

Shearer, M. S., and Shearer, D. E. "Parent Involvement." In *Early Childhood Education for Exceptional Children;* ed. J. Jordan, A. Hayden, M. Karnes, and M. Wood. Reston, Va.: Council for Exceptional Children, 1977.

Sprigle, H. *Inquisitive Games: Discovering How to Learn.* Chicago: Science Research Associates, 1969.

Thorum, A. R.; Sterns, E. C.; Harms, K. L.; Van Vliet, D.; and Martinez, G. *Instructional Materials for the Handicapped: Birth Through Early Childhood.* Salt Lake City, Ut.: Olympus Publishing Co. 1976.

Thurstone, T., and Lillie, D. *Beginning to Learn: Fine Motor Skills.* Chicago: Science Research Associates, 1970.

Utley, J. *What's Its Name: A Guide to Speech and Hearing Development.* Urbana, Ill.: University of Chicago Press, 1968.

Van Etten, C. *Directory of Selected Instructional Materials.* Reston, Va.: Council for Exceptional Children, Head Start Information Project, 1974.

Wabash Center for the Mentally Retarded, Inc. *Guide to Early Developmental Training.* Boston: Allyn and Bacon, 1977.

Wepman, J. *Auditory Discrimination Test.* Chicago: J. Wepman, 1958.

Wiegerink, R., and Parrish, V. "A Parent-Implemented Preschool Program." In *Teaching Parents to Teach,* ed. D. L. Lillie and P. L. Trohanis with K. W. Goin. New York: Walker and Co., 1976.

Wood, M. M., and Hurley, D. L. "Curriculum and Instruction." In *Early Childhood Education of Exceptional Children,* ed. J. B. Jordan, A. Hayden, M. Karnes, and M. Wood. Reston, Va.: Council for Exceptional Children, 1977.

Zigmond, N., and Cicci, R. *Auditory Learning.* San Rafael, Calif.: Dimensions Publishing, 1968.

II. Teaching with Impact

Adults who care for children have a responsibility for setting a climate conducive to learning: Spontaneity, creative planning, feelings of humor and good will, and an abundant zest for life by both children and teachers make the curriculum come alive. This can happen where children are treated as individuals worthy of respect and consideration, where a real interest is shown in dealing with the child's feelings, where children are encouraged toward self-help, and where affection and understanding make it possible for children to meet new challenges.

Teachers who are flexible, creative, and responsible find opportunities to offer children choices, listen to them, question them in ways that will deepen their understanding, encourage children to consider others, and ultimately enable children to become problem solvers. These children learn to make decisions, at their level of understanding, and to accept responsibility for their choices. Crazymaking will be replaced by accurate, rational interpretations of reality.

Adults who create a nurturant atmosphere and give attention to all areas of the children's learning—social, emotional, physical, and intellectual—and who are themselves involved in the continual process of their own learning and growing, can and will teach with impact, as we see in each of the three articles in this section.

Davia M. Veach

Choice with Responsibility

We often tell a child precisely where he goofed.

Parents and teachers of young children generally agree that the stage should be set for children to make wise choices and accept responsibility during the early and middle childhood years. However, we often tell a child exactly what to do. If he does it "wrong" the first time, we tell him precisely where he "goofed," so that next time he will be able to make a wiser decision. As parents and teachers we need to ask ourselves, "Is this really the way to help a child grow toward making wise choices and behaving responsibly?"

Young children can be expected to show some evidence of independent thinking, following through with a task, dependability, self-confidence, and willingness to admit mistakes. Each of these characteristics is in some way related to making wise choices and behaving responsibly. Yet, these desirable outcomes do not just happen. They are learned. Furthermore, they are learned mostly from parents and teachers. Our crucial concern comes in how the goal is reached.

Choice with Responsibility Rightfully Belongs to the Child

Parent or teacher reactions can definitely determine the value of the learning experience inherent in the following incident.

Tim, Jamie, and John (ages four, five, and six) were on their way to the ice cream stand when they stopped by the wishing well at the corner of the park. Jamie's family was new in town and he had never seen a wishing well before. He expressed his amazement at seeing nickels, dimes, and pennies on the bottom of the well. Tim, who had thrown many nickels and pennies into the well, said, "Yeah, you make a wish and throw in your money and your wish will come true." Jamie pondered for a moment, trying to sort out the new information. Then he asked, "If I throw my money in, can I get anything I want?" Tim nodded. However, John, who had also thrown pennies into the well, quickly added, "No, that's just pretend, your wish really won't come true."

Jamie stood there for a few seconds with his hand in his pocket fingering his only quarter which was just enough to buy one ice cream cone. Then he gripped the quarter tightly, withdrew his hand from his pocket, and said in a hesitating voice, "I wish for two ice cream cones," and threw his money into the water.

A child in Jamie's position is likely to be upset when he faces the consequences of his decision. But surely his perceptions will become sharper, and his thinking more

45

logical if he is expected to accept the responsibility for his act. Adults often react with a feeling of pity in these situations. However, Jamie definitely will not learn to accept the responsibility for his behavior if someone always gives him another quarter or if, out of pity, he is promised a new toy or a special treat. If this happens continuously in Jamie's life, will he ever stop throwing his money into the wishing well?

Jamie does not need someone to say, "I told you so," "You should have known better," "I'm sorry," or "Next time you'll know." All he needs is someone to listen as he tells his story about losing his quarter and not getting an ice cream cone. One might say, "You must have been so mad at yourself when you realized you had thrown away your quarter and couldn't get any ice cream." A statement such as this encourages Jamie to talk about his upset feelings. It is nonpunitive and does not fault him for his unwise decision. It also lets him know that someone understands how he feels. As a result, Jamie's hurt can ease a great deal and he can take a giant step toward wiser decisions and more responsible behavior.

There Must Be a Gradual but Continuous Assumption of Responsibility

Freedom of choice and the assumption of responsibility for choices must be gradually expanded in view of a child's physical, social, emotional, and intellectual growth. Two-year-old children can decide whether they want a chocolate cookie or a vanilla cookie. Five-year-olds can decide which clothes to wear or which toys to play with. Preteens can decide upon the time, food,

Davia M. Veach, Ph.D., is Assistant Professor of Early Childhood Education at Wichita State University, Wichita, Kansas. She has also taught and directed programs for young children.

decorations, and friends for a pajama party or an outing. Teenagers can decide whom to date, whether or not to cheat on an exam, cut class, or leave school. However, teenagers are not going to be equipped to make logical decisions if they have never had the chance to decide whether they wanted a chocolate cookie or a vanilla cookie. Neither are they equipped to analyze all available data if they were never allowed to accept the responsibility for their selection when they found out they did not like chocolate.

The age at which a child is allowed to make various choices and accept the consequences of those choices depends upon the child's developmental level. For example, two-year-old children are not ready to accept complete freedom in deciding where to play. They may decide to play in the street and of course they are not yet capable of realizing the possible consequences of that decision.

A teacher once told me, "But when I do give the children some freedom and tell them to choose an activity, they don't know what to do. They always end up asking me." It is quite true that children who are accustomed to having decisions made for them may become frustrated and may not

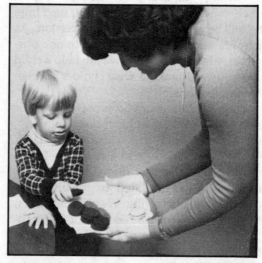

DAVIA M. VEACH

Two-year-old children can decide whether they want a chocolate cookie or a vanilla cookie.

Five-year-olds can decide which clothes to wear.

know what to do if suddenly they are given the responsibility of making an independent choice. Whatever their reaction, it is unlikely that they will use the opportunity constructively. Children must become accustomed to thinking, deciding and choosing independently on a gradual basis. No one can take a child from a point he or she has not yet reached.

Choice with Responsibility Is a Learning Process

One major reason for allowing children to make choices and accept responsibility for those choices is to enable them to gain experience in making their own decisions. The following example illustrates some of the values of this decisionmaking process.

At age six, Karen was given $3.00 each Monday as an allowance. She could buy small toys, play items or use the money for personal entertainment. One Monday afternoon Karen saw a set of doll clothes that cost $2.87. Without deliberation she bought the set. The next afternoon a friend invited her to the Thursday matinee. Karen wanted to go but she did not have any money.

This is an excellent opportunity for Karen to learn about decisionmaking, if she is allowed to accept the responsibility for her

predicament. She must first recognize the problem, ask herself how the problem can be solved, and come up with possible solutions. The amount of adult guidance Karen will need will depend in part upon her prior experience in solving her own problems. As Karen thinks of alternatives, the following possibilities may seem feasible: (1) stay at home, (2) ask for more money, (3) ask for an allowance advance, (4) borrow from a friend, or (5) earn some money.

As children grow toward wise decisionmaking they will learn to think independently, stay with the task long enough to look at all sides of the issue, analyze the possible effects of each alternative, and then accept the consequences of their decisions. If a mistake has been made, the child must be able to admit the error and have self-confidence to start again and proceed logically.

Inauthentic Choices

While providing children with opportunities for making choices with responsibility, it is important to avoid offering inauthentic choices, as in the following situations.

Choice without responsibility: This was discussed in the example of Jamie and the wishing well. If he never has to accept the responsibility for his behavior he will have no need to stop and think about consequences before he acts. Choice without responsibility leads to irresponsibility.

Unreal choice: If adults have already decided the issue before asking, even young children soon come to recognize that the choice is really not theirs. This type of choice can lead to distrustfulness and feelings of unimportance and apathy on the part of the child.

Unlimited choice: When children are allowed to make decisions in areas they are not equipped to handle, they are almost sure to experience disappointment and defeat. Children can learn a great deal if they have to accept the responsibility for throw-

47

ing their daily or even weekly allowance into the wishing well. But the disadvantages can far outweigh the advantages if, at the age of five, they have to accept the responsibility of throwing a whole month's allowance away. Young children can be given only small amounts of their allowances at one time. This way their disappointments will not be so long lasting that the whole teaching-learning process is defeated. Unlimited choice or freedom without limits is almost certain to result in frustration and confusion for the child.

Adults Have Responsibilities, Too

Providing children with opportunities to make choices and accept responsibility is not an easy task. The following characteristics seem to be necessary on the part of adults in order for a child to become a responsible self-directing individual.

The adult must be flexible: Adults must realize their own biases and not let these interfere with the children's decisions. (If there are reasons children should not have a choice, do not give them a choice. If there are limits to their choices, state these clearly.)

The adult must be creative: Children often need adult guidance in realizing the many possibilities of choice.

The adult must be responsible: When children are given a choice they need an adult who will support their decision and assist in implementation if necessary. It is also essential that adults make logical decisions and accept responsibility themselves.

If children are allowed to make choices and accept responsibilities that are right for their developmental levels, the values inherent in wise choices and responsible behavior can be vividly manifested in their daily activities and reactions to others. Allowing children to make choices and accept the responsibility for those choices is one of the most important things adults can do in fostering children's growth and development.

Robert F. Marcus and Marion Leiserson

Encouraging Helping Behavior

Practical suggestions for encouraging helping behavior through classroom climate, structure, and activities and materials.

Children are first helped by their parents who give love, affection, and respect and who care for basic biological needs. This period of dependence upon parental assistance lasts far longer in humans than in almost any other species of animal life. Gradually children's need for parental sustenance diminishes as they become more self-reliant, while the need for emotional support both in health and security, as well as in sickness and fear, never completely disappears. Having been *given to*, children become able to *give*; giving and receiving are central to affectional relationships during and after childhood. The child meets other needs through solitary enjoyment and opportunities for aesthetic expression. Thus individuality in children's behavior and concern for the welfare of others is developmentally normal. Willingness to differ and stand alone and willingness to work together for common purposes are complementary aspects of social consciousness.

What Is Helping Behavior?

Dictionaries define help as making it easier for a person to do something by sharing the labor or giving relief to one in need. Help also means making it easier for something to happen or develop. Helping behavior includes any behavior which is an attempt to ameliorate distress in another (e.g., rescuing, removing cause of distress, defending) or which facilitates another's work or play activity (e.g., sharing materials, giving information). Motivation for such behavior might be selfish, and instituted for personal gain, or altruistic.

Naturalistic studies of helping behavior have made the distinction between helping with a task (task help) and helping with another's distressed feelings (psychological help). Whiting and Pope's (1973) cross-cultural study of preschool and elementary school children distinguished between "offering help" (food, toys, tools, one's labor) and "offering emotional support" (giving consolation, encouragement, physical comfort, or reassurance). Severy and Davis (1971), using teacher ratings and direct observation measures of the helping behavior of preschool and elementary school retarded and normal children, factor analyzed their measures of helping behavior. Two factors were labeled *task-helping*— "task-helping" and "opportunity to help with a task"; two others were labeled *psychological helping*—"showing concern" and "comforting and reassuring." Hartup and Keller (1960) also studied the giving of comfort, reassurance, affection, praise, or help in preschool children but called these *nurturant* behaviors.

It is also important to note the use of the related term *altruism*. Yarrow, Scott, and

Waxler (1973) point out that altruistic behavior is not specific but includes helping, sharing, defending, rescuing, sympathizing, and other behaviors, all characterized by unselfish motives. (The laboratory setting was created to minimize the possibility of gains for the child.) Staub (1971a) studied children's responses to audiotaped cries of distress coming from another room. Explicit rules permitting helping responses led to greater altruistic behavior than the absence of such rules. Friedrich and Stein (1975) evaluated children's responses to a ripped greeting card supposedly made by a child who earlier had failed in the card's construction. Exposure to prosocial models plus training resulted in optimal learning of helping behavior of this kind.

Potential Advantages of Helping

Helping behavior in children and adults has received considerable interest in the last six years (Bryan 1975; Bryan and London 1970; Rushton 1976), but the potential advantages of encouraging helping behavior in young children have yet to be examined. What might children learn from helping others or from being helped by others? What significance might helping have for children, the classroom, or even society?

A personal benefit to the child who helps others would be the sense of competence in assisting others. White (1960) and others have referred to a key motivational disposition which is central to psychologically healthy development. "Effectance motivation" is the desire to feel potent and competent in dealing with one's physical and

Robert F. Marcus, Ph.D., is Assistant Professor, Institute for Child Study/Department of Human Development, University of Maryland, College Park. He is a former school psychologist.

Marion B. Leiserson, M.Ed., is Lecturer, The College of Home Economics, University of Iowa, Iowa City. She is a former nursery school teacher and director.

social worlds. Ideally, children become increasingly able to meet their own needs and to change those aspects of their world that are dissatisfying. This is in contrast to the child who feels that whatever he or she touches leads to disaster and who is a passive (reactive) agent in his or her own development. The isolate, for example, has little chance to feel effectance in dealing with people and fails to reap the motivational benefits of working cooperatively with others.

Children who do not help also have no chance to gauge the needs of others for help. Sensitivity to the "need for help" cues others give is probably an outcome of the shift from an egocentric concern for one's own needs and perceptions to a sociocentric concern for others' needs. The beginnings of friendships may entail a reciprocal trading of help, and one would find it difficult to imagine a lasting friendship that is not characterized by such mutuality. Helping may be perceived by friends as a reliable alliance in times of stress and as a sign of affection.

There are also advantages in learning to receive help from others. It is likely that every child will meet situations in which he or she needs comfort or support or help with a task. The child or adult who is unwilling or unable to accept help from others is likely to suffer needlessly, or to cause suffering in those people who are close. Coping with life's stresses is made easier when others lend a hand.

Encouragement of helping behavior may also mean gains for the classroom and the society as a whole. Our society has a history in which both help in times of distress and rugged individualism have been valued. Neighbors often responded to a misfortune such as a barn burning down by helping raise a new one, but otherwise neighbors did not wish to intrude on one another's independence. Lately there has been concern about bystanders not responding in emergencies, such as in the Kitty Genovese murder in New York City. Have we gone

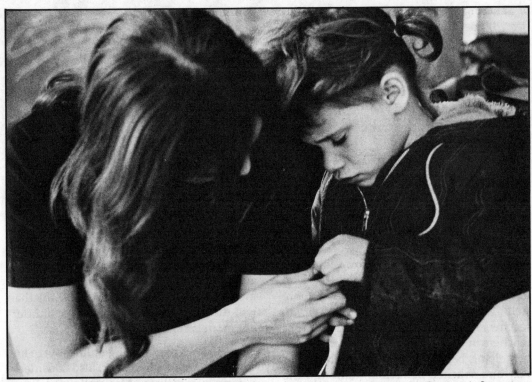

Having been given to, children become able to give.

too far in the direction of independence and noninterference? When responsibility is evaded, the result may be the mushrooming of violence and, possibly, moral decay within the society.

The benefits to the classroom as a mini-society are at least twofold. The kind of atmosphere that is likely to arise from greater helping behavior is likely to be friendlier and more supportive. The relationship between classroom achievement and a positive (e.g., warm, helping) classroom climate has been demonstrated (Gazda et al. 1973). There are also a number of classroom chores such as cleanup and setting tables for snacktime that become more manageable if children "pitch in."

Research on Helping and Altruistic Behavior

Studies on helping and altruistic behavior have focused upon laboratory methods, almost to the exclusion of direct naturalistic observation (Bryan 1975; Rushton 1976). Bryan concludes that "confidence in the relevance of laboratory findings to other settings remains a matter of faith" (p. 142). Laboratory methods usually attempt to isolate highly specific influences over helping or altruistic behavior, and the children do not have a chance to interact with the recipient of the assist, who is a stranger. Measures of altruistic behavior are often those we are unlikely to see in the classroom, thus adding to the artificiality of the findings of laboratory experimentation.

Rushton (1976) has presented a detailed examination of correlations between different kinds of altruistic behaviors in the laboratory and between laboratory behavior and observations in natural settings. Generally, he found that correlations between various laboratory tasks of altruistic behavior correlated about .30. Only one study by Yarrow and Waxler (1976) calculated correlations between laboratory tests of sharing and comforting to naturalistic measures of sharing and comforting combined (r=.29). Because such findings have not clearly shown the relationships between laboratory and naturalistic behaviors, experimental studies should be viewed only as suggestive of forces promoting altruism and helping behavior.

Naturalistic Studies of Helping Behavior

A recent study by Marcus (1977) on task and psychological helping behavior of 19 preschool children over a period of two months found that helping behavior is reciprocated. The correlation between the total help given and received by each child was .80, indicating that those children who gave more help tended to receive more help. Children who gave more help to teachers tended to receive more help from teachers in return (r=.57). These measures of helping behavior included both voluntary and solicited behaviors, although the former were far more numerous. When directed help was examined alone, the correlation between directed help given and received was .00. This suggests that children who give help to others without being asked are more likely to have their behavior reciprocated.

The children in the above study were also given a test of sociometric status. Children who received greater psychological help from others and who received a greater amount of help solicited by them or by others for them were found to be less popular. This confirmed earlier research by McCandless, Bilous, and Bennett (1961), in which low sociometric-status children showed greater emotional dependency than higher status children, and Moore and Updegraff's (1964) finding of a negative correlation between sociometric status and the amount of affection and support-seeking directed toward adults. Children who are frequently in need of emotional support and who must have help solicited for them are likely to be regarded negatively by other children.

Modeling Effects

The effects of models as they influence the aggressive and prosocial behaviors of young children have a lengthy history of theoretical formulation and subsequent research (Bandura 1969; Bryan 1975). Children will initiate acts of rescue of another child in distress (Staub 1971b), and will donate money to a charity (Schwartz and Bryan 1971) when these behaviors have been modeled for them. The effects of modeling were enhanced when the models made it clear to children that their intent was to donate to a charity (Grusec 1972). More nurturant or warm models are likely to be more potent influences upon children and will more likely lead children to show more rescue behavior (Staub 1971b) than will the same behavior by cold or indifferent models.

A number of modeling studies were limited to charitable behavior, also considered a form of altruism. Midlarsky and Bryan (1972) found that models who showed pleasure right after donating to a charity or right after performing a selfish act led children to donate a lot or a little to the charity, depending upon which modeled behavior they saw highlighted with delight. Presbie and Coiteux (1971) found that first grade children were more likely to imitate either selfish or generous behavior when the models praised themselves following the action *or* when the experimenter praised the models.

Research on children's behavior has also focused upon a pervasive source of modeling influences—televised models. An earlier interest in the effects of televised violent models upon children's behavior has given way to a more positive concern for the constructive influences television might have upon children (Stein and Friedrich 1975). A series of studies of the effects of viewing episodes of the "Mr. Rogers' Neighborhood" program on the child's learning of such behaviors as sensitivity to others' feelings, helping, cooperation, etc., have shown that such televised models do have an impact upon young children.

Friedrich and Stein (1973) found that showing sequences of programs to pre-school children resulted in an increase in prosocial behavior in the classroom for lower socioeconomic status (SES) children. They also found that kindergarten children who saw four episodes of "Mr. Rogers' Neighborhood" learned several prosocial lessons, including the importance of "helping a friend" (1975). Review of the television stories afterwards, hearing the stories read aloud, or seeing puppets act out the drama also enhanced the children's prosocial learnings. Shirley (1974) found that middle SES children did not increase in cooperation and helping behaviors after viewing such programs but did increase their sharing behavior.

Classroom Climate

Schmuch and Schmuch (1975) state that "even the most casual observer of schools can perceive the difference in feeling tones of different classrooms. Some are quiet, formal, and tense while others are pleasant, active, and exciting" (p. 23). Although the definition of a positive or negative classroom climate has been somewhat abstract and vague, the authors indicate that a positive classroom climate is one in which (1) students expect one another to do their best and support one another; (2) teacher and students share influence over one another; (3) norms support work activity and acceptance of individual differences; (4) communication is open and not one-way; (5) there is a high level of liking for the group and for one another; and (6) the group examines methods of working together in more satisfying ways (p. 24).

Teachers are an important force in shaping the classroom climate because they model helping behaviors, help curb aggressive behaviors, and provide a warm and secure environment in which children can learn prosocial behavior.

Yarrow, Scott, and Waxler (1973) conducted an experimental study of teacher warmth as related to children's learning of concern for others. The study involved 104 preschool children who were taught by either a nurturant or a nonnurturant adult to respond altruistically to pictures, miniature models, and real life distress situations involving the experimenter. Half the adults were trained to be nurturant (defined as initiating friendly interaction, offering help and support freely, giving sympathy and protection, expressing confidence in the child's abilities, giving praise frequently, and responding to the child's bids for attention). The other half of the adults were trained to be nonnurturant (defined as maintaining a reserved attitude, disregarding or critically evaluating the child's approaches or achievements, giving many directives, maintaining an aloof supervisory role, and not becoming involved in the child's play). The adults taught the children to be altruistic by illustrating awareness of distress, showing sympathy for and giving help to the victim, and showing their personal pleasure in the comfort and relief that resulted from the help. Half the children were trained by using the miniature toy dolls while the other half were trained using the dolls, pictured distress situations, and real life behavioral incidents. Both experimental groups gave more help to the miniature dolls and expressed more sympathy for the victim than did the control group children. The experimental group receiving all three treatments did show more concern for the pictured distresses and gave more helping responses to "real life" distress events *only* if they had been trained by a nurturant adult!

Staub (1975) cites four reasons why parental nurturance has been found to be related to the development of prosocial behavior:

- Nurturance makes a child feel comfortable and secure and is likely to reduce his self-concern. As a result he may be more willing to initiate action when someone needs help;

53

- Nurturance is likely to create a positive inclination toward other people. Someone who has had affectionate, warm relationships with others is likely to help people more;

- Nurturance may improve learning because of the positive emotional involvement it produces . . . tension, fear and anxiety . . . interfere with learning;

- Parental nurturance has long been regarded as an important source of identification with parents, of wanting to be like the parents. . . . If a parent himself behaves prosocially, children may be more likely to imitate that behavior if they identify with the parent. (p. 3-4)

Prosocial learning within the classroom is surely related similarly to teacher nurturance.

White and Lippitt's study (1960) of the effects of three styles of adult leadership (autocratic, laissez-faire, and democratic) on groups of preadolescent boys indicated that the classroom climate was markedly different in each. Autocratic leadership was related to high competitiveness, hostility, and dependence upon the teacher; while democratic leadership was related to openness, friendly communication, and independence. Rutherford and Mussen (1968) found that nursery school boys who were highly competitive in a "racing game" were less likely to share with their friends than the less competitive boys. Finally, Henry (1953) vividly describes the attitude organization of some elementary school classrooms in which the teacher had set child against child by profusely criticizing their ideas and encouraging students to criticize one another. Scapegoating and extreme competition for the teacher's approval limited the amount of helping within the classroom.

Role Playing

Piaget's conception (1932) of a shift from egocentrism to a reciprocal perspective during the elementary school years suggests that prosocial behavior would rely on the child's perception of the needs of another. Opportunity to play the role of another (to be both the recipient and giver of help) has been suggested as a means of heightening the perception of others' needs, if not actually leading to a developmental shift.

Staub (1971b), using role playing situations in which children played both helper and helpee, trained children under six years of age to show a number of helping behaviors. This training led children to demonstrate greater altruism in similar situations.

Friedrich and Stein (1975), in a study mentioned earlier using films of "Mr. Rogers' Neighborhood" with young children, required some children to reenact the show's prosocial content in puppet play or in reading stories about the shows. Particularly for boys, the puppet role play episodes heightened the learning of such behavior.

Planning the Learning Environment

Helping can be taught as a central factor in living, and teachers should be aware of ways to encourage such behaviors in the school environment. In setting the stage for helping behaviors, the teacher needs to consider the following factors: classroom climate, structure, and activities and materials.

Classroom Climate and Modeling

The teacher serves as a model for altruism in helping children both verbally and nonverbally. By expressing the need for cooperation and by behaving in ways that help children feel warmth and affection, the teacher sets the atmosphere for helping behaviors. In an environment where helping behaviors are encouraged, the teacher—

1. Establishes rapport by communicating nonverbally with a smile, an arm around a shoulder, or by holding a

By expressing the need for co-operation and behaving in ways that help children feel warmth and affection, the teacher sets the atmosphere for helping behaviors to occur.

Lynne Bruna

child. When communicating verbally, the teacher stoops or bends down to talk at eye level. The teacher extends a hand to a child who is a little hesitant about joining a game.

2. Helps each child feel a sense of belonging by singing songs and playing games to learn everyone's name.
   "Let's sing about Davy's brown pants."
   "Who is wearing the blue and red striped shirt?"

3. Helps children understand routines and expectations so they feel secure.
   "After snack time we will get ready to go outdoors."
   "When you are finished with your picture, it is time to go to the rug for a story."

4. Acknowledges children when they give comfort to another.
   "That was thoughtful of you to bring Mary inside when she hurt her hand."
   "Thank you for helping Tony with his boot. It's easier when someone helps pull it."

Nonverbally the teacher smiles as Elena helps Nicky zip her jacket.

5. Interprets a child's feeling and tries to clarify a child's intent so that children can receive help.
   "Chris has his arm around you because he thinks it makes you happy."
   "Tina was trying to help you read the chart. When she put her arm on your back, she was trying to help you get closer."

6. Expresses positive encouragement of independence as well as helping after having assisted a child several times.
   "I think you are able to put your coat on by yourself today."
   "Scott, you were able to put your coat on today without anyone's help! It must make you feel happy."

7. Notices when a child needs to limit the amount of time spent in helping peers or the teacher.
   "I'll take care of washing off these tables. Perhaps you'd like to play

in the fire station with Tom."
"You helped Debbie with the puzzle. Now you can choose something you want to do."

8. Clarifies ideas about similarities and differences in skin color, ethnic background, family customs, and values to increase children's tolerance for differences.
   "Andrei's skin is darker than yours, but you both have brown eyes."
   "Rina's mother is helping to make some Baratha. It's a kind of bread she learned to make when she was growing up in India."

9. Suggests and encourages ways for children to help each other.
   "If you hold one end of the table, it will be easier to carry."
   "If you help Dwayne carry the plank, he can finish the roof on his house."

10. Praises a child who helps, or comments when a child praises him- or herself.
    The child might say with delight: "I helped Alicia with her picture and it was fun!"
    The teacher reinforces:
    "I'm glad you seemed to enjoy helping her."

11. Praises self when help has been offered to provide a model.
    "I'm glad I helped you carry the rocking boat. It's too heavy for one person to move."

12. Helps children with difficult tasks.
    Teacher helps a child tie a shoe which has become untied.

Classroom Structure

Structure refers to the way the teacher sets the stage for learning through a variety of experiences. The experiences are extended and enriched by making comments, asking questions, or listening, and are adapted to what is known about children's growth and development. The teacher needs to make expectations clear and is ready to prohibit, redirect, and talk with children about unacceptable behavior. Some programs give directed guidance with set plans and rules. In others, children are encouraged to make decisions about whom they want to work or play with or what materials they want to use. Rules are formulated as awareness grows about how certain behaviors affect others, or they are formulated in regard to safety. Within the structure of the classroom, some interactions become routines and the teacher—

1. Allows children to have opportunities to set tables for snacks and pass out food.
   "Bobby's name is on the chart today to set the tables, and Jenny is going to pass the crackers."

2. Authorizes ways for children to be responsible for putting away toys and materials.
   "It's time to clean up now. You and Kelly may carry the paste to the shelf while I put away the paper."

3. Asks the children to help give directions to others.
   "Will you please tell Karen and Ann that it's time to go indoors now."

4. Provides play areas in the room where small groups can work together. As children interact, the teacher suggests ways to help each other.
   "Margery wants to help with the block building. Can you show her a place where she can build?"
   "Steven wants to be in the restaurant. Can you help him find a way to be a cook?"

The teacher may approach some of these routines in the following ways to encourage helping: The teacher—

5. Implies ways children can help by suggestions and questions.

> "Amy's painting drips when she tries to carry it alone. Can you find a way to help her get it to the drying rack?"

> "Alan had trouble climbing on the tower outside. If you had been near him, what would you have done to help him?"

6. Encourages children to play and interact with each other.

> "When you were playing your ball game, you were helping each other. I saw Shawn throw the ball to Kevin so that he could run to the fence."

> "The table is easier to carry when several people help."

7. Deals with behavior regarding its effect on other people and safety.

> "It isn't safe to climb on the wall. Can you help remind Michael, too?"

> "You told Rhonda you didn't like it when she hit you. We need to help John understand that it hurts when he kicks."

8. Reinforces helping with comments about successful cooperation.

> "All your ideas have helped make the plans for the party."

> "Our room is ready now for the children this afternoon. They appreciate it when you put materials away so that they can find them."

Classroom Activities and Materials

A school environment has different areas of interest where children can work and play together and use a wide variety of materials. The teacher plans what materials will be used and invites children to try the materials. Helping can be encouraged as children work on block structures, use the dramatic play area, cook together, work with manipulative materials, saw and hammer at the workbench, and use an assortment of art materials. Outdoors, children can be urged to help each other develop skills in throwing balls, climbing, and following directions for simple games. The teacher observes and waits to see if children help each other before stepping in with a comment about helping. When personal interchanges are allowed and encouraged among individuals and the teacher is consistently helping children feel like capable human beings, both the teacher and children are able to reach out and assist one another. Some activities and materials to encourage helping are—

1. Reading and telling stories about helping and pointing out situations when help occurred.

> After reading the book, *Mike's House*, the teacher might ask, "How did the police officer help Robert during the blizzard?"

2. Making up songs about helping, using familiar tunes. The teacher might begin by singing, "Old MacDonald helped a boy walk across the street," then asks, "What could Old MacDonald help someone else do?"

3. Using puppets to act out situations where help is needed.

> "My puppet is trying to climb down from the jungle gym and can't get down. What could your puppet do to rescue my puppet?"

4. Acting out situations through creative dramatics.

> "It's hot in here today, and I can't open the window because it's stuck. Can you show me a way to help open it?"

5. Dictating stories to the class or teacher about someone who has helped.

> "Let me write down the story about how you helped your Daddy."

6. Drawing pictures and dictating a story to a classmate who is ill.

"Carol has been ill with tonsillitis. What do you think we should say in our letter to her?"

7. Baking a cake to celebrate a child's birthday.

"I'm glad we helped make Eric's birthday cake. He is four years old today."

Conclusion

Many questions remain for both researchers and practitioners regarding the development of helping behavior in young children.

- What is the role of helping activity, of helping and being helped in the overall emotional development and health of the child?

- Are competitive and prosocial behaviors incompatible with one another, or because they are both traditions within our society, can children learn to behave in both ways when each is appropriate?

- What is the role of peer helping in the cognitive development and academic learning of the child?

- What are the roles of helping and being helped in the forming of friendships and in the maintenance of friendship relationships in early childhood?

References

Bandura, A. "Social Learning Theory of Identificatory Processes." In *Handbook of Socialization Theory and Research*, edited by D. A. Goslin. Chicago: Rand McNally, 1969.

Berkowitz, L., and Daniels, L. "Affecting the Salience of the Social Responsibility Norm: Effects of Past Help on the Response to Dependency Relationships." *Journal of Personality and Social Psychology* 68 (1964): 275-281.

Bryan, J. H. "Children's Cooperation and Helping Behaviors." *Review of Child Development Research* 5 (1975).

Bryan, J. H., and London, P. "Altruistic Behavior by Children." *Psychological Bulletin* 73 (1970): 200-211.

Friedrich, L. K., and Stein, A. H. "Aggressive and Prosocial Television Programs and the Natural Behavior of Preschool Children." *Monographs of the Society for Research in Child Development* 38 (1973): 1-64.

Friedrich, L. K., and Stein, A. H. "Prosocial Television and Young Children: The Effects of Verbal Labeling and Role Playing on Learning and Behavior." *Child Development* 46 (1975): 27-38.

Gazda, G.; Asbury, F.; Balzu, F.; Childers, W. C.; Dessille, W.; and Walters, R. "A General Review of Related Research Literature." In *Human Relations Development: A Manual for Educators*. Boston: Allyn and Bacon, 1973.

Grusec, J. E. "Demand Characteristics of the Modeling Experiment: Altruism as a Function of Age and Aggression." *Journal of Personality and Social Psychology* 22 (1972): 139-148.

Hartup, W. W., and Keller, E. D. "Nurturance in Preschool Children and Its Relation to Dependency." *Child Development* 31 (1960): 681-690.

Henry, J. "Attitude Organization in Elementary School Classrooms." *American Journal of Orthopsychiatry* 27 (1953): 117-133.

Marcus, R. F. "A Naturalistic Study of Reciprocity in the Helping Behavior of Young Children." Paper presented at the Society for Research in Child Development biennial meeting, New Orleans, March 1977.

McCandless, B. R.; Bilous, O. B.; and Bennett, H. F. "Peer Popularity and Dependence on Adults in Preschool-Age Socialization." *Child Development* 32 (1961): 511-518.

Midlarsky, E., and Bryan, J. H. "Affect Expressions and Children's Imitative Altruism." *Journal of Experimental Research in Personality* 6 (1972): 195-203.

Moore, S. G., and Updegraff, R. "Sociometric Status of Preschool Children Related to Age, Sex, Nurturance-Giving, and Dependency." *Child Development* 35 (1964): 519-524.

Piaget, J. *The Moral Judgment of the Child*. New York: Harcourt, Brace, and World, 1932.

Presbie, R. J., and Coiteux, P. F. "Learning to Be Generous or Stingy: Imitation of Sharing Behavior as a Function of Model Generosity and Vicarious Reinforcement." *Child Development* 42 (1971): 1033-1038.

Rushton, J. P. "Socialization and the Altruistic Behavior of Children." *Psychological Bulletin* 83 (1976): 898-913.

Rutherford, E., and Mussen, P. "Generosity in Nursery School Boys." *Child Development* 39 (1968): 755-765.

Schmuch, R. A., and Schmuch, P. A. *Group Processes in the Classroom*. 2nd ed. Dubuque, Iowa: William C. Brown, 1975.

Schwartz, F., and Bryan, J. H. "Imitative Altruism by Deaf Children." *Journal of Speech and Hearing Research* 14 (1971): 453-461.

Severy, F. J., and Davis, K. E. "Helping Behavior among Normal and Retarded Children." *Child Development* 42 (1971): 1017-1031.

Shirley, K. W. "The Prosocial Effects of Publicly Broadcast Children's Television." Doctoral dissertation, University of Kansas, 1974.

Staub, E. "Helping a Person in Distress: The Influence of Implicit and Explicit 'Rules' of Conduct on Children and Adults." *Journal of Personality and Social Psychology* 17 (1971a): 137-144.

Staub, E. "Child in Distress: The Influence of Modeling and Nurturance on Children's Attempts to Help." *Developmental Psychology* 5 (1971b): 124-133.

Staub, E. "The Use of Role Playing and Induc-tion in Children's Learning of Helping and Sharing Behavior." *Child Development* 42 (1971c): 805-817.

Staub, E. *The Development of Prosocial Behavior*. Morristown, N.J.: Silver Burdett, 1975.

Stein, A. H., and Friedrich, L. K. "Impact of Television on Children and Youth." *Review of Child Development Research* 5 (1975).

White, R. W. "Competence and the Psychosexual Stages of Development." *Nebraska Symposium on Motivation*. Lincoln, Nebr.: University of Nebraska Press, 1960.

White, R., and Lippitt, R. *Autocracy and Democracy*. New York: Harper & Row, 1960.

Whiting, B., and Pope, C. "A Cross-Cultural Analysis of Sex Differences in the Behavior of Children Aged Three to Eleven." *Journal of Social Psychology* 91 (1973): 171-188.

Yarrow, M. R.; Scott, P. M.; and Waxler, C. Z. "Learning Concern for Others." *Developmental Psychology* 8 (1973): 240-260.

Yarrow, M. R., and Waxler, C. Z. "Dimensions and Correlates of Prosocial Behavior in Young Children." *Child Development* 47 (1976): 118-125.

Charles A. Smith and Duane E. Davis

Teaching Children Non-Sense

Crazymaking (Bach and Wyden 1968; Bach and Goldberg 1974; Wahlroos 1974) refers to a variety of communication styles utilized by one individual to inhibit another person's rational understanding of reality. The victims of crazymaking become confused and uncertain of their own experiences because of distorted feedback; they begin to doubt and mistrust their own perception of what the world is like and eventually develop *non*-sense, the inability to recognize and deal with personal and interpersonal reality.

Crazymaking and Reality Construction

Rather than being born with an understanding of how the world operates, children must experience and construct reality as they interact with their environment. One aspect of mastering reality involves learning about the nature of **things** ("What is that?"). For example, children learn that certain animals at certain times are dangerous, and that some objects will break when dropped.

This article is based on a keynote address by Charles A. Smith at the Minnesota AEYC Conference, October 1975, in Minneapolis.

Another important aspect of reality construction involves learning about **people** ("Who are they? How are we going to relate to each other?"). For example, children learn that people have different values and generally prefer to be treated with gentleness. This particular process of growth involves a movement from egocentric to sociocentric thinking (Piaget 1965).

A third important goal involves getting in touch with **personal** reality ("Who and what am I?"). For example, children learn that they have emotions, that they experience pain, that their blood will not "leak" out if they have a cut, that they have a name and belong to a family, etc.

Learning about reality depends on feedback from **things** (e.g., the child observes a glass breaking) and **people** (e.g., the child hears another say, *"I do not* like to be hit!"). This feedback can be either supportive or distortive. **Supportive** feedback is a clear,

Steve Herzog

accurate, rational representation of reality. **Distortive** feedback, however, is a confusing, inaccurate, and irrational misrepresentation of what is real. **Crazymakers** are distortive forms of feedback from people.

The basic and necessary ingredients in a crazymaking relationship (Bach and Goldberg 1974) include:

1. An emotional dependency and vulnerability of at least one person in the relationship;
2. An unequal power balance;
3. A socially traditional role relationship which provides the opportunity for crazymaking to be masked by "good" intentions;
4. Resentment, hostility, and/or alienation within the controlling person who is generally unaware of his or her unreasonable behavior.

Each of these factors are especially relevant and lethal in parent-child and teacher-child relationships. Adults may exploit a child's natural dependence and need to be wanted and accepted; they may also deny a child the opportunity to confront the irrational behavior. In moments of thoughtlessness, though, most of us can be guilty of crazymaking in various forms and degrees toward children whose lives we touch. Nevertheless, if crazymaking communication is a pervasive norm in their lives, some children will withdraw from or distort a confusing reality and develop severe emotional problems.

Children depend on adults to help clarify and reaffirm their experiences with the world. Unfortunately, this sensitive awareness of self and others is easily sabotaged by adults who frequently seem determined

Charles A. Smith, Ph.D., is Assistant Professor and Director of the Child Development Center, Texas Tech University, Lubbock, Texas, and a former teacher of four-year-olds.

Duane E. Davis, M.A., is an elementary teacher in the Northern St. Paul-Maplewood, Minnesota, Public Schools and a former elementary counselor.

to peddle a phony image of reality to willing and receptive young minds. We must stop this destructive response by becoming more aware of our own crazymaking habits and by investing the time and effort to help children develop a more rational understanding of reality.

Types of Crazymakers

The following list identifies the types of responses that prevent children from constructing an accurate understanding of reality. Although some of these forms of communication may resemble each other, each type of crazymaker illuminates a different aspect of irrational communication. Also, the amount of confusion experienced by victims may vary somewhat from one crazymaker to another.

Disconfirming (discounting). Confirmation is a process through which individuals are recognized, acknowledged, or "endorsed" by others. A response to another that is relevant to the other's needs "confirms" the other and supports that person's feeling of being OK (Laing 1961). Disconfirming, however, ignores the needs and wishes of others by "putting down" or discounting their feelings or thoughts. Disconfirming also includes *conditional* acceptance: "I will like, love, or accept you only if you. . . ."

Example: An excited preschooler runs to his teacher to show her a worm he has found.

Boy: "Teacher, look at this fat worm I found!"
Teacher: "It's time for a snack and you're dirty. Go wash your hands."

Example: After a rather hectic ordeal to get the children seated for music time, the teacher positions himself near a record player and holds up two records he was planning to play.

61

Teacher: "Would you like to hear these records during rest today?"

Children: (Most do not respond, but a few say "No.")

Teacher: (With a broad smile on his face) "Okay, I think you'll like them." (Proceeds to play the records.)

Mind Threatening. One of the most frightening experiences a child can have is to be threatened with bizarre, senseless consequences by an adult. Unreal threats are especially mystifying because of the child's limited understanding of reality and readiness to believe everything a controlling adult says.

Example: A young girl who had been rather troublesome at bedtime was told by her parents that if she didn't behave ". . . the boogeyman is going to come and get you during the night." The child responded by quieting down and going to her room without protest. Recently, however, she has been troubled by nightmares and bed-wetting.

Example: The father of a four-year-old boy recently responded to his son's fighting with a younger brother with the statement: "If you don't stop hitting your brother, I'm going to beat your head in!" Although the fighting stopped, the little boy developed a fear of his father, expressed both by nightmares of being hurt and an actual withdrawal from him.

Young children do not disregard what the adult says as exaggerations. "What *is*

this 'boogeyman'? What is he going to do to me? Would father really beat my head in? Will he hurt me in other ways too?" Although adults readily understand the real intent behind these statements, mind threats are no laughing matter to children.

Strategic Failing. This crazymaker involves two necessary features or strategies: The controlling adult *demands* that the child do something he or she is not capable of doing and then *punishes* the child for failing to successfully complete the task. The child is in a total "no win" situation.

Example: After reading "How to potty-train your child in five days" in a popular magazine, mother initiated a rather structured toilet training schedule for her ten-month-old. The child is confused about her mother's intentions and expectations and is biologically unable to gain necessary control over the muscles involved. Recently the mother has been scolding her daughter for having wet diapers.

Example: Four-year-old Billy is attending his sister's wedding ceremony. He has experienced a structured morning and, feeling both anxious and excited about the event, he begins to fidget. Father demands that ". . . he behave himself." After a brief period of nonactivity, the little boy begins to squirm again. The father gives him a sharp slap.

Masking. Masking (Lidz et al. 1958) is an attempt by a controlling person to conceal some disturbing situation within the group by acting as though a problem did not exist.

The individual who resorts to this crazy-maker relies on intimidation and uncertainty to enlist the cooperation of group members in ignoring or masking the obvious. Out of an ill-conceived desire to be "protective" the masking adult will sometimes overlook the child's need to understand what is happening. As with the other crazymakers, children begin to doubt the trustworthiness of their own perceptions.

> *Example:* One child in a preschool group has an obvious physical disfigurement. Several of the children seem curious, while others are somewhat frightened regarding the physical problem. The teacher firmly avoids discussing or dealing with the matter out of a misguided concern for ". . . hurting the poor child's feelings."

> *Example:* Ann has returned to school after the recent death of her father.
>
> Child: "Teacher, Ann is crying."
> Teacher: "Don't worry. I'm sure everything is OK; go back and play now."

Mixing Messages. A person who denies a feeling which others can clearly observe is communicating a mixed message. The victims are lured into a trap (Briggs 1970) involving two messages: one based on what the other *says* (e.g., "I'm *not* angry.") and another which contradicts the first in terms of *tone* or *body language* (e.g., loud voice, clenched fist). Mixing messages is a result of believing that an underlying feeling is unacceptable and that admitting or acknowledging the feeling will have dangerous consequences. Yet feelings are very difficult to hide from others. Children, for example, may be very aware of their teacher's anger despite any attempts to appear cool and calm.

If they accept the adult's false front as reality, children may distrust their own real experiences. Children may also substitute their own personal concerns to reduce their confusion. For example, they may conclude that their teacher is angry with them for something they did (which may not actually be the case). Mixing messages creates a climate of masks that teach distrust.

> *Example:* A child approaches a teacher who is obviously very sad, almost to the point of crying.
>
> Child: "Teacher, why are you so sad?"
> Teacher: "What? Oh, I'm not sad. I feel fine."

> *Example:* A four-year-old boy has thrown his lunch on the floor during a heated conversation with another child. The teacher (who has had a bad day) removes the child from the table. As she carries him to the office, she smiles and says rather sweetly, "Now Chad, you know you're not supposed to do that." But the teacher's tight grip, abrupt handling, and clenched teeth convey something else. After being seated, Chad asks, "Mrs. Brown, why do you hate me?" Mrs. Brown responds, "Why honey, you know that isn't so."

Double Binding. This crazymaker subjects others to incongruent or conflicting demands. Victims are doomed to rejection because they are in a "no win" situation. If one command is obeyed, then another is disobeyed. Double binding differs from mixing messages in that the double bind involves conflicting *commands*. The necessary ingredients of a double bind (Watzlawick et al. 1967; Bateson et al. 1963) are:

Sandy Felsenthal

Example: A child is feeling hostile toward the teacher. The teacher approaches and the following exchange occurs.

Teacher: "What's wrong? Tell me how you feel." (Command 1)

Child: "You are a bum teacher."

Teacher: "Now you shouldn't say things like that." (Incongruent command 2)

Faced with this type of bind, the child may escape the teacher's anger only by becoming skillful in hiding true feelings. But then again, the teacher might show disappointment in the child's unwillingness to reveal those feelings.

Example: It is late in the school year, and the teacher has just told the children he would like to have them take more responsibility in caring for things in the classroom, since they are now big enough to help him. Later that day, Ann sees an opportunity to be helpful by watering the plants. As she starts to water the first plant, the teacher rushes over and says, "Oh, no! I'll do that. It's too difficult for you." It becomes quickly apparent that the teacher is unwilling to allow any significant responsibilities for the children. Because the teacher was not specific about the things the children could help him with, Ann becomes very confused. She may feel she is in trouble if she helps and in trouble if she doesn't help.

1. Two or more persons are involved in an intense relationship with a high degree of physical and/or psychological value for one or more of them.

2. The less powerful individual is confronted with two incongruent directives. For example: "I order you to disobey me." Negative commands can be expressed through action or be implicit in the situation of interaction as well as being directly expressed through words. Punishment is expected regardless of the response.

3. A third injunction or demand is also present that prevents the victim from escaping the interaction.

The double bind is particularly disruptive if it occurs frequently with children.

Guiltmaking (scapegoating). In this crazymaker one person is blamed for the personal problems, concerns, or "hang-ups" of another. Individuals who scapegoat may select another person to be the recipient of their own negative dealings toward themselves. Instead of assuming responsibility for their own weaknesses, they may project their problem onto another, blaming others for their own destructive or ineffective behavior. The victim then develops an exaggerated and destructive sense of his or her impact on others, generating a fear of self-expression (Bach and Goldberg 1974). Scapegoaters thus create the illusion that they are actually the victims.

Example: A young child approaches the teacher and asks for some glue for an art project. The teacher, who has just finished a rather bitter fight with another teacher, ignores the request. The child continues to ask for the glue. Finally, the teacher explodes in a rather hostile outburst.

Teacher: "No glue! Stop bugging me!"

Child: (Cries)

Teacher: "See! Now you *made me* lose my temper!"

Example: A teacher is on a short walk through the neighborhood with a group of young children. One child has been particularly difficult for the teacher to handle.

Teacher: "All right, I guess we will all have to go back to the school. It seems as if some of us don't know how to behave ourselves on a walk."

Psyching-out (mind reading, jumping to conclusions). This crazymaker includes unrealistic and totally unfounded interpretations or predictions about the behavior of others. Psyching-out may also include accusing others of vicious or sinister motivations for their actions (Wahlroos 1974). Adults who are involved in psyching-out make the false assumption that they know what is going on in the other's mind.

Example

Child: "Dad, can we go to the fair this weekend?"

Father: "No, dear, it's so crowded you wouldn't like it."

Child: "I wouldn't? Oh, Dad, can we go anyway?"

Father: "No, *you know* the last time we went to the fair you just didn't like it!"

Child: "I didn't?"

Example: Child sadly walks into room.

Child: "Tommy (his older brother) got to go to grandma's. I didn't get to go."

Teacher: "I bet you're really angry with Tommy."

Example: Mother has repeatedly asked her toddler not to open a certain drawer. Despite her requests, the child continues to stand on her tiptoes to open the drawer.

Child: (Opens drawer)

Mother: (Frustrated) "Sally, why are you trying to get my goat?"

False Harmonizing. False harmonizing describes group relationships which are based on facade or pretense. In false harmonizing the emphasis is on presenting an image of satisfaction at the expense of allowing true feelings and needs to emerge in the relationship (Wynne et al. 1958). In contrast, genuine harmony and mutuality provide an opportunity for persons in the group to develop a sense of their own meaningful identity, which is also acknowledged by the others in the group. As growth and change occur, the group helps its members affirm their own sense of well-being. There is a recognition, exploration, and negotiation of differences and disagreements. For example, teachers can give children the opportunity to discuss classroom problems and identify potential solutions. Disagreement is seen as an opportunity to get to know and reach out to others. In false harmonizing all disagreements with the adult controller's definition of a happy group are actively if not openly discouraged.

> Example: A teacher talks about her class in glowing terms: "Oh, they're such a wonderful group. They don't give me any trouble." A visit to the class gives the initial impression that everyone is extremely well behaved. But everything is too right. There is an absence of spontaneity, novelty, humor, and zest as children move about. A weary sense of oppression hangs like a heavy blanket over the entire group. The classroom is physically enriched but emotionally stifled.

> Example: A teacher approaches a child who is getting rather loud in his play and says, "Now Jamie, WE always use our quiet voices when WE are in school." The response is both confusing and oppressive. Is the statement an accurate reflection of the child's reality? Not really. Jamie has observed this teacher yelling many times in the classroom. The teacher also creates the illusion of togetherness and

agreement by using the impersonal term "we."

Emotional Blackmailing. This crazy-maker is a form of benevolent violence where one person threatens another with the withdrawal of love, affection, or interest in order to manipulate the other's behavior. This tactic is especially threatening because it disrupts another's need for security in a relationship.

> Example: A child is continually disrupting the activities of the other children, and the teacher is feeling frustrated with her inability to handle the problem. Suddenly the child deliberately knocks down another child's block tower. The teacher forcefully removes the child from the situation and says, "If you keep on being nasty, I don't want you to come to school. I will send you home."

> Example: A child has been caught taking some candy from another child in the classroom.

> Teacher: "I am very ashamed of you because you stole this candy. People don't like little children who steal."

Bugging (interrogating). This crazy-maker (Egan 1970) refers to the use of the repeated and/or meaningless questioning of a person who is experiencing a problem. Questions are asked to show "interest": "How do you feel? When did it happen? What did you do?" This holds the victim as the center of attention and reduces the possibility of meaningful and potentially threatening conversation. Bugging or interrogating is often used in connection with preaching or lecturing and can be very irritating to others. Good questions can be very insightful and deeply supportive if they are sincere and lead to deeper involvement, but bugging ensures emotional distance and does not bring about a resolution of the problem.

> *Example:* Ken was hiding in a makeshift tent during snack period. The teacher peeked inside and said, "Looks like you don't want to eat lunch today." Ken responded with a rather "put-on" sarcastic tone, "All the teachers come up to me and say, 'What's the matter, Kenneth, what's the matter?'" Ken had been sitting in his tent all day because he felt sad that some special packages had not yet arrived by mail at home. After discussing the problem for a minute, his spirits brightened and he joined the rest of the children. Ken was disgusted with the well-intentioned but interrogating student teachers who were more concerned with identifying his motives than dealing with his current feelings. They probably would have been more successful if they had just sat quietly next to him.

> *Example:* Karen began crying as soon as she came into the classroom.
> Teacher: "Karen, what's wrong?"
> Karen: (No response)
> Teacher: "What happened? Did you get hurt?"
> Karen: "No."
> Teacher: "Did someone take something from you?"
> Karen: "No."
> Teacher: "Did something bad happen at home?"
> Karen: (No response)
> The teacher and Karen continue to play this interrogating game until one of the two becomes tired and walks away.

Shunning (nonengagement, emotional withdrawal). A shunning response involves the "cold-shoulder" treatment of silence, ignoring, sulking, or pouting. Probably one of the greatest needs of all humankind is to have one's existence and significance acknowledged by another person (Wahlroos 1974). To have other people act as though we did not exist can be the cruelest of all experiences. Children have an obvious need for recognition, especially from parents and teachers. Unfortunately, many children discover that the only way they can get attention is to misbehave.

> *Example:* A teacher has decided to ignore the disruptive behavior of a child. Regardless of what the child did, the teacher would turn away. Later in the day, the teacher finds color crayon marks all over the papers on his desk.

> *Example:* A kindergarten teacher has been avoiding a certain child. Whenever she is in the child's presence, she feels uncomfortably "turned off," and talks to the child only when necessary. The child initially made overtures of friendship to the teacher but has now given up after the repeated rebuffs. Recently the child has been complaining about stomachaches.

Thinging (childism, racism, sexism). This crazymaker is present in a dehumanized interpersonal relationship characterized by treatment of victims as if they were objects, commodities, or status symbols rather than persons with unique needs and special backgrounds. Overcrowded class-

rooms and bureaucratic management techniques make "thinging" a common experience for those involved in many school situations.

> *Example:* At the end of his first year in the public school, Paul was given an IQ test. Because of the low score, he was "held back." The new teacher was informed of the test results and later was overheard to remark that Paul was one of her "slow" children. Paul is confused when he learns that he will not be going to school with the rest of his friends.

Door Slamming (sidetracking, derailing). Door slamming involves shifting the focus during a problematic confrontation to prevent the resolution of a conflict (Bach and Goldberg 1974). The natural flow of energy being channeled into the encounter is disrupted, and the victim becomes confused and frustrated. Door slamming can

be the result if teachers try distraction at inappropriate moments.

> *Example:* During outside play, a toddler makes an attempt to climb up a slide for older children, but her teacher picks her up and carries her to another more suitable piece of equipment. The child gets up, however, and begins to run to the slide. The teacher then carries her to the sandbox and tries to interest her in digging. After a brief involvement, the child makes another attempt to go to the slide. This time she begins to cry when the teacher intercepts her.

In this case it was important for the teacher to try to communicate to the child the motives for her intervention. Without some explanation ("I cannot let you climb up this slide. Climbing this is dangerous."), the distraction does not make any sense to the child. As far as she is concerned the adult's behavior is bizarre and unreasonable.

The Prevention of Crazymaking

Since crazymakers are more likely to occur in relationships characterized by a power imbalance, as in child-adult interactions, one strategy for reducing their occurrence is for adults to share as much control as possible with children. Sharing control means the adult must be ready to deal with conflict in an open and forthright manner. Adults can strive to enable children to become decision makers rather than dependent and conforming automatons. On the other hand, they must also acknowledge the exact nature of the power structure in the relationship, since some decisions cannot be left to children and some rules must be appropriately enforced.

Crazymaking is also a potential in relationships where power imbalances are hidden and disguised behind the facades of equality (Bach and Goldberg 1974) and when one person assumes a complete understanding of what is going on in the mind of another person. Adults should recognize that children are people, individuals worthy of the same type of respect and consideration granted to any adult. Finally, crazymaking is a potential in relationships where individuals have unrealistic expectations toward others and for themselves (Smith 1974). Unreasonable self-demands (e.g., "Good teachers do not get angry with children.") immediately create an artificial relationship which will ultimately have to be maintained by crazymakers (e.g., "No! I'm NOT ANGRY!").

The most productive response to the discovery of our own crazymaking habits involves gentle self-acceptance combined with self-determined change. Certainly irrationality is not something to be admired. But true self-renewal will occur only if we recognize our inevitable destiny to be imperfect. We must not forget that, like the children we serve, we too are involved in a continual process of growing up. 🗗

References

Bach, G. R., and Goldberg, H. *Creative Aggression: The Art of Assertive Living*. New York: Avon Books, 1974.

Bach, G. R., and Wyden, P. *The Intimate Enemy: How to Fight Fair in Love and Marriage*. New York: Avon Books, 1968.

Bateson, G.; Jackson, D.; Haley, J.; and Weakland, J. "A Note on the Double-Bind—1962." *Family Process* 2 (1963): 34-51.

Briggs, D. C. *Your Child and His Self-Esteem*. Garden City, N.Y.: Doubleday, 1970.

Egan, G. *Encounter: Group Processes for Interpersonal Growth*. Belmont, Calif.: Brooks/Cole, 1970.

Laing, R. D. *The Politics of Experience*. New York: Ballantine Books, 1967.

Lidz, T.; Cornelison, A.; Carlson, D. T.; and Fleck, S. "Intrafamilial Environment of the Schizophrenic Patient: The Transmission of Irrationality." *Archives of Neurology and Psychiatry* 74, no. 3 (1958): 305-316.

Piaget, J. *The Moral Judgment of the Child*. New York: Free Press, 1965.

Smith, C. A. "Peopleteaching: A Personalized Approach to Teacher Education." In *Teacher Education*, edited by B. Spodek, pp. 35-44. Washington, D.C.: National Association for the Education of Young Children, 1974.

Vogel, E. F., and Bell, N. W. "The Emotionally Disturbed Child as the Family Scapegoat." In *The Psychosocial Interior of the Family*, edited by G. Handel, pp. 424-442. Chicago: Aldine, 1967.

Wahlroos, S. *Family Communication*. New York: Macmillan, 1974.

Watzlawick, P.; Beavin, J. H.; and Jackson, D. D. *Pragmatics of Human Communication*. New York: W. W. Norton, 1967.

Wynne, L. C.; Ryckoff, I. M.; Day, J.; and Hirsch, S. I. "Pseudomutuality in the Family Relations of Schizophrenics." *Psychiatry* 21 (1958): 205-220.

III. Language Arts in the Curriculum

Learning to read remains one of both parents' and teachers' foremost concerns. Articles in this section address the questions of when and how language arts skills are most appropriately included in the curriculum, beginning with a statement developed by several major educational associations.

Children's use and understanding of one or more languages opens the door to a more complete view of their world and enables them to communicate more meaningfully. Fostering good language must be an integral part of the total curriculum. Reading and telling stories, plus use of a wide variety of materials, experiences, and opportunities, will enable children to communicate not only what they know but also what they feel.

Language develops in an atmosphere where the language children bring to the school with them is accepted and respected, where children are allowed to experiment with words as well as with things, and where there are significant people who not only encourage language experiences but also who listen to what the child is communicating both verbally and nonverbally.

The following articles reinforce and expand these ideas and more.

Reading and Pre-First Grade

A Joint Statement of Concerns about Present Practices in Pre-First Grade Reading Instruction and Recommendations for Improvement

Pre-first graders need . . .

opportunities to express orally, graphically, and dramatically their feelings and responses to experiences.

opportunities to interpret the language of others whether it is written, spoken, or nonverbal.

Teachers of pre-first graders need . . .

preparation which emphasizes developmentally appropriate language experiences for all pre-first graders, including those ready to read or already reading.

the combined efforts of professional organizations, colleges, and universities to help them successfully meet the concerns outlined in this document.

Concerns:

1. A growing number of children are enrolled in pre-kindergarten and kindergarten classes in which highly structured pre-reading and reading programs are being used.
2. Decisions relating to schooling, including the teaching of reading, are increasingly being made on economic and political bases instead of on our knowledge of young children and of how they best learn.
3. In a time of diminishing financial resources, schools often try to make "a good showing" on measures of achievement that may or may not be appropriate for the children involved. Such measures all too often dictate the content and goals of the programs.
4. In attempting to respond to pressures for high scores on widely-used measures of achievement, teachers of young children sometimes feel compelled to use materials, methods, and activities designed for older children. In so doing, they may impede the development of intellectual functions such as curiosity, critical thinking, and creative expression, and, at the same time, promote negative attitudes toward reading.
5. A need exists to provide alternative ways to teach and evaluate progress in pre-reading and reading skills.
6. Teachers of pre-first graders who are carrying out highly individualized programs without depending upon commercial readers and workbooks need help in articulating for themselves and the public *what* they are doing and *why*.

Recommendations:

1. Provide reading experiences as an integrated part of the broader communication process that includes listening, speaking, and writing. A language experience approach is an example of such integration.
2. Provide for a broad range of activities both in scope and in content. Include direct experiences that offer opportunities to communicate in different settings with different persons.
3. Foster children's affective and cognitive development by providing materials, experiences, and opportunities to communicate what they know and how they feel.
4. Continually appraise how various aspects of each child's total development affects his/her reading development.
5. Use evaluative procedures that are developmentally appropriate for the

children being assessed and that reflect the goals and objectives of the instructional program.

6. Insure feelings of success for all children in order to help them see themselves as persons who can enjoy exploring language and learning to read.
7. Plan flexibly in order to accommodate a variety of learning styles and ways of thinking.
8. Respect the language the child brings to school, and use it as a base for language activities.
9. Plan activities that will cause children to become active participants in the learning process rather than passive recipients of knowledge.
10. Provide opportunities for children to experiment with language and simply to have fun with it.
11. Require that pre-service and in-service teachers of young children be prepared in the teaching of reading in a way that emphasizes reading as an integral part of the language arts as well as the total curriculum.

Alan Borrud

12. Encourage developmentally appropriate language learning opportunities in the home.

This statement was developed by

- **American Association of Elementary/Kindergarten/Nursery Educators**
- **Association for Childhood Education International**
- **Association for Supervision and Curriculum Development**
- **International Reading Association**
- **National Association for the Education of Young Children**
- **National Association of Elementary School Principals**
- **National Council of Teachers of English**

Single copies of this statement available free with a self-addressed, stamped envelope. Bulk copies available at cost. International Reading Association, 800 Barksdale Road, Newark, DE 19711.

Judith A. Schickedanz

"Please Read That Story Again!"
Exploring Relationships Between Story Reading and Learning to Read

If a child has ever asked you to reread a favorite story, then you may find yourself rereading this article—it's just for you!

In searching for explanations for why some children learn to read without apparent difficulty early in elementary school while others do not, reading researchers have looked at children's experiences at home, prior to school entrance. A common finding in this research has been that children who learn to read easily in school are the same children whose parents have read to them at home (Durkin 1966; Sakamoto 1977; Sheldon and Carrillo 1952; Sutton 1964). Because the evidence from this research is correlational, we cannot be certain whether it is the story reading itself or some other associated factor that helps these children learn to read. Nevertheless, reading to young children is often recommended as a critical experience, and parents and teachers alike are encouraged to read to children as often as they can (Department of Education and Science 1975; Durkin 1970).

Surprisingly though, parents and teachers rarely ask *why* they should read to children. Perhaps the question never arises because it makes such good sense that reading to children should be related to later reading ability. It is important, however, to know why reading to children makes a difference because unless we can answer this question, we have little to guide us in determining how best to read

to young children, or in deciding what additional experiences we might provide to help children learn to read.

In this article, some of the common explanations for the effects of story reading will be discussed, and an alternative explanation, along with implications for classroom practices, will be presented.

Common Theoretical Explanations

Several theoretical explanations for the observed relationship between extensive story reading at home and later reading achievement can be found, including:

- **Identification and social-learning modeling:** Children are thought to adopt behaviors of the parent because they wish to become like the parent. If parents read in the presence of their children, their children are likely to try to read, too (Elkind 1974; Gordon 1976).

- **Direct reinforcement:** Children are thought to receive many reinforcements in

Judith A. Schickedanz, Ph.D., is Assistant Professor, Early Childhood Education, Department of Childhood and Curriculum, Boston University, Boston, Massachusetts. She is a former teacher of preschool children.

the reading situation (e.g., attention, physical contact, verbal praise). Because of this positive reinforcement children are thought to approach reading situations as a way to maintain reinforcement obtained there. In time, the reading situation itself would become reinforcing. Helping children learn to "love" books or to develop an "enjoyment" of books as preparation for later reading instruction seems to be based in part on this explanation (Durkin 1970; Flood 1977).

• **Emotional security and confidence:** The warmth of the story reading situation, as well as the generally positive affective climate created by parents when they read to their children, is thought to support the child's emotional well-being, and to build his or her confidence. Therefore, children approach the reading situation because they have developed good feelings about reading and are not afraid of it (Department of Education and Science 1975).

• **Language development:** The reading process is viewed here as basically a language-prediction process. The language learned from the stories themselves, as well as from discussions of the stories with parents, is assumed to make it easier for children to learn to read (Durkin 1970; Flood 1977; Smith 1977; Olson 1977).

• **Book knowledge and knowledge of reading:** Children are thought to gain basic understandings such as "books have beginnings and endings," "print is read from left to right," "when one reads, one says what is printed in the book," etc. (Durkin 1970).

Inadequacy of Common Explanations

Most of the common explanations for why reading to children should be beneficial are based on, or are at least consistent with, a learning theory model of learning. Specifically, the first three explanations stress the importance of motivation and reinforcement derived *externally* from the learning act itself. In addition, they assume

that story reading serves as *preparation for* instruction in reading that is to occur at some later time, not that it is itself a situation in which actual instruction can and does occur.

This "readiness" view of story reading is consistent with a learning theory model: Learning is viewed as linear or additive, accruing slowly, bit by bit through the establishment of "associations" or "bonds." In a learning theory model, the story reading situation would probably not even be suspected as a possible source of actual reading skills, because it would be viewed as too complex, disorganized, and unstructured for such learning to occur. It is not surprising, therefore, that benefits from the experience have been assumed by many to be ones that render the child receptive to and motivated for actual reading instruction that will take place *later* in school.

The language explanation assumes that reading is primarily a language process. While there is wide support for this view, even its most ardent advocates do not say language is all there is to reading. Goodman and Goodman (1977), for example, suggest that readers use three systems: grammatical, semantic, and graphophonic. While the language explanation does assume that children learn something about the reading process itself from being read to, it stresses only the contributions to the grammatical and semantic systems. Because there is evidence that children can also learn letter-sound associations primarily from story reading experiences (Forester 1977), the language explanation is incomplete.

The book knowledge and knowledge of reading explanation, like the language explanation, is different from the others in that it suggests that children learn something about reading from the story reading situation itself. This explanation, however, is rarely extensively developed. Authors only mention it, and then stress the affective effects of story reading through comments such as, "Reading to children is primarily for enjoyment, and anything that detracts from that goal should be by-passed" (Durkin 1970, p. 84). Yet, it is precisely this last, less well-developed explanation that may be particularly interesting and fruitful to explore, because it is consistent with cognitive theory.

A Cognitive Explanation for the Effects of Story Reading

A cognitive explanation focuses on the story reading situation itself as a source of data from which children construct knowledge about rules that govern the reading process. In a cognitive theory of learning, the learner is viewed as active, both in terms of motivation and construction of knowledge. Learning is conceived structurally as schemes or representations of experiences that become reorganized and more highly differentiated as learning progresses (Piaget 1963). Access to complex raw data, or what teachers call "real experiences," is necessary for a learner to develop schemes.

Reinforcement in the cognitive model is thought to be "inherent in the act of information-processing itself" (Hunt 1965). The child engages in activities not for the purpose of gaining external reinforcement (e.g., praise, attention, affection) but because he or she finds the activities interesting.

What data about reading are made available in the story reading situation? What schemes might children construct? How might early schemes become reorganized into more complex schemes?

With respect to the development of knowledge about letter-sound associations, for example, schemes might develop as follows:

Scheme I: Memorized Story Line

In the story reading situation, the reader makes the story line accessible to the child. When the same story is repeated many times (which usually happens), children learn it "by heart." Learning stories "by heart" when they are read can be viewed as a cognitive scheme. The scheme is not the story line of an individual story but the general idea that story lines can be remembered, and general strategies for doing this. Children would then apply this scheme to several, or even many, books that they could learn "by heart."

Scheme II: Locating Print in Books

The story reading situation also helps children locate print in books. Sometimes parents point out words to their children as they read them stories. Even if they do not, children can probably learn which words appear on particular pages through observing when the parent says certain words. In addition, children's "by heart" versions of the story line include not only the words but the phrasing of the story, which they may be able to associate with the turning of pages. These associations would help them "line up" their "by heart" rendition of the story with the words printed in the book. Children probably also associate pictures with certain words that have been read. They know that when the parents say a certain line, a certain picture appears on the page. The picture can then be used to locate the page where a part of the story line that the child knows is printed.

In all of these ways, children probably can determine what the printed words in a book say, and they can then become familiar with how the words look. "Reading" at this point might be "by sight," while earlier it would have been "by heart."

Scheme III: Matching Letters and Sounds

Once the child knows the story "by heart," and also knows the same printed words "by sight," he or she can observe letter-sound correspondence. A third scheme, consisting of the general idea that there is a pattern or some regularity in the correspondence between letters and sounds might possibly develop as a consequence. When a certain degree of learning of this kind has taken place, "reading" using phonics rules can occur.

It should be noted that Scheme III involves a unique interaction between the child and a book, and does not involve a story reader. Scheme III, however, is a product of two earlier schemes that *are* dependent on the story reader.

Each of the above schemes could be expected to take considerable time and experience to develop. The reader need only consider the fact that it takes an infant about two years to develop a complete concept of the object (Piaget 1963) and about six years to develop concepts of conservation, classification, and seriation (Inhelder and Piaget 1964; Piaget 1965) to appreciate how long it might take a child to develop an understanding of letter-sound associations.

Implications of the Cognitive Model for Classroom Practice

If knowledge of letter-sound associations can be constructed by children in a fashion similar to that proposed above, then some ways of reading to children should be more effective than others. Suggestions for possible effective techniques follow.

• **Story reading, to be most effective, should take place in a situation that allows the child to see the print in the book.** Reading stories to large groups of children, or even to relatively small groups (six to eight children), may not give the access to print needed to learn words "by sight."

• **Turning the pages of the book may help children learn the phrasing of the story,** which may, in turn, help them match their "by heart" story line with the printed words in the book. This may be one strategy children use to learn words "by sight." Again, individual or very small group story reading situations would be necessary.

• **The same story should be read to children many times** because repetition is required for construction of the story line. The amount of repetition necessary for individual children to construct the story lines of a particular book would be expected to vary. The "match" between the linguistic abilities of a child and the language in the book may determine in part how much repetition is required. The experiences a child brings to the book would surely also influence the child's comprehension of what it says, and this, too, would probably play a part in determining the amount of repetition necessary for a child to construct the story line "by heart."

It would be important, then, to pay particularly close attention to children's pleas to hear a particular story and to read it again. It is impossible to exhibit this kind of responsiveness when reading to a group of children, because children are different; the book one child wants and needs to hear may not be at all suitable for the others. Again, then, reading to individual and small groups of children would seem to be much more effective.

• **Adults should point out, at least occasionally, where in the book words that "say" what they are reading appear.** Adults should probably also pose questions to the child, such as, "Where do you think it says, 'MEEOW!' on this page?" or "Where do you think it says, 'Will you please come to my birthday party, Peter?' on this page?" Obviously, children would need to be very close to the book to become involved in answering such questions.

• **Listening posts** may be used most effectively when children have individual books of the stories they hear to follow along in.

• **Children would need free access to books** that are read to them at times *in addition* to the story reading time itself. Such access would be critical for children to practice matching their "by heart" story lines with printed words, and for integrating their "by heart" and "by sight" versions to abstract rules about letter-sound associations. Mere access to books that have not been read may not be particularly useful, and no access to books that have been read would limit learning terribly.

• **Observation lists** used to keep records of children's progress should include items such as the following:
—Child chooses frequently to look at storybooks during a free-choice activity period.

Children who pretend to read familiar stories to themselves, other children, stuffed animals, or dolls are exhibiting progress toward learning to read. Why is this environment conducive to that progress?

—Child asks adult to reread stories often.
—Child pretends to read familiar stories to him- or herself, to other children, or to stuffed animals and dolls.
—Child corrects the adult when he or she alters the story line of a familiar story.
—Child turns pages for adult reader on the basis of phrasing clues only.
—Child asks what the words in a favorite storybook say.

• **Teachers should encourage children to compose stories** that the teacher can write down. These experience stories would be easy for children to read "by heart" because they composed them. Stories of individual children, rather than total-group experience charts, are likely to be more effective in promoting the development of schemes described above.

Summary and Conclusions

If the view presented describes with reasonable accuracy what indeed does occur, then it is clear that the *how* of story reading is critically important. Even programs in which story reading occurs on a daily basis may not be very effective if the stories are always read to the entire group or if the same books are not frequently repeated or if children do not have access to books that are read.

The effects of story reading at home may be quite strong, while the effects of even frequent story reading at school may not be. At home, the child is usually on the reader's lap where he or she can see the print and turn the pages of the book; in the classroom children often are seated far from the book in groups of twenty or more, a situation that limits both physical and visual contact with the book. At home, the child usually chooses the books to be read, thus ensuring repeated access to the same books; in the classroom children often do not select the books that are read to them. At home, a child has easy access to his or her storybooks at other times than when the parent is reading; unfortunately, at school there is often only a short time when children have access to books. In far too many classrooms, books are kept high on shelves or on the teacher's desk, out of the children's reach.

The issue of whether or not young children should be taught "reading skills" also emerges out of this discussion. The real issue is not whether children do or do not need to learn reading skills, but rather, *how* children come to know the skills that indeed are necessary if they are to learn how to read. In a learning theory model, the teacher teaches the skills directly, in one way or another. In a cognitive approach, teachers provide experiences that make knowledge about the reading process accessible to children who are thought literally to construct the skills for themselves. While skills are not directly taught, teachers must pay close attention to the kinds of experiences that are provided.

The cognitive model also suggests possible remedial procedures for children who encounter difficulty in the elementary school. A direct skill-teaching situation may be successful with children who have had all the necessary experiential background, such as having been read to at home by their parents, before they are taught to read in the school situation. They probably already know, at least on an intuitive level, the very skills that they are being "taught," and have learned to use others as well. Thus, they master the phonics training quickly. Because these children are often the best readers, teachers believe erroneously that it is the phonics training that is responsible.

Children without this background, however, may become terribly lost, not knowing the source of these rules. For these children, the cognitive model would predict that no amount of phonics drill or training would be effective, not because it is too "hard" or "advanced," but because the information is too simple, i.e., data-starved. It is isolated from the data-rich context of real reading materials.

Children experiencing this difficulty may profit from the procedure found to be effective by Chomsky (1975). She was able to help four third graders who were having great difficulty learning to read, despite hours of phonics drill, by having them memorize storybooks! Although she attributed her success to the confidence gained by the children in their ability to read, it might also have been due to the knowledge of the reading process itself obtained in the story reading situation described above.

Some possible directions for research are also suggested. We need answers to the question: "What does reading look like before we recognize it as 'real' reading?" We know what behaviors are typical of young children on tasks of conservation and classification, for example, and we know how these behaviors change qualitatively over time. But we do not have comparable descriptions of behavior for early reading.

Instead, we have knowledge about children's ability to recognize or manipulate isolated elements thought to be related to the reading process (e.g., alphabet recognition, recognition of rhyming words, etc.). This is very different from knowing how they understand the process of reading as a whole. To use mathematics as an example, it is the difference between knowing that a child can recognize the numerals one through nine and knowing the child still confuses space with number (says there are more cubes in a row when they are spread out than when they are close together). These two pieces of information are likely to lead us to different conclusions if we are trying to determine if such a child is "ready" for instruction in operations on number, e.g., addition, subtraction, etc. They become critical in determining how we might attempt to help such a child come to understand addition.

The few researchers who have suggested that cognitive skills are involved in learning to read (Dimitrovsky and Almy 1975; Elkind 1974) have assumed that these consist of the logico-mathematical concepts of conservation and classification. What I am suggesting is that structures unique to reading might also develop. The schemes outlined above might possibly be examples of children's early understandings of the reading process. Of course, any theoretically-based hypotheses such as those suggested above need rigorous empirical confirmation.

Finally, the discussion presented here provides an interesting basis for speculation about the relationship between affect and cognition. If the story reading experience is to result in the cognitive learnings outlined above, a closeness between the adult reader and the child is required. In other words, a story reading situation that is loaded with positive affect (e.g., individual attention, physical contact, verbal praise, etc.) is the same situation that is loaded with information for the child. Part of the "loading" no doubt results because the adult is in a situation where he or she can be responsive to an individual child's behavior. The adult can be directed by the child to back up or to go forward, to repeat, to answer questions, and so on.

It may be that a child's affective tie to an adult is influenced by the adult's responsiveness to the child's cognitive needs. It has been well-documented in relation to infants, for example, that they like best those adults who are most responsive, i.e., who play with them, etc. (Rheingold 1956; Schaffer and Emerson 1964). It has been suggested by others that infants may like these adults best because they know that with them around they can get interesting things to happen (Schickedanz and Goldstein 1977).

Affect and cognition, then, may truly interact with each other. If this conception is at all accurate, ideas such as "we should limit goals of the preschool to emotional development and leave cognitive development to the elementary school" need to be reconsidered. ⊻

Preparation of this article was supported in part by Grant No. G007-605-403 from the U.S. Office of Education to the Boston University Pre-Elementary Reading Improvement Collaborative.

References

Chomsky, C. "After Decoding, What?" *Elementary English* 52, no. 6 (March 1975): 288-296, 314.

Department of Education and Science. *A Language for Life*. London: Her Majesty's Stationery Office, 1975.

Dimitrovsky, L., and Almy, M. "Early Conservation as a Predictor of Later Reading." *Journal of Psychology* 90 (1975): 11-18.

Durkin, D. *Children Who Read Early*. New York: Teachers College Press, 1966.

Durkin, D. *Teaching Them to Read*. Boston: Allyn & Bacon, 1970.

Elkind, D. "Cognitive Development and Reading." *Claremont Reading Conference Yearbook* 38 (1974): 10-20.

Flood, J. "Parental Styles in Reading Episodes with Young Children." *The Reading Teacher* 35 (May 1977): 864-867.

Forester, A. "What Teachers Can Learn from 'Natural Readers.'" *The Reading Teacher* 31 (November 1977): 160-166.

Goodman, K. S., and Goodman, Y. "Learning about Psycholinguistic Processes by Analyzing Oral Reading." *Harvard Educational Review* 47 (August 1977): 317-333.

Goodman, K. S., and Goodman, Y. "The Psycholinguistic Nature of the Reading Process." In *The Psycholinguistic Nature of the Reading Process*, ed. K. S. Goodman. Detroit: Wayne State University Press, 1968.

Gordon, I. "Parenting, Teaching, and Child Development." *Young Children* 31, no. 3 (March 1976): 173-183.

Guinagh, B., and Jester, R. "How Parents Read to Children." *Theory into Practice* 11 (June 1972): 171-177.

Hunt, J. McV. "Intrinsic Motivation and Its Role in Psychological Development." *Nebraska Symposium on Motivation* 13 (1965): 189-282.

Inhelder, B., and Piaget, J. *The Early Growth of Logic in the Child*. New York: Norton, 1964.

Olson, D. "From Utterance to Text: The Bias of Language in Speech and Writing." *Harvard Educational Review* 47 (August 1977): 257-281.

Piaget, J. *The Child's Conception of Number*. New York: Norton, 1965.

Piaget, J. *The Origins of Intelligence in Children*. New York: Norton, 1963.

Rheingold, H. "The Modification of Social Responsiveness in Institutional Babies." *Monographs of the Society for Research in Child Development* 2, no. 63 (1956).

Sakamoto, T. "Beginning Reading in Japan." Paper presented at the International Reading Association annual meeting, May 1977, Miami, Fla.

Schaffer, H. R., and Emerson, P. E. "The Development of Social Attachments in Infancy." *Monographs of the Society for Research in Child Development* 29, no. 94 (1964).

Schickedanz, D., and Goldstein, G. "The Relationship Between Moderate Novelty and Effectance Motivation in Determining Children's Visual Attention and Instrumental Behavior." Paper presented at the Eastern Psychological Association annual meeting, April 1977, Boston, Mass.

Sheldon, W., and Carrillo, L. "Relation of Parents, Home, and Certain Developmental Characteristics to Children's Reading Ability." *Elementary School Journal* 52 (January 1952): 262-270.

Smith, F. "Making Sense of Reading—and of Reading Instruction." *Harvard Educational Review* 47 (August 1977): 386-395.

Sutton, M. "Readiness for Reading at the Kindergarten Level." *The Reading Teacher* 22 (January 1964): 234-239.

John Lee Sherman

Storytelling with Young Children

Fairy tales can have a powerful formative role in children's emotional development argues Bettelheim in *The Uses of Enchantment: The Meaning and Importance of Fairy Tales.* His book has inspired a wonderful renaissance of the use of fairy tales in classrooms, but he also argues that just reading a fairy tale isn't quite enough. According to Bettelheim, "To attain to the full its consoling propensities, its symbolic meanings, and most of all its interpersonal meanings, a fairy tale should be told rather than read" (Bettelheim 1976, p. 150).

All types of stories, whether fairy or folk, myth or fable, modern or ancient, gain in meaning and effect when *told* to young children. Furthermore, the medium of the storyteller—as opposed to books, recordings, television, or movies—is developmentally the most appropriate way for children first to be exposed to narrative literature.

The Importance of Storytelling for Young Children

Storytelling, the original form of narrative art, goes back to the beginnings of human history. It is found in all cultures at all historical periods and exists today with great vitality in the face of heavy competition from other forms of narrative art. Much of the storytelling of today is informal—the sort that goes on at the dinner table about a wonderful fishing trip or about a recently seen movie. Just as it was humanity's first narrative art, so should it be each individual's, for storytelling has special meaning and importance for young children.

The storyteller produces narrative literature in its most direct form. No technology comes between creator and audience. The storyteller's voice, expressions, gestures, and imagination are immediately accessible to children. Consequently the children can apply their full range of human understanding and observational skills. Young children know people better than they know words or pictures; consequently storytelling is the first way in which they can fully understand and appreciate narrative art.

Storytelling is also a reciprocal interaction between teller and audience. As Bettelheim suggests, ". . . the telling of a fairy story should be an interpersonal event into which adult and child enter as equal partners, as can never be the case when a story is read to a child" (Bettelheim, p. 152). The audience reacts to the storyteller, and the storyteller in turn reacts to the audience; the story is molded anew with each telling through this dynamic interplay. This interaction is appealing and important to young children, for it implies a personal relationship with a caring adult.

Flexibility is another aspect of interaction. As the skillful storyteller Ruth Sawyer writes, "There is a kind of death to every story when it leaves the speaker and becomes impaled for all time on clay tablets or the written and printed page" (Sawyer 1965, p. 59). A story can be modified at each telling, ensuring a living artwork adjusted to meet the needs of each moment and place. The story can be shortened or lengthened, speeded up or slowed down; parts can be left out or added, endings changed, and concepts

Photograph on p. 83 by Sandy Felsenthal

81

explained as necessary within the fabric of the tale to ensure understanding and enjoyment.

Because the narrative comes through the medium of a person, storytelling also provides the opportunity for identification and subsequent modeling of a creative act. There is a large gap between a child's capacity to experience a book, recording, TV show, or movie and his or her ability competently to create a similar experience. Storytelling can be mastered by young children; many three-and most four-year-olds can do a creditable job of retelling a familiar tale or making up a highly imaginative story. My experience has been that children who are told stories begin to tell more stories on their own. The African writer Birago Diop claims he owes his own writings to his family *griot* or storyteller:

> If I have not been able to reproduce, in what I set down, the atmosphere in which I had luxuriated as a young listener, nor describe those tentative, quivering, contemplative people about me, it is because I have become a man, therefore an incomplete child, and being thus reduced, am incapable of re-creating the marvelous. It is especially because I lack the voice, the verve, and the art of mimicry of my old Griot.
>
> (Diop 1964, p. 93)

High quality narrative art in any medium is vitally important to children's social, emotional, and intellectual development. Quality stories present children with new and deepened experience, pleasure, values, life-sustaining myths, and symbolic interpretations of existence. Storytelling can add one important dimension. It can produce personal narrative art—stories created about people, creatures, events, and places that children

John Lee Sherman, Ed.D., is Nursery Teacher and Curriculum Coordinator, Francis W. Parker School, Chicago, Illinois. His experiences include Head Start, elementary, and university teaching.

know. Storytelling can add the element of personalization to the field of children's literature.

There are also a number of practical reasons for storytelling with young children. Storytelling is a useful tool for teachers and parents because it is portable entertainment. The storyteller has all the equipment needed at a moment's notice. When the school bus breaks down, the museum opens late, naptime or bedtime arrives, or the children are fighting in the back of the car, the storyteller can spring into action. A storyteller, but not a story reader, can maintain eye contact with children, and effectively control a wiggly group. Furthermore, storytelling allows a teacher flexibility in choosing narrative materials which can bring to life other curriculum areas. For example, a study by older children of Eskimo life can be enriched through Eskimo tales. Many of the available collections of traditional stories are not written for children but can be adapted for telling.

Suggestions for Storytelling

Storytelling is an art, but its most meaningful modern form is as a popular amateur art. To be personal, intimate, and flexibly appropriate, it needs to occur between adults and children who know each other. My introduction to storytelling was in a graduate course on children's literature with the wonderfully enthusiastic Charles Reasoner. He was pure ham, shamelessly brazen in his willingness to tell the silliest children's stories to university scholars. I learned from him that what you need most of all to tell stories to young children is enthusiasm for the art of storytelling and love for the stories you tell. You don't need a good voice, dramatic training, a spontaneously creative imagination, a movie star's looks, or an elephant's memory.

Assuming that you possess the enthusiasm, the next thing you need is a

story to love. Find a tale for which you have feeling and understanding. The great heritage of traditional spoken materials—folk tales, fairy tales, myths, sagas, religious stories, and fables have been shaped as oral narratives by countless retellings. One point to remember when searching through traditional material is that it often reads poorly because stylistic elements of oral and written narratives differ greatly. For example, oral works thrive on bare-bones plots and frequent repetition of descriptive phrases and rhythms. But storytelling should not stop with the traditional tales. Ross suggests,

> When we think of the storyteller and his story, we tend to think of folk tales and fairy tales; these are the commodities he trades in. But such a view stunts our possible growth in our craft. The range of stories available to us should include anything and everything which we have tasted and touched, felt and seen and heard. In short, all life experiences, whether they come from reading, or listening, or from doing or from imagining are sources for stories.
>
> (Ross 1972, p. 28)

Traditional Stories

The preparations you will follow differ slightly depending upon whether the story comes from a book or other medium, from your own experience, or from your imagination. Let's begin by looking at the steps involved in telling a story found in a book or other medium.

It makes sense to use traditional folk or fairy tales for your first attempts at storytelling. They were designed for it. After you have chosen a story, the next step is to learn it. *Do not memorize the story.* Reciting a story verbatim is not storytelling, and it takes forever unless you possess an exceptional memory. Instead, try rereading the story three or four times over a period of several days. If the story comes from a movie or TV program, try replaying the show in your head. The object is to learn the story, to know its plot, characters, and spirit.

There is one exception to the rule on memorization. Occasionally there are rhymes, special beginnings, or endings that are worth learning. For example, "Jack and the Beanstalk" would not be the same without "Fe, fi, fo, fum, I smell the blood of an Englishman!" The traditional ending for "The Three Billy Goats Gruff" which goes, "Snip, snap, snout, this tale's told out," is also nice. The beginning of the Buddhist tale, "The Hare That Ran Away" is worthwhile, "And it came to pass that the Buddha was reborn as a lion. Just as he had helped his fellow men, he now began to help his fellow animals." There are many more, usually quite brief. They take only a short time to learn.

Take time to think about and feel out the mood of the story. Is it frightening, funny, sad, or silly? Young children enjoy all types. If you can focus on the mood, it will help you paint your word pictures with just the right colors.

Next go over the action line until you are sure of it. After sitting with the story for several days, you should know the plot sequence well, but it is important to check. Frequently you'll find some twist, section, or detail that you need to get straight.

Storytellers create each story anew from their own inner visions. Take time to imagine the setting. Visualize your own pictures for each story. What kind of forest is Little Red Riding Hood walking through? What kind of flowers does she stop to pick along the way? What does grandmother's house look like? What does the inside of her room look like? Use the richness of your own experience to make inner visions of the tale and then draw upon them during the telling. Above all, "Storytelling is a sharing of experience. The more of his own experience the teller brings to the story, the richer the story" (Sawyer et al. 1962, p. 33).

A story tends to get richer, more subtle, and better the more you tell it; however,

I find it difficult to repeat a story without a week's break. It loses its freshness. One of the great benefits of being a teacher storyteller is that each year you get a different group of young children to whom the stories you know and love are new. In preparing to retell a story, you can follow the same steps as for a new story but at an accelerated pace. Reread it once and think it through. Your original work on the story will come back plus new insights and images. If you tell a story over a number of years, you will feel it growing and becoming as real a part of your background as things you have actually experienced.

Personal Experience Stories

The next in order of ease of telling are personal experience stories. These are stories that have really happened to you or to the children in your audience. Preparing a personal experience story is a bit different from the traditional type. You do, however, start at the same place, by choosing a tale that you have a feeling and understanding for. Pick out an experience: something that happened to you, perhaps a childhood anecdote, or something that happened to your own child or your class.

Next consider the mood. How did it make you feel when it happened? What mood do you want to convey in the telling? Think about the message or theme of the experience. If you can isolate central elements, it will help you winnow out extraneous details and give your narrative dramatic life and engrossing plot movement.

Remember that a personal experience story is a true story. Color it to fit the mood of your telling and exaggerate different elements to enhance the plot, but stick to the truth. That's where the story draws its life. Children love to hear this type of tale, and they will often spontaneously help in the telling when it's an experience in which they were involved.

An important benefit is that children clearly witness the creation of narrative art.

Personal Imagination Stories

The storyteller can also call on pure imagination by inventing stories. For many, this is the most difficult type of story to tell. It calls for a quick tongue as well as confidence in one's storytelling ability.

The preparation of the personal imagination story differs markedly from either the traditional or personal experience story. You usually do not know the plot before you begin the narrative; the story evolves during the telling. (If you write a story first and then tell it, you are working from a written narrative, only it is more personalized because you wrote it.)

Begin by choosing a topic for the story. One method is to select a special character. If you choose a character you feel comfortable with, you can use that character again and again in many different tales. I have one friend who tells stories about the adventures of the Talking Baby and another who made up a creature called the Bionic Worm. The character I enjoy telling about is the Big Man. I am six foot two, weigh two hundred pounds, and teach four-year-olds, so the Big Man is a character into which I can project many of my own feelings. Because you make up the plot as you go, all you can really think about in advance is the personality of your central character. How does she, he, or it look, act, sound, and behave?

Another way to select a topic for a personal imagination story is to use real events and people as the basis for the narrative. For example, you can tell a story about a little girl, little boy, or class of children who happen to look, act, and be about the same as the children to whom you are telling the story. When telling this type of personal imagination story, I recommend that you don't give the characters names; instead call them "the little girl" or "the four-year-old class," etc. This heightens the audience's sense of identification in the narrative. One of the best naptime or bedtime stories I've encountered is simply telling the class's or family's adventures for the day with imaginative additions. For example,

> It was a beautiful Tuesday morning in October and the four-year-old class decided to walk to the zoo. They packed a picnic snack of apples, pineapple juice, and wheat crackers and hiked to the zoo. The first thing they did was say, "hello" to the seals. Do you know what happened next? A baby seal said "hello" right back to them, etc. . .

A great advantage of this type of personal imagination story is that the storyteller has a framework for invention. It is rather like jazz musicians using the melody and harmonic structure of a song but improvising their own sections.

Once you select the topic, the next step is to tell the story. Don't panic. You are not alone. You have your topic, your experience as a storyteller, and an audience that is going to help you shape the tale through their reactions to it.

The tragic flaw in the personal imagination story is that the spontaneity that makes it thrilling also makes it hard to retell. It can be difficult to recall what you invented, and you often find yourself in the bind of recreating instead of creating anew so that the retelling lacks vitality. In general I have learned to treat these stories like rare magical flowers that bloom once, then disappear forever. Fortunately, one of the nicest features of personal imagination stories is that they lend themselves to being serialized. Like old Flash Gordon movies, they can always end with "To be continued."

Techniques and Devices

There are a number of techniques and devices useful to the storyteller that hold true for any type of tale. The physical setting in which the story is told is important. Get as close to the audience as you can and make sure you see everyone's face, unless of course it is naptime or bedtime. A special ritual can add mystique to the setting. A candle can be lighted, incense burned, or a stuffed animal visitor brought out. I wear a multicolored knit cap, which I call a story cap, and assure children that it fills my head with stories. I also claim they must be quiet so I can hear the stories to tell them.

Part of the physical setting is the audience itself. Even during the best told and most engrossing story, there are children who may need help controlling themselves. Since you are close to your audience and have face to face contact, much of this work can be done with your eyes or a simple shake of the head. Sometimes, however, you need to stop the story and deal with the problem. If I have to interrupt a story more than two or three times, I usually figure something is wrong with the story, the telling, or the audience, so I'll stop for the day. Remember, storytelling is an exchange of gifts. It is a gift of preparation and imagination from the storyteller to the audience and a gift of shared appreciation from the audience to the storyteller. Gifts need to be exchanged in an atmosphere of mutual respect.

Some storytellers believe traditional stories need to be retold with strict adherence to plot, details, and language. There is a lot to be said for this approach, and as an adult audience we would be poorer without it; however, it does not make sense for teachers or parents telling stories to young children. Stories frequently benefit by changes. For example, there are relatively few old tales that present women in positive dynamic roles. You can alter the plot so that Little Red Riding Hood's angry mother breaks in and kills the wolf.

Likewise the details and concepts in old stories are often too obscure for young children to understand. Many of the old versions of "Little Red Riding Hood" make use of a locking mechanism on grandmother's door. Grandmother says, "Pull the bobbin and the latch opens," giving the wolf the secret. If you can find an old latch with a bobbin to illustrate this point, then use it. Otherwise it makes sense to have grandmother say, "The key is under the mat, dear."

It does make sense to work at preserving traditional details in a story when you are telling it in conjunction with a social studies project. Then the story can serve to put into context the terms and concepts the children are studying. The important thing to remember is that you need to make the story live both for yourself and for the audience. Do what you feel will best accomplish this.

The storyteller's instrument is his or her voice. Make it loud, soft, fast, or slow to enhance the story. Try consciously cutting down on your use of connecting sounds like *or*, *er*, and *a*. Be silent if you are thinking of what to say next. Silence in the form of a pause is a key technique in using the voice. Famous professional storyteller Marie Shedlock writes, "First and foremost, as a means of suddenly pulling up the attention of the audience, is the judicuous art of pausing" (Shedlock 1951, p. 53).

Voices within a story can be done in several ways. If you are good at mimicry or dramatic impersonation, give each character a distinctly recognizable and appropriate voice. Fortunately, there is no need to do this. You may simply use your speaking voice for all the characters in the story. By slightly altering volume and speed, you can easily separate two characters in a dialogue. Accent and dialect are controversial issues. My personal rule is that I have the right to use my own ethnic dialect and accents, but I do not have the right to use other people's. In general the use or omission of dialect and accent does not dramatically affect a story for young children.

Gestures and facial expressions are also important storytelling devices. Since storytellers are usually seated or at least stationary, the gestures used to enhance a narrative need to be circumscribed and rather subtle. But gestures do help, and at times they even take the place of words. In a recorded version of the Spanish story "The Flea," Ruth Sawyer says, "And he caught the flea like so!" (Sawyer, n.d.). There is a slight pause and then the sound of hands slapping together. Just listening to the record gives one vivid picture of her catching that flea. Facial expressions also seem most effective when kept subtle. I find they come naturally with the story, particularly with dialogue. The important thing is to relax and allow your face to mirror your words and inner feelings.

Frequently a story will benefit from a brief introduction or an after-story follow-up. Before you begin your tale, think about the age and experience of your audience. Are there important words or concepts that need to be described? Is the background of the tale of interest to the children? Where does the story come from? Is it old or new, real or make believe? In telling the traditional tale "The Tinder Box," it is important to explain what a tinderbox was and what it looked like. An artifact related to a story can serve as a wonderful introduction. A real tinderbox, or samples of straw, sticks, and a brick for "The Three Little Pigs" might do the job. The artifacts can be left for closer examination after the storytelling.

Another approach to introducing a story is to ask a leading question that will help children focus on a particular aspect of the narrative. For example before telling "Hansel and Gretel," you might ask the children to think about meanness. Ask them to listen and try to decide who is the meanest person in the story.

Likewise there are many ways to follow up a story. One is to discuss the leading question posed in the introduction. Remember the best questions for discussion are open ended with no correct answer. Who really is the meanest person in "Hansel and Gretel"? Is it the witch who wants to eat them, the stepmother who wants to get rid of them, the father who goes along with the stepmother and loses the children in the forest, or Gretel who pushes the witch into the oven and burns her to death? Another follow-up is simply to ask children who they liked or didn't like, or how the story made them feel. You can also ask if the story reminds them of some other stories. Another approach is to let children retell the tale themselves in some manner. One is to draw pictures. Another is to have story characters available as felt board figures, dolls, or puppets. An interesting approach is to give children their own time to retell stories to the class. This often works best when each child who wants to participate retells a brief section of the story.

A few words need to be said about imagination and honesty. In a strange way imagination is honesty when telling stories to young children. You are the creative force behind each story you tell, whether it is traditional or personal in its origins. Don't stretch for the fantastic, the bizarre, or the unique in image, gesture, or language. If you are in touch with yourself and tell the story directly, without self-conscious mannerisms such as sarcasm, your honest feelings about the material will produce a narrative of great imagination. You will create a work of shared pleasure and experience—the ultimate objectives of the use of imagination in narrative art.

Conclusion

Listening to storytelling is an important developmental experience for young children. It is the first form of narrative literature they can fully understand and in which they can participate. In storytelling lie the roots of all other narrative art forms. There are a number of different types of stories to tell young children. The easiest for the novice are the traditional oral tales. Stories of personal experience offer the unique contribution of building narrative art from children's own worlds, and personal imagination stories provide a shared adventure in the use of creative imagination.

Narrative art, and storytelling in particular, is the sharing of pleasure and experience between audience and artist, but it is only in storytelling that the creative artist and the medium come together at the moment of performance in the person of the storyteller. The greatest pleasure in storytelling for a teacher or parent lies in being a storyteller. The rewards are satisfying and usually self-generating. Once you start telling stories to young children, you're hooked.

The recompense for a story well told is great. "Tell it again," "That's a good story," "Do you know some more stories like that?" is pay enough for the effort it takes to prepare and tell a story to young children. The spontaneous laughter, the moment of absolute silence at the story's end, the immediate response, send one out further to perfect his art: by self-criticism of one's accomplishments, by considering new ventures in one's tellings, by further study of story art from great storytellers themselves.

(Jacobs 1965, p. 19)

References

Bettelheim, B. *The Uses of Enchantment: The Meaning and Importance of Fairy Tales.* New York: Knopf, 1976.

Diop, B. "Stories Which Cradled My Childhood." In *African Heritage*, ed. J. Drachler. London, England: Collier Books, 1964.

Jacobs, L. "Telling Stories to Young Children." In *Using Literature with Young Children*, ed. L. Jacobs. New York: Teachers College Press, 1965.

Ross, R. *Storyteller.* Columbus, Ohio: Merrill, 1972.

Sawyer, R. *Ruth Sawyer, Storyteller.* Two-record album. Weston, Conn.: Weston Woods Studios, n.d. Number WW701 and WW702.

Sawyer, R. *The Way of the Storyteller.* New York: Viking, 1965.

Sawyer, R.; Haviland, V.; Baker, A.; Coughlan, M.; and Fenwick, S.I. "The Golden Sounds of Storytelling." In *Compton's Encyclopedia Reprint: Reading and Storytelling.* Chicago: F. E. Compton Co., 1972.

Shedlock, M. L. *The Art of the Storyteller.* New York: Dover, 1951.

Janet Gonzalez-Mena

English as a Second Language for Preschool Children

English as a second language (ESL) programs sometimes leave much to be desired. Many seem to be designed for efficiency, assuming that language is something that can be lifted out of life (out of context) and instilled in a child. Language acquisition, however, particularly in preschool age children, is a very complex mixture of inherent linguistic and cognitive phenomena, developing within a constantly changing situational context. Greater understanding is needed of some of the more important aspects of second language learning in the young child.

Any second language program for young children should be based on the following principles:

1. Children are motivated to learn a second language because of language relationships.
2. Young children need a total development program within a language program.
3. Children learn by doing.

Establishing a Language Relationship

The first problem confronting any foreign language teacher is how to get the students to speak the target language. A three- or four-year-old child does not have the motivation of an adult who is leaving for Spain in six months and is enrolled in a Spanish class. After all, the child has a means of communicating that is comfortable and familiar. Why would any child want to struggle to learn another language? The answer is simple. Young children will struggle, in fact, they will put forth great effort, *if* they feel a need. How can a teacher help the children feel a need? The teacher can establish an English language relationship with each child.

Many teachers of ESL say over and over to their children, "Speak English! Speak English!" They may even explain in the child's native tongue why it is important to learn English. All this becomes unnecessary with the establishment of an English language relationship between teacher and child, and undue frustration will be largely eliminated.

The concept of language relationships can be easily observed in anyone who speaks more than one language. Perhaps an example would best explain it.

Juan came to California from Mexico ten years ago. He and his wife always speak Spanish to each other though both have learned English. Juan also speaks Spanish to his good friend, Jaime, but to Jaime's wife he speaks English because she was born in Texas. Although she speaks Spanish fluently, she is shy about it because people from Mexico have laughed at her accent and vocabulary.

89

Juan is taking an English class. During the coffee break (when the language relationships become obvious), he speaks Spanish to Luis, who is from Chile. He speaks English to Pierre, a fellow student from France. At the restaurant where he works, he speaks English with the cook, an Anglo, and Spanish with the waiter, a teenager recently arrived from Mexico.

Juan does not have to make decisions about which language to speak—it is an automatic reaction. If he speaks English with someone with whom he has a Spanish-language relationship, he may very likely feel strange and uncomfortable. Language teachers need to know about this feeling. Better yet—they should have experienced this feeling themselves.

Every effort should be made to minimize such a linguistically-induced, negative psychological state in the students, whether adult or child. The best way to make the student comfortable when speaking the target language is to establish a language relationship in that language from the beginning.

My own experiences have convinced me of the importance of the language relationship in motivating the child. I have found that the children identify me as an English-speaking person who speaks Spanish. At first totally monolingual children say everything to me in Spanish, but as they develop English skills they begin to utilize the English they know, using Spanish only to sup-

Janet Gonzalez-Mena, B.A., is an instructor in child development at Canada College in Redwood City, California. A former nursery school teacher, she taught English as a second language in the Cuauhtemoc Home Centered Bilingual Preschool Program.

plement what they cannot yet express. I have not had to say, "Speak English," because children try to use all the English they know when speaking with me. This would not be true if I tried to teach English using Spanish as the vehicle. I have seen teachers do this: "Dime *car*" ("Say *car* for me"). Unfortunately, to communicate with this teacher, the child will use Spanish, saving English for the English lesson. There is more than one way to handle this problem of two languages. The method of separating the languages by teachers is but one of several approaches. See Andersson and Boyer (1970) for a typology of bilingual education.

The issue of ESL-only versus ESL as part of bilingual education must be confronted. In the ESL-only approach, children may have no adult in school with whom to have a native language relationship. However, this two-way linguistic thrust is needed if they are to continue to grow and develop in their native language. Otherwise, the children either speak English entirely, or use English exclusively for thinking, logical and intellectual processes, keeping the native language for their homes. These children do not become true bilingual speakers since they acquire no words, tools, or skills for higher thinking in their own native language (Manuel 1965, p. 118).

The above is one of several strong arguments in favor of bilingual education as opposed to only ESL. The United States needs truly bilingual adults, and our education system has not only failed to produce bilinguals, but has actually discouraged the development of the native language in children who began school speaking a language other than English.

the child may be left floundering in a new language. Research indicates that children who are secure in the development of their first language acquire a second language faster and better (John and Horner 1971).

Children Need a Total Development Program

Young children are not only in the midst of their language development, but also in the midst of their total development. They are forming concepts (which may or may not be considered as separate from language) and acquiring other cognitive skills such as problem solving. Children are learning to interpret the messages from the five senses and developing perceptual skills. They are, of course, also developing motor skills (which can be tied to perceptions and called perceptual-motor skills). For the adult, one of these areas may be isolated and taught separately—such as language. Isolating one skill from the others would be doing the child a disservice since they are so closely tied into one another, if not inseparable.

Moreover, a bilingual program tends to have a positive effect on the educational longevity of low-income children whose dominant language is other than English. Many of these children fall behind in school and eventually drop out (Andersson and Boyer 1970). The proponents of bilingual education believe that the child's first language and the child's self-esteem are so tied together that they cannot be separated. If the native language of the child is replaced by English (which very often happens), it is as if to say that the child's native language is not as good or not useful. Because language is an integral part of personality, any affront to language is a blow to self-esteem (Cohen 1970).

The young child who has not yet developed in the area of language, who is still in the process of incorporating the internal structure of a first language, should not be hindered in that development. In other words, if growth in the first language is cut off in midstream,

For example, suppose your objective as an ESL teacher is to teach the English word for triangle. To adult students you have to do nothing more than draw one, and tell them *triangle*. You could also mention the native language word for it (although language interference might result if the word is similar, e.g., if you say *triangulo* and *triangle* together for the Spanish speakers, they may say "tree-angle" or "try-angoolo"). But little else is usually necessary. The point is—the adult has the concept; all that is needed is the English label for it.

However, young children may not have the concept or the label in any language. In fact, they may not even be able to perceive a triangle as yet; they may see no difference between a square and a triangle. They may feel no difference if given a block with three corners or one with four corners. What young children need are many experiences with triangles while acquiring the label. They need to make triangles with crayons and clay, fit them together as in playing with puzzles and blocks, touch, manipulate them . . . even eat them (as in half a sandwich). Then when a label is attached, the children have experiences upon which to base the concept. If a label is given to a piece of paper cut with three corners, how do children know whether or not the paper is the defining characteristic, or the color, weight, or size? Children *build* the concept "triangle"—it is not instilled in them. Once they understand the concept, they have little difficulty labeling or using two labels such as *triangle* and *triangulo*.

Children Learn by Doing

The above example also illustrates the third principle necessary for an early childhood ESL program: Children learn by doing. How else can children gain experiences as a basis for language development? They can explore, experiment, find out for themselves. Piaget's work indicates that the child needs "active, self-discovery, inductively oriented learning experiences whereby . . .[the child] is able to perform transformations on materials from the environment" (Evans 1971, p. 235). Only after performing physical actions on

JOYCE HAHN

physical objects can children then move to mental action on objects. Learning is interacting with the environment, not remaining passive and being told. If this assumption is basic, the ESL teacher will not hold up a picture of a ball and say, "Repeat after me, 'This is a ball.'" Yes, the adult can get children to react to a picture of a ball with "This is a ball." But unless children have concrete experiences such as rolling balls, sucking on a jawbreaker, or making snowballs, they are just parroting. They are like machines spitting out that which has been programmed in.

We acquire meanings to words through their connotations, not their denotations. Connotations consist of all the feelings, verbal and nonverbal, that surround a word (and are different for each person), while denotations are the definitions of the word. Holt (1969) states that he has a vocabulary of about 25,000 words, yet he has probably looked up fewer than 50 words in the dictionary in his life. He gained the denotations from the connotations which were derived from his personal experiences. *"Language is caught, not taught"* would seem to be a good motto for ESL teachers.

Additionally the social development of children cannot be ignored, or children will be greatly hampered in other developmental areas. I would suggest that social development and ESL be tied together by insuring social interaction between the ESL child and other children who speak English. Moreover a program based on the assumptions and principles described here will provide opportunities for social interaction which may strengthen social growth and development.

Summary

The adults in a foreign language class already have achieved full language development. The job of the teacher is to work around any inhibitions and help the students acquire a second language (or third or fourth). What the teacher does in the classroom probably has little effect on the students' native language(s) except perhaps to add some insights.

Conversely, young children are in the midst of their development—not only in language, but also in conceptual growth, cognitive skills, perceptual-motor development, etc. Furthermore, children have not built up the walls of inhibitions to protect themselves psychologically. They are eager to learn, and their mistakes can help them learn.

Young children have been experimenting with sounds since they were tiny and in most cases are more than willing to continue trying. What children need are the opportunities to hear and use the target language; it does not need to be "dragged out" of them. Young children do not need to be motivated. As long as children speak with a person with whom they have an English language relationship, they are most willing to speak English. A child who is asked to play cars by two English-speaking friends is going to speak English with them. No one needs to stand over the children and remind them to speak English.

In too many programs the total focus is on the level of achievement in language skills alone. We teach and evaluate in the cognitive area, completely skipping over the affective aspects. How does each child feel about this new skill and the culture to which it is tied? That is a question that should be asked. How did the child feel about his or her native language upon entrance to the ESL program? Have the child's feelings about this native language changed? Has the native language taken a backseat position in the child's life? Evaluating the affective domain is difficult, but it is no less important than the cognitive domain (Nida 1965).

Educators must recognize the value of the wholeness of experience (Holt 1969; Hymes 1968). The world should not be broken up into little pieces, taken apart, called by different subject names, and taught for fifteen minutes at a time. When the world is artificially broken into segments, it is difficult for children to put it back together again as a whole. Children can live a whole experience in a second as well as a first language. They take in what they can

93

handle at one time, and that which begins to make sense. They learn by being immersed in the experience rather than having it broken up into little pieces The teacher's function is to provide experiences which enable children to learn. *Children learn language best in real situations with concrete experiences.* ▼

References

Andersson, T., and Boyer, M. *Bilingual Schooling in the United States*. Austin, Tex.; Southwest Educational Development Laboratory, 1970.

Cohen, A. *Points of Interest about Bilingual Education with Specific Reference to the Spanish Speaking of the Southwest*. Mimeographed, 1970.

Evans, E. D. *Contemporary Influences in Early Childhood Education*. New York: Holt, Rinehart and Winston, 1971.

Gonzalez-Mena, J. *Program for English Experiences: English as a Second Language for Preschool and Kindergarten*. Silver Spring, Md.: Institute of Modern Languages, 1975.

Holt, J. *The Underachieving School*. New York: Pitman Publishing Corp., 1969.

Hymes, J. L. *Teaching the Child Under Six*. Columbus, Ohio: Merrill Publishing Co., 1968.

John, V. P., and Horner, V. M. *Early Childhood Bilingual Education*. New York: Modern Language Association of America, 1971.

Manuel, H. *Spanish-Speaking Children of the Southwest—Their Education and the Public Welfare*. Austin, Tex.: University of Texas Press, 1965.

Nida, E. A. *Some Psychological Problems in Second Language Learning: Teaching English as a Second Language*, edited by H. B. Allen. New York: McGraw-Hill, 1965.

IV. Ideas for Learning Activities

The poem at the beginning of this section sets the stage for the ways children learn and points out the kinds of questions that teachers of young children are called upon to answer regarding their programs. This section is filled with ideas that enable teachers to add richness to their plans for children. While many materials and activities are selected primarily to foster cognitive development, they enhance other areas of development simultaneously.

Alert teachers observe the ways materials are used—or not used—by the children. They arrange and rearrange the materials and activities to keep the children's interest alive. Different ideas permit the children's play to take on new forms and encourage children to discover their own ideas. The program extends its value as teachers and parents share their own heritage. The food, the games they played as children, and other cultural traditions and values can be passed on to children. Teachers, parents, and children all learn from each other in this type of program.

A four-year-old, preparing to go home from a play session where parents and children had explored many art activities together, told his mother, "I had the best time in my whole life." As the ideas in this section are put to use, we can truly share with children some of the best growing and learning times of their lives.

Play Today?

You say you love your children,
And are concerned they learn today?
So am I—that's why I'm providing
A variety of kinds of play.

You're asking me the value
Of blocks and other such play?
Your children are solving problems.
They will use that skill everyday.

You're asking what's the value
Of having your children play?
Your daughter's creating a tower;
She may be a builder someday.

You're saying you don't want your son
To play in that "sissy" way?
He's learning to cuddle a doll;
He may be a father someday.

You're questioning the interest centers;
They just look like useless play?
Your children are making choices;
They'll be on their own someday.

You're worried your children aren't learning;
And later they'll have to pay?
They're learning a pattern for learning;
For they'll be learners alway.

Leila P. Fagg, M.S., received her degree from Indiana State University in elementary education. She has previously taught both kindergarten and primary groups and is currently teaching first grade in Paris, Illinois.

Alice Whiren

Table Toys:
The Underdeveloped Resource

Today, in most child care centers, the observer may see shelves with toys near a grouping of tables. The number, variety, and condition of these materials varies widely, as does the way in which they are used. What are some of the considerations that teachers need to make as they plan to improve the effectiveness of this aspect of their program?

Selection

Choosing table toys is the first step of planning. Each year the market is flooded with new educational toys that increase the number of alternatives available. Rather than providing a list of specific toys by name and manufacturer, let us examine four common categories of table toys: *coordination activities, construction activities, reconstruction activities,* and *classification activities.* Each group of materials offers different potentials for learning. Some materials may fit into more than one category, though references are made for the most frequent or common experience of the child.

Common *coordination activities* are the sewing cards, busy box, lacing shoe, button frame, and latch and catch box. The outstanding characteristic of this group of materials is that each is designed to provide practice involving a motor task that may be difficult for the child. It should be noted that all of the coordination activities are developed to enable the child to become self-sufficient in his day-to-day environment. Skills developed through these coordination activities have an essentially practical value to the child and his family.

98

Paul J. Cryan

Michelle Florman

Construction activities, however, are designed so that the end product or result is deliberately left undetermined by the materials used. Interlocking blocks, colored cubes, hammer and nail, magnetic shapes, and many others comprise this group. Children explore two and three dimensions of space, combine shapes to create new forms, use imagination to enhance their structures with special meanings relevant to themselves. They learn through experience the relative characteristics of wood, plastics, foam, or metal. They become sensitive to texture and color

of the materials. But, perhaps most important, the child learns that *she can control the material* and that his or her behavior determines the process and the product. The opportunities for learning are so numerous in these open-ended materials that they cannot be adequately listed here.

Reconstruction activities involve self-correcting materials that can be taken apart and reassembled. The degree of difficulty of these materials is so varied that some toys in this category are designed for infants (graduated boxes) and others are designed for teenagers (some model boats and airplanes). Among the most common reconstruction activities for preschool children are those that are graduated in size, such as stacking cups and those that must fit together: all puzzles, the mailbox, and similar inset toys.

The task for the child is to observe the assembled toy, to manipulate the

Alice Whiren, M.S., following the completion of an Advanced Certification in Early Childhood Education from the University of Illinois, Urbana, became an Instructor in Family and Child Sciences at Michigan State University, working as a coordinator of the laboratory preschool and teaching undergraduate teacher preparation courses.

pieces in order to take it apart, then reassemble them in the appropriate sequence or position so that the toy is in its original condition. Even the simplest toy in this category requires visual memory, assessment of size, shape, color and function, persistence, and motor coordination to complete the entire task. Having a variety of these materials at several levels of difficulty enables the child to develop skills and competencies that could be difficult to reproduce elsewhere in the program. Perhaps this is why children show such pleasure in their accomplishments as they exclaim, "Look, see what I did! I did it myself!"

The last category of table toys are those that are, or can be, *classification activities.* This would include all of the materials that require matching, patterning, and grouping, and most games. Some of the more commonly seen materials in this category are dominoes, lotto, board games, peg boards, and beads. Perhaps the criteria for including materials in this category

Donna J. Harris

is more a matter of *how* materials are used than the structure of the materials themselves. Beads are illustrative of this. Frequently, they are used as a coordination activity with the child

Cecil Cohen

100

stringing them at random. This is the first step, but the child may also sort beads as to color and form and string them in simple or complex patterns. It should be noted that the most economical use of resources is to use old toys in new ways and save limited funds for the truly new and different materials. *Many of the newly produced "educational" toys are variations of the basic activities inherent in all classification materials.*

The ideal number and distribution of table toys varies according to the number of children in the center, the number of rooms in which these toys are used, the storage and display space available, and the length of time children are in the center. A minimum guideline that has been helpful is one per child. If there are 10 percent coordination toys, 40 percent construction toys, 40 percent reconstruction toys, and 10 percent classification toys, the activities generally meet the developmental needs of most three- and four-year-old children.

If there are several groups of children in a center, each having independently equipped rooms and a central storage area where table toys can be selected, the variety available to any one group of children may be increased through a toy rotation procedure. It is particularly helpful to have a separate collection of table toys that are used *only* in the late afternoon of full-day programs. It regenerates interest in the activities that otherwise might become overfamiliar. It is always wise to reserve some toys and equipment for rotation in *any* preschool setting.

Display

The storage and display of these materials is, in many ways, as impor- tant as the number and variety available. Below are some suggestions that you might find helpful.

1. Select toys from your supply for classroom use for the day.

2. Place them on shelves at the child's eye level. *Avoid over-crowding* the shelves.

3. If the children do not tend to select materials from the shelves, place one or two toys on the tables before they arrive.

4. Store pieces of each set together. Cardboard shoe boxes, plastic shoe boxes, and plastic dishpans can be labeled and are useful storage containers.

5. Maintain all materials in good condition. Materials should be complete so that each child can be successful in his play. Do not display incomplete toys such as puzzles with missing pieces or bells without clappers.

6. Rotate toys regularly. Never put *every* table toy you possess on the children's shelf at once—even if you have a limited supply.

7. Allow the children to use the toys during free play. Each free play period should be about one to two hours in any one block of time.

8. Provide comfortable seating, good lighting, and an area clearly separated from other activities.

The way all materials are displayed determines (1) the attractiveness of the activity to the children, (2) their use of the materials, and (3) influences the way *they* take care of them.

Examples of Toy Selection for Two Days

15 children–Day 1

1 puzzle	4 to 5 pieces
1 puzzle	6 to 10 pieces
2 puzzles	11 to 15 pieces
2 puzzles	over 15 pieces
1 set	space wheels (interlocking pieces)
1	threading block
2	lacing boards
1	magnetic shapes and board
1 set	"Pegit Numbers" (wooden board with printed numbers, plus appropriate number of holes for pegs)
1 set	lotto (such as community helpers)
1 set	100 beads, 3/4″ size in assorted shapes and colors. 3 strings.
1	"Kitty in the Keg"

15 children–Day 2

Puzzles remain the same in number and pieces, but change pictures

1 set	"Shapeez" (instead of space wheels)
1	latch and catch board (instead of threading box)
2	lacing boards
1	magnetic shapes and board
1 set	"Pegit Numbers"
1	lotto (such as go-together lotto)
3	pegs and boards, with large pegs and holes (instead of beads)
1	stacking cups (instead of "Kitty in the Keg")

Planning for Increased Teacher Effectiveness

Planning for increased effectiveness with table toys is the key for encouraging learning with these materials.

If the adult knows in advance some of the alternative types of play that are possible, appropriate comments can be added to the spontaneous learnings of the child. It is obvious that some of the alternatives listed below for beads are more difficult than others. This is one reason why stringing beads is appropriate for children from two to six years old. Children need practice to consolidate their learnings. Later, with encouragement, they will move to more complex tasks with the same material through their explorations.

The child may:

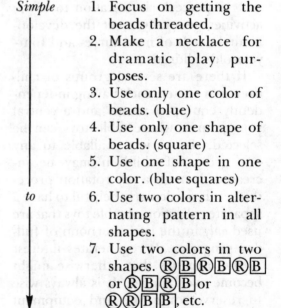

Simple

to

Complex

1. Focus on getting the beads threaded.
2. Make a necklace for dramatic play purposes.
3. Use only one color of beads. (blue)
4. Use only one shape of beads. (square)
5. Use one shape in one color. (blue squares)
6. Use two colors in alternating pattern in all shapes.
7. Use two colors in two shapes. Ⓡ Ⓑ Ⓡ Ⓑ Ⓡ Ⓑ or Ⓡ Ⓑ Ⓡ Ⓑ or Ⓡ Ⓡ Ⓑ Ⓑ, etc.
8. Develop a complex pattern of color and shape.

Guidance in Table Toy Area

Knowing the possibilities of any

material is important, but planning for the guidance of the child's behavior and general use of materials is as important. Complaints that the children tear up the materials, lose puzzle pieces and, in general, lay waste to the entire area are common. Such problems are the result of insufficient planning as to the appropriate limits for the children, rather than destructiveness of the children.

It is important for one of the teachers to be near the children while they are playing and follow through with individual children who may have forgotten the limits. Be explicit and positive. Praise children who are behaving in the desired manner.

For some construction activities, one set of materials, such as space wheels, are just enough for one child and sharing these with two or more others will inhibit each child's potential. This does not necessarily hold true if the children are working cooperatively on one construction.

General limits for manipulative toys include keeping pieces of toys (such as parts of puzzles) together and in the manipulative toy area, i.e., "on the rug" or "at the table." All toys are used carefully and reasonably by the children.

Teacher-Child Interaction

There are basically four kinds of teacher-child interaction that lead the child in learning some of the possible concepts through the use of table toys. The most important and frequent experience for preschoolers is *exploration*. It enables the children to utilize their information, imagination, and ability to organize their behavior in a happy and relaxed way. The child solves many problems independently and tests out his or her own level of competence. During the exploration phases, it is the adult's responsibility to (1) provide a comfortable working area; (2) make sure it is free from disruptions and interference from others; and (3) see that the children have space in which to work and time enough to complete their experience. The adult, of course, allows exploration within accepted limits established for the activity.

Expansion occurs when the adult puts into words what a child has done, "You used all the red beads," or comments on the way the child is experimenting in order to solve a problem, "You are trying to find the round piece for the squirrel's head." Expansion is used to call attention to important information and to provide words useful to the child in a meaningful context. Teachers focus on these behaviors after the child has had previous experience with the material and during his or her further explorations.

Teacher-initiated activity is frequently an invitation to the child to explore new materials. There are usually several children who through habit or choice play house or play with blocks day after day. The teacher may introduce the child to some other activity because of his or her assessment of the child's developmental needs and interests.

Another example of teacher-initiated activity: The teacher suggests a new, more complex level of exploration, "John, what would happen if you tried this . . . (giving a sequence of red, yellow, blue beads)?" Though the intent is to guide the child's behavior, the teacher does not force the child's activity or decide what should happen.

This type of guidance is perhaps the distinguishing characteristic between *teacher-initiated behavior* and *teacher-directed behavior*. In the latter, the teacher gives directions which the child is expected to carry out. A common example is establishing the rules for games such as lotto, dominoes, Raggedy Ann, and others. Here is an example: "This is a picture of a giraffe. In lotto games, you match the picture just like it on your card." (Demonstrate.) "Now you find a picture of a zebra on your card." (The child does it.) "Good!" The teacher-directed method is used frequently and many times inappropriately. It should, however, be the least frequently used technique if children are to become increasingly independent and self-directed.

Each child, though, needs a variety of experiences with the same materials over an extended period of time to enable him or her to utilize all of the possibilities of the table toys available. Over time the child may use a toy frequently and still learn new things because he or she has grown and changed so that his or her level of play is increasingly complex.

Val Kositsky

What in the World Is Cooking in Class Today?

Multiethnic Recipes for Young Children

Cooking as a learning tool has become an everyday affair in many early childhood classrooms. Hopefully, times have passed when a teacher might be questioned by a mother, for having had a child prepare a gelatin dessert, with "How many four-year-olds have to make their own dinner?" The chances are greater that appreciative "oohs" and "aahs" will come from delighted parents receiving a still-warm loaf of multigrained bread, ground and kneaded by their child's hands.

The preschool program has broadened the cooking itinerary to encompass food preparation, beginning with the planting of the seed and ending with the feasting on the finished product. It has moved from the world of prepackaged mixes and other convenience foods to the world of recipes more representative of our multiethnic population. A closer examination of the "melting pot" concept has led to the more realistic generalization that likens Americans to a tossed salad in which a great variety of ingredients are combined in a single bowl. Each ingredient, however, retains its own identity. A satisfying way for children to learn about and appreciate differences in American eating practices is for them to participate in multiethnic food projects. So, let's sample what's cooking in class today!

Foods Inherited from the American Indian

Many of the foods important to our diets are of American Indian origin. Barbecued meats, steamed lobster, succotash, spoon bread, cranberry sauce, sweet and Irish potatoes, tomatoes, avocados, peppers, pineapples, pumpkins, squash, wild rice, maple sugar, corn, and mincemeat pie have been inherited from Native Americans.

The Indian foods and recipes we use today come mainly from five areas. From the Southwest, the Pueblo tribes, the Papagos (Bean People), and the Hopis grew peppers and beans to be made into savory chili, soups, guacamole, and barbecue sauces. The Tlingit, Kwakiutl, Salish, and other tribes of the Northwest smoked and broiled many kinds of marine food taken from the waters of the Pacific Ocean and western rivers. The nomadic Plains Indians, such as the Sioux and the Cheyenne, roasted buffalo over campfires. The Cherokees and other tribes of the South prepared fragrant soups and rich stews. They also baked the same type of cornbread we make today. Fireless cooking in earthen pits for baking foods like clams and beans was done by the Indians of the East coast: the Narrangansetts, Penobscots, Powhatans, and Iroquois.

Most Indians regarded corn as a gift from the gods to be treasured and surrounded with sacred ceremony. Although tribes had various ways to say the word for corn,

Barbara Stross

they meant the same: "our life." Writings by Governor Bradford of the Massachusetts Bay Colony tell how corn saved the Pilgrims from starvation. An Indian chief, Squanto, taught early colonists how to insure an abundant crop by planting a fish head for fertilizer along with the kernels in a mound of dirt.

Corn is an ingredient used in a variety of American Indian and Mexican dishes. Although its exact origins have not as yet been determined, botanists believe corn may have originated in Mexico or South America. As one of the most important plants domesticated by the Indian, corn was roasted, shelled, dried, ground, and stored. When tribes traveled or hunters pursued game, the dried kernels were carried along in corn husk bags or deerskin parfleches for a quick meal.

Piki, the traditional bread of the Hopis, is made with a souplike batter from finely ground blue Indian corn and water. The piki breadmaker dips a hand into the loose batter and swipes it deftly over a very hot stone griddle. It quickly bakes into a translucent sheet of bread and is lifted off. A second layer is placed on the hot rock and then covered with the first. The two are rolled together to form a crisp, tender corn-flavored bread. Sometimes they are rolled around a piece of meat, goat's milk cheese, or piñon nuts.

Val Kositsky, M.A., is Instructor in Early Childhood Education at Merritt Community College and the University of California Extension; a teacher, Parent-Nursery Schools, Berkeley Unified School District; and a consultant in nutrition education.

Within the scope of the preschooler's culinary skill is a Navaho version of bread, *pahnelaquaz*, known also as stick or fry bread. With precautions it can be made in the classroom on a hot plate. A small saucepan is half-filled with cooking oil and heated to about 350°F (177°C). The temperature is right if a small piece of dough sizzles and bubbles upon contact with the oil.

For each child-sized bread, mix the following ingredients in a small bowl or cup:

2 tablespoons flour
¼ teaspoon baking powder
pinch of salt
2 teaspoons water (enough to make a workable dough)

The dough is patted and shaped with floured hands into a flat, thin pancake. Using a slotted spoon, this is lowered gently into the hot fat. A clean stick or fork holds the bubbling cake under the oil until it is lightly browned on both sides. It is carefully lifted out, drained on a paper towel, and eaten warm and crisp.

Indian shuck bread is another food which can be made in the classroom. While a corn husk is soaking in cold water, the cook mixes the following ingredients in a small bowl:

3 tablespoons cornmeal
⅛ teaspoon salt
⅛ teaspoon baking powder
1 tablespoon hot water

The stiff batter is spooned onto the drained and dried corn husk. The husk is folded over to form a sealed package and tied with string. This is boiled in a pot of water for about 10 minutes. After it is removed from the pan, the string cut, and the husk opened, the tasty cornbread is ready to eat plain or with syrup. It may have originally been baked in the hot ashes of an open fire and thus became known as *ash cake*.

Young children can make blackberry, blueberry, currants, or gooseberry *preserves* by harnessing the radiant energy of the summer sun. They can wash and measure about 4 cups of berries, combine them with 3 cups of sugar and 2 tablespoons of lemon juice. This mixture should stand in a 4-quart saucepan for about an hour before it is boiled vigorously for 4 minutes. After cooling for 30 minutes, it is poured into shallow pans to a depth of ⅓ to ¾ inch. A clear plastic or glass cover with an inch opening along one side to permit evaporation is placed over each pan. The covering concentrates the heat of the sun like a lens when placed in the full sun. The contents should be stirred gently every hour until the fruit is plump and the juices are the consistency of corn syrup. Depending on your local sun power, the process will take from 2 to 10 hours. (Seattle's sun took 10 hours to Phoenix's 2.) If you should run out of sunshine, the preserves can be brought

Barbara Stross

107

indoors overnight to stand at room temperature until the next sunny day. What is not eaten can be stored in clean jars and refrigerated.

Indians balanced their diets by eating fresh greens. *Dandelion leaves* are still fairly available even in urban areas. Children can pick them where it is known that no poison sprays have been used. After washing, the leaves are snipped with blunt-nosed scissors into small pieces. Combined with equal parts of oil and vinegar, these greens make a snappy, slightly bitter salad. Another Indian dish mixes crumbles of fried bacon with the prepared leaves.

For soothing and medicinal drinks the Indians made teas. The roots of the young dandelion and the red sassafras were dug, dried, and then steeped in boiling water. Sassafras tea is called *Ga-Na-A-Da Dai*. More to children's taste might be tea made from the leaves of a mint plant grown in a jar of water or the school garden.

Mexican Cookery

Mexicans have utilized the land and the sea for sustenance. The earth provided materials for their clay cooking and eating utensils. The conquering Spaniards introduced cattle, poultry, and sheep to Mexico, but meat continues to be a premium food. Beans serve as a primary protein source. Rice and corn, an occasional meat treat, spicy chili and tomato sauces, fresh fruits and vegetables also make up the daily diet.

The Indian staple of corn plays an important role in Mexican cookery. There is evidence that the ancient Mexican Indian enjoyed popcorn as we do today. Chilies and beans have been basic to Mexican cuisine for many centuries. However, the mainstay of the Mexican diet is a thin corn or flour pancake, the *tortilla*.

The tortilla is present at every meal and snack. It is eaten hot or cold, plain or with other foods, acting as a scoop. Rolled around a spicy mixture of meat or cheese the tortilla becomes the *taco*. Covered with

a nippy sauce a taco is known as an *enchilada*. Flour tortillas filled with beans are called *burritos;* one containing melted cheese, a *quesadilla*. When a thick tortilla forms the platform for chopped cooked meat, poultry, grated cheese, shredded lettuce, chili sauce, or guacamole, it is known as a *chalupa*.

Corn kernels were dried in the sun, soaked in limewater to make them soft, and ground in a hollowed-out stone (metate) to form a paste called *masa*. Lumps of this dough were slapped back and forth between the hands to make a thin pancake and baked on a stone slab heated by a charcoal fire. Today, prepared fresh masa or packaged "instant" masa can be purchased at the food store. Tortillas come ready-made canned, frozen, or boxed.

A metal or wooden press and a heated griddle make it possible for young children to prepare their own tortillas. To make a *corn tortilla*, the cook will break off a piece of prepared masa about the size of a walnut. This is placed in a press between pieces of plastic wrap and flattened. It is cooked on a heated grill or iron fry pan until lightly browned on both sides. If a press is not available, the pancake can be formed with a rolling pin or pressed flat with the palm of the hand.

When instant corn tortilla flour is used, the child will mix 4 tablespoons of it with 1 tablespoon of lukewarm water in a small bowl. This dough is turned out onto a waxed paper square, kneaded lightly, patted, pressed, or rolled into a thin flat circle and cooked as above.

About 400 years ago in Mexico, Montezuma introduced the Spanish explorer, Cortez, to *xoco-latl*, his favorite drink, made from a paste of roasted cocoa seeds ground up with water, spices, and pulverized vanilla pod. The mixture was beaten until foamy and then eaten with a jeweled spoon or drunk from a golden goblet.

To mix this bitter drink, make a paste with 2 teaspoons of plain unsweetened cocoa and 3 teaspoons of cold water added a few drops at a time. Then ½ teaspoon of vanilla extract and ½ cup of cold water are added. This mixture is beaten by an egg beater or twirled by a "Molinillo" (a primitive, decoratively carved wooden stick) to a frothy consistency, while the person chants "Bati, bati, sho-co-lat-tie."

Black-American Foods

For the contemporary Afro-American, soul food provides a lasting link with the African past and forms a bond with other Blacks. Soul cooking is a style of food preparation brought to America mainly from West Africa by African slaves. Field slaves in America, forced to live in isolated, segregated groups, prepared foods as they had in their home countries. Living in close proximity to members from many different African tribes, they had the opportunity to sample and exchange a variety of recipes which forms the basis of the present international African cuisine.

During the long, hard workweek, tired slaves had to rely on quick cooking methods like frying to prepare food, but on holidays and weekends more time could be spent fixing traditional stews, roasts, and sauces. Although the important African ingredient, palm oil, was not available, pork fat issued by slave owners was used to flavor sauces, vegetables, rice, meat, and fish, and for deep-fat frying. Barbecue sauces, peppery and flavorful, were served with meats.

A *barbecue sauce* to be brushed on chicken, spareribs, or pig feet as they are charcoal broiled at school can be made by combining equal amounts of catsup and cider vinegar, with prepared mustard and drops of Red Devil or Tabasco sauce added to taste.

Pig feet and tails, hog's maws (stomach), chitterlings (intestine), and hocks (thighs) are prized parts of succulent soul dishes. To make *pig tail stew* have the children wash and dry 2 to 3 pounds of pig tails, then cut them into 2-inch pieces. These are browned in 1 tablespoon of hot lard heated in a heavy

large pot. The children can also prepare 2 chopped onions and 2 minced cloves of garlic to add to the pig tails. Two cups of canned tomatoes, 2 cups of beef broth, 2 cups of water, 1 to 2 bay leaves, and 1 teaspoon of salt are then put into the pot, brought to a boil, covered, and simmered gently for about 45 minutes. During this time have the children wash and cut up 4 potatoes, slice 4 carrots, and shell 2 cups of peas. These are added to the stew which is cooked about 15 to 20 minutes longer until the meat and vegetables are tender.

Corn appears in soul food primarily in the form of cornmeal hominy (prepared by leaching kernels with lye) and grits (ground from hominy). This staple forms the basis for cooked cereal, cakes, breads, and dumplings. Cornbread used to be baked in the fields on the back of a hoe heated on an open fire. In the classroom *hoecake* can be made by having the child mix 2 tablespoons of white cornmeal with a pinch of salt and 1 tablespoon of boiling water. Formed into a pancake it is cooked slowly on a heated greased griddle until browned on both sides, and served with syrup or molasses.

Corn pone is a more nutritious version of this cornbread, containing 2 teaspoons of beaten egg and substituting milk for the water. In Africa, the cornmeal paste was wrapped in banana leaves and baked on hot ashes. In America, cabbage leaves were used instead in preparation of these *ash cakes*. Another version is to drop spoonfuls of the cornmeal batter carefully into deep hot fat and cook until golden-brown puffs to make *hush puppies*.

Leafy green plants such as cabbage, kale, collards, mustard, turnip, dandelion, pigeonweed, cowslip, rape, and land cresses can be cooked as greens and seasoned highly or combined with smoked or salted meat. *Gumbo z'herbes,* found in Creole cooking, is a dish made of wild and cultivated greens which originated in the Congo.

When cooking ham hocks with *greens,* first cook two or three ham hocks, 1 cut-up onion, 2 teaspoons salt, and ½ teaspoon pepper in a large pot of water for two

Barbara Stross

hours. Meanwhile, the children can wash three bunches of collards and mustard, leaf by leaf, and then strip off the stems. Add the leaves and a large diced bell pepper to the ham hocks and cook for another hour and one-half, until the meat is tender. Served with rice, this dish makes a wholesome meal.

On New Year's Eve it is a tradition with some Black Americans to serve a meal of *greens* and *Hopping Johnny* (black-eyed peas cooked with ham hocks and rice) which represents an abundance of money and good luck for the coming year.

Various types of peas and beans brought from Africa were cultivated around the borders of cotton and corn fields, becoming known as "field peas." These were preserved by sun-drying, then soaked and slowly simmered with pieces of salted or smoked meat or combined with rice and vegetables for hearty one-pot meals.

A delicious dish of *peas and rice* can be prepared in the classroom. While one-half pound of minced bacon is simmered in 1

quart of water, soak 2 cups of dried black-eyed peas. Peas are drained and any discolored ones are discarded. The peas, 1 chopped onion, 2 teaspoons salt, ¼ teaspoon pepper, and 1 more quart of water are added to the bacon. The pot is covered and cooking continues until the peas are tender (about 30 minutes). The mixture is stirred frequently and water added as needed. A cup of rice is added and cooking is complete in about 15 more minutes.

Peanuts grown extensively in the South and in Africa are popular and nutritive ingredients for sauces and stews. Raw peanuts obtained from natural food stores can be planted and later harvested in the classroom for use in various recipes.

Zucchini with peanuts is an adaptation of an African dish. Slices of 6 washed zucchinis are stirred into 2 to 4 tablespoons of melted margarine, covered to steam in their own liquid for about 5 minutes, then garnished with ground peanuts and red pepper flakes.

Okra, native to Africa, is an important ingredient in the making of different kinds of *gumbo*, a stew that approaches the consistency of the thick Louisiana soil known as "gumbo." The origin of the word gumbo may have been derived from the African term for okra, "kingombo" or "ngombo." In the South the word means "all together" or "all at once." So gumbo can also be a dish composed of a potpourri of ingredients (turkey, chicken, rabbit, fish, crab, shrimp, oysters, etc.) seasoned with okra or gumbo file made from dried sassafras leaves. There are as many versions of *gumbo* as there are people making it.

Another link between sixteenth century Africa and twentieth century Black-American diet is the frequent use of yams and sweet potatoes. They can be boiled, fried, baked, or roasted.

For a simple *sweet potato pie*, each child spoons some of the following filling into a small aluminum foil tart pan lined with a circle of unbaked pie crust. For the filling, bake 2 large sweet potatoes or yams until soft. The children can peel and mash them in a large bowl. Add 1 cup fresh or canned milk, ½ cup sugar, ¼ pound melted margarine or butter, one egg, and ½ teaspoon nutmeg. Raisins may be added, or the pie may be topped with marshmallows. Bake the pie at 375°F (190°C) until the filling is set, about 20 to 30 minutes.

Foods from the Orient

Each Oriental group has its own distinct customs and habits, but rice forms the basis of most meals. In Japanese and Chinese cookery it is served boiled, fried, steamed, and in combinations with vegetables, fish, meats, or shellfish. It may be made into gruel, rice-water, rice-wine, and flour baked into noodles. This grain provides the calories, while soybeans provide the protein for both cuisines.

To cook *rice* the Chinese way, put 1¾ cups cold water for every cup of rice into a heavy pot with a lid. Bring the water to a rolling boil, cover, and turn the heat as low as possible. Don't peek for 20 minutes, then remove the cover. If the rice looks dry and has volcanolike holes, it is done. To form a crisp crust, leave the pot of rice on low heat for an additional 4 or 5 minutes.

Chopsticks are used for eating instead of knives and forks. The Japanese brought them along when they left China centuries ago for their present homeland. With practice, chopsticks make good eating utensils. They are held in one hand so that one stick is stationary and the other moves much like pincers to pick up small pieces of food. The food bowl is held close to the mouth and the chopsticks are used to convey the contents quickly to the mouth. Ingredients for all recipes are cut into bite-sized pieces so that no knives are needed.

To eat in traditional Japanese manner, the children should remove their shoes and sit on large flat pillows or on grass mats at low tables. The foods are arranged on individual trays. The Japanese prepare an odd number of dishes (3 or 5) for regular meals and 7 or more for special occasions. Many foods are pickled in brine, only slightly cooked, or served raw. Much cooking is done at the table over charcoal. When ready to eat, the diner bows and says, "I start eating." According to tradition it is not polite to eat without eating rice, nor is it polite to eat fewer than two bowls of rice at a meal. If a third bowl is desired, a fourth must also be eaten. *Green tea* is drunk from handleless cups throughout the meal. Pickles are the final dish. The eater then bows and says, "Goshiso sama" (It was quite a treat) at the end of the meal.

Sushi, a cooked short-grained rice seasoned with a little mild vinegar and sugar and shaped into small, firm balls, is the Japanese equivalent of a sandwich, good for school lunches and picnics. One type, *onigiri,* is a rice ball with bits of salted salmon, pickled plums, cod roe, cooked carrots, or other ingredients inserted into its center. To form the ball, have the children wet their hands in a bowl of salted water and then push the chosen tidbit into the middle of a handful of rice before shaping. For variety they could pat on a coating of black or white roasted sesame seeds or wrap the ball in a strip of seaweed called *nori.*

Very hot tea poured over leftover rice with a pinch of salt added makes a dish called *chazuke.*

Tempura is one of the most popular Japanese dishes. It is said to have been in existence during the Tokugawa period (1600-1853). It consists of seafood, vegetables, or meat coated in batter and deep-fried in oil. To make the batter have the student use a chopstick to stir in 1 tablespoon water and 2 teaspoons beaten egg into 2 tablespoons flour. It should be lumpy. Strips or square pieces of vegetables, like carrots, string beans, or green pepper, are strung onto an 8 to 10 inch bamboo skewer and then dipped into the batter. The skewered food is cooked in hot oil heated in a small saucepan. When the batter is slightly browned the morsel is ready to dip into *tensugo* sauce (equal parts soy and mirin, a mild rice vinegar) and eaten.

Teriyaki is a method of broiling foods directly over a charcoal fire. Small pieces of boneless chicken, prawns, firm-fleshed fish, beef, lamb, and vegetables are marinated in a mixture of soy and mirin for about 30 minutes. The cook selects the pieces desired and strings them onto an 8 to 10 inch bamboo skewer. The loaded stick is placed on a grill over a medium hot fire and rotated every few minutes for even cooking.

The cuisine of China is among the most varied in the world. There are five important schools of Chinese cooking. Of these schools Cantonese has been the most familiar in the United States, but in recent years the elegant types from Peking, Shanghai, Yang Chow, and the spicy Szechuan are becoming known. Wheat is used in the northern provinces while rice is the important staple of the South.

The wok is the chief Chinese cooking utensil. It is a shallow, round-bottomed frying pan. An iron cookpot is often used for steamed dishes.

Chinese meals are served communally, like a hot buffet; the family meal will consist of 4 or 5 dishes while banquets could have as many as 30! Each diner has a bowl and set of chopsticks. Food is taken from the platters in the center of the table, always serving from the near side of the common dish. At the end of the meal hands are wiped with a clean cloth wrung out in hot water. At a ceremonial banquet a guest, having finished, says to the others, "Eat at your leisure" and may then leave the table. Chopsticks are left crossed over the empty bowl. As a polite farewell gesture, the host will lift these chopsticks saying, "I hope you walk in safety."

Soup is served throughout the meal as a savory liquid while quantities of rice and other foods are eaten. Sometimes more than one kind will be served at a meal.

With the aid of an old-fashioned food grinder, *egg fu yung* can be easily made by the young child. For one serving the cook will combine 3 tablespoons of beaten egg and ½ teaspoon of soya sauce in a small bowl. This dish is placed directly under the grinder to catch the ingredients being ground (1-inch piece of celery, 3 small shrimp, and 2 inches of green onion). The mixture is stirred and poured into a greased, heated fry pan or wok until set. It is turned to brown on the second side. If no grinder is available these ingredients may be chopped up with a paring knife or cut up with scissors.

To prepare *tea eggs,* one egg is boiled for each child for 10 minutes and then soaked in cold water. With a spoon the shell is tapped lightly to make small cracks. Now 3 tablespoons of black tea, 2 tablespoons of salt, and 2 tablespoons of soya sauce are added to the water, and the eggs boiled again for 20 minutes. When the shells are removed a pretty pattern remains on the egg white. Cut into quarters the egg is ready to eat.

Leftover rice can be combined with many different ingredients to make *chao fan,* a typical dish served on Chinese trains. Heat 1 teaspoon of oil in a wok or skillet, then add 1 teaspoon minced green onion and 1 beaten egg. When the egg has become well scrambled, stir in 1 tablespoon chopped ham and 1 tablespoon cooked peas and cook until hot. This is served over ½ cup of cooked rice.

Won tons are a great favorite. The "skins," 3-inch squares of thin noodles, are available fresh or frozen at many food stores. Fillings vary. For 3 or 4 won tons, have the child combine 1 tablespoon raw hamburger with ½ teaspoon soya sauce, 3 cut-up bean sprouts, and ⅓ teaspoon minced green onion. A teaspoon of this mixture is put in the center of each won ton noodle. The noodle is folded in half to form a triangle and the edges dampened to make them adhere to each other. Now the ends of the triangle are moistened and brought together. Won tons can be deep-fat fried for 1 to 2 minutes or simmered gently in chicken soup.

Soybeans, the most versatile and popular

Asian vegetable, are used for bean paste, curd (*tofu* in Japanese), soya sauce, and producing bean sprouts. To grow *bean sprouts* in the classroom, cover the bottom of a baking pan with four layers of burlap. Sprinkle about ½ cup of mung beans over the fabric. Saturate with water, pouring off any excess. Water daily. Keep in a dark place until sprouted, then move to a sunny spot. They are ready to eat in five to seven days when they are about one inch long. Rinse in a colander to remove husks, dry well, then store in a plastic bag in the refrigerator.

Conclusion

By preparing and eating different ethnic foods in the classroom, children can experience the flavors of a multitude of cultures which make up America. Through first-hand activities, they can discover meals other than those idealized by TV advertising. They will be exposed to many ingenious ways to use foods that people from various backgrounds have developed. Young children thus can have a taste of the world through their multiethnic cooking experiences.

References

Berry, E. *Eating and Cooking Around the World*. New York: John Day Co., 1963.

Doi, M. *Japanese One-Pot Cookery*. Tokyo, Japan: Kodansha International Ltd., 1966.

Kluckhohn, C. *The Navaho*. New York: Doubleday & Co., 1962.

Kositsky, V.; McFarlane, B.; and Swenson, M. *I Made It Myself Cookbook*. Berkeley, Calif.: Merritt Publishers, 1973.

LINC Leadership Development Program. *Idea Exchange, Native Americans*. Greensboro, N.C.: Learning Institute of North Carolina (LINC), 1973.

Ma, N. *Chinese Cookbook*. Tokyo, Japan: Charles Tuttle Co., 1960.

Mendes, H. *The African Heritage Cookbook*. New York: Macmillan, 1971.

Meyer, C. *The Bread Book*. New York: Harcourt Brace Jovanovich, 1971.

Murphey, E. *Indian Uses of Native Plants*. Fort Bragg, Calif.: Mendocino Historical Society, 1959.

Peter Maurin Neighborhood House, *West Oakland Soul Food Cookbook*. Oakland, Calif.: Peter Maurin Neighborhood House, 1960.

Pueblo Indian Cookbook. Santa Fe, N.M.: Museum of New Mexico Press, 1972.

Sunset Books Editors. *Oriental Cook Book* and *Mexican Cook Book*. Menlo Park, Calif.: Lane Books, 1974.

Walter, E. *American Cooking: Southern Style*. New York: Time-Life Books, 1971.

Wilms, B. *Crunchy Bananas*. Santa Barbara, Calif.: Peregrine Press, 1975.

Dorothy T. McDonald
with Jonny H. Ramsey

Awakening the Artist:
Music for Young Children

A visitor to any center for early childhood education in this country would probably hear music of some kind. Children like to sing; they like to play musical instruments; they like to listen to records. Teachers of young children generally include musical activities daily for the pleasure they give, for the release from tension they can often provide, and for aid in developing cognitive skills in many curricular areas. Most teachers, however, find it necessary to proceed by instinct; there is little information about the kinds of musical experiences that are appropriate for the young child, the methods and techniques which might be helpful in planning musical activities, or the criteria which might be applied when choosing musical materials for young children. From study of the research and theory about the musical development of young children, we have formulated the following guidelines for teachers to use in planning for one of children's most meaningful human experiences—responding to and making music.

Learning to Listen

From studies of infant responses to music, a first guideline seems appropriate:

Music should be included daily for infants as well as for older children. The presence of music, whether through recordings or the teacher's singing or playing, can awaken early responses to musical sound and can encourage infants to *learn to listen*.

Noy (1968) described music as an auditory channel of communication and emotional exchange between the infant and the outside world. McDonald (1970) also suggested music's importance in the emotional well-being of children; she wrote about children selecting a familiar song or composition, heard in the home, as a *transition tune*—something of the child's world which helps the child alleviate anxieties and makes acquaintances with the outside world more pleasurable. Michel (1973) reported that children receive and respond to music at a very early age—"at two months [an infant] will lie motionless, with fixed attention to the sound of singing or playing of an instrument" (p. 17). It would appear that musical experiences can and should be purposefully planned even for infants.

A baby seldom is thought of as a singer. Ostwald (1973), however, noted that even infants attempt to vocalize musical intervals at an early age. Described as a period of *vocal contagion*, this stage can begin before the second half of the first year. He cited studies by Mead of cultures where nurses are specifically instructed to encourage infants' vocalizations by mimicking the babies' sounds.

Dorothy T. McDonald, Ph.D., is Associate Professor, Music Education, Elementary Education Division, University of Iowa, Iowa City, and a former music teacher in Iowa, Illinois, and North Carolina.

Jonny H. Ramsey, M.A., is a consultant and Assistant Director of a related-arts curriculum development project at Pennsylvania State University, State College, and has taught music at the University of Iowa and in the Virginia public schools.

Thus, the presence of music in the first year, when the child is primarily a receiver of music, appears to be an important prerequisite to participation in the music-making process. *Receiving* evolves to *sound-making* and, subsequently, to *music-making*.

Learning to Sing

As young children become interested in participating in making music, certain questions arise. At what pitch levels can they sing most comfortably? Are there certain melodic patterns which children sing easily? What kinds of musical experiences could help them achieve accuracy and "tunefulness" in singing?

Sally Gale

A second guideline, based on studies of young children's singing, is:

Singing should be included in the daily activities of preschool children, but expectations of achievement should be based upon knowledge of the developmental nature of this ability. Songs for classroom use should be chosen with careful consideration of tonality, range, melodic configurations, and vocal developmental stages of the children.

Singing attempts have been reported in children as young as four to six months of age (Michel 1973). From six months to one year, babies try out clearly audible musical intervals, usually within a range of three to five tones (Shuter 1968). Around the age of

two, before many children will attempt to join in group singing, *chanting*, a form of spontaneous singing, is often heard among children at play. Many children experiment with familiar word patterns by giving them a tune—*language-related chants*—while others like to repeat a melodic pattern, experimenting with tonal sounds (Simons 1964). Often chants do not seem rhythmically related to the physical activity they accompany. The melodic patterns reported by observers appear to be those commonly found in songs of the child's culture (Scheihing 1952). Ascending and descending scale patterns, falling minor thirds, fourths, and fifths seem to be frequently used intervals. One of the most commonly heard melodic patterns in play activities is the familiar *teasing chant*—two falling minor thirds separated by the upper neighbor of the higher tone ("sol-mi-la-sol-mi"). The familiar song "Rain, Rain, Go Away" uses this pattern for the entire song. Perhaps *musical conversations* can be created by teacher and child using this common pattern.

At what pitch levels do young children sing easily? Cooper (1973) has reported that two-year-old children seem to sing most comfortably in a range from D_4 to A_4*—a range of five diatonic tones above middle C. Songs such as "Go Tell Aunt Rhody," the chorus of "Jingle Bells," "Twinkle, Twinkle, Little Star" (six tones), and "This Old Man" (six tones), long favorites with children, can be pitched to fit comfortably in this range; these songs also employ the melodic patterns cited above.

As children grow, their vocal range expands. Simons (1964) reported, in the spontaneous singing of children nine to 31 months of age, a usable range from C_4 to C_5.

---

*Middle C on the piano keyboard is identified as "C_4"; the pitches identified with subscript "4" lie in the octave above middle C. Pitches identified with subscript "3" lie in the octave below middle C; pitches with subscript "5" lie in the octave above third-space C (treble clef).

in twins and A^b_3 to B_4 in singletons. Kirkpatrick (1962) reported that the range used most frequently by five-year-old children extended from G_3 to B^b_4. Over half the children tested had extensive ranges from F_3 to E_5; however, approximately 20 percent had limited ranges from B_3 to $F^\#_4$. From a comparison of these ranges, it seems that even for children who have wide singing ranges, tones in the relatively low range below middle C become usable as soon as, or before, those in a relatively higher range (above A_4 or B_4).

When learning songs (imitative singing), however, the requirements of matching tones and words result in more restricted ranges (Jersild and Bienstock 1935). Drexler (1938) found that the most frequently used range of three- to six-year-old children was from C_4 to $D^\#_5$, but that the lower pitches were sung more easily. Young (1971) and Smith (1963) reported similar findings.

These researchers also reported certain sequential stages in the development of tuneful singing. While great individual differences exist among children, and no age seems significantly related to each stage, teachers may observe the following growth pattern. First, young children attempt to use the range of their speaking voices to reproduce songs. Next, they might exhibit inconsistent melodic direction. Gradually gaining vocal control, they may become accurate directionally, but inaccurate in interval reproduction. The hoped-for final stage is the accurate reproduction of a melody within a given tonality.

Maturation appears to be the most significant factor in range development; Boardman (1967) and Smith (1970) found that first grade children who had received early group training in singing, as well as those who had not, had more difficulty with upper range accuracy than with lower tones.

When choosing songs for beginning group singing, teachers might be advised to include many songs in ranges from approximately B_3 to A_4. Perhaps the concept of tuneful singing—important to all subsequent musical experiences—may be formed more easily in songs of this limited range.

Hermanson (1972) suggested that teachers teach songs using voice rather than piano; in her study, pitch accuracy was best when the children imitated a woman's voice and worst with a piano. One finding of a larger study by Sergeant and Roche (1973) drew attention to the matter of pitching songs in a consistent manner (each time a song is sung, it is sung in the same tonality). In their study, children three or four years of age tended to remember and reproduce songs at the same pitch levels in which the songs were learned.

Studies of techniques for helping children discriminate melodic intervals—a skill important in singing accuracy—provide a third guideline.

Visual, verbal, and motor cues may be effective in helping young children develop concepts of melodic interval and direction.

Yendovitskaya (1971) designed a pitch discrimination training program for three- and four-year-old children in which the subjects were taught to represent melodic intervals with matching arm amplitude; wide intervals were represented with arms far apart, narrow intervals with arms close together. He found that the physical representation was prerequisite for these children's successful identification of paired pitches as same or different. Repina trained children to associate low and high pitches with pictures of large and small animals. Williams (1932) used the piano keyboard as a visual cue in helping young children acquire concepts of melodic direction (tones moving "upstairs" or "downstairs").

In a similar manner, a teacher may provide visual cues, such as moving the hands up and down with the tones of a song or playing the melody on songbells held vertically. The inclusion of songs whose lyrics describe direction ("number songs" might fit in this category) or suggest directional physical movement ("I Put My Arms Up High") can provide experiences with the concept of melodic direction.

Ellen Levine Ebert

Learning to Move

To a young child, melody and movement are closely related; studies of children's spontaneous singing have shown that songs often grow out of motor activities. Studies by Greenberg (1972), Romanek (1974), and Belyayeva-Ekzemplyarskaya show that concepts of beat, tempo, and dynamics may develop before those of pitch, melody, harmony, and form. However, most young children need experience with rhythmic movement before they are successful in duplicating or synchronizing movement with music. One of the first spontaneous rhythmic activities among children is producing a *beat* (Shuter 1968). These regular, unaccented pulsations are quite fast in tempo ($\quarternote$ = 120 to $\quarternote$ = 176) (Scheihing 1952; Simons 1964) and little attempt is made to synchronize them with those of other children. When accents appear, they are often irregular and experimental in nature. At three years of age, the ability to synchronize beat with music for a controlled duration of time begins to develop (Christianson 1938); at age four, interest in dramatizing ideas in music appears; at age five, most children are able to march, clap, and otherwise keep time with music at relatively fast tempi (Jersild and Bienstock 1935).

117

Training does not seem to improve these skills significantly; maturation is the most important factor. Therefore, a fourth guideline for planning rhythmic experiences might be expressed:

Rhythmic activities should start with exploration rather than duplication. Synchronization training is less important then opportunity to explore movement and rhythm.

Fingerplays, action songs, and musical games provide many exploratory experiences with rhythmic expression. Songs such as "This Old Man," "Jim Along Josie," "In and Out the Window," and "Little Rabbit in the Wood" are but a few which can be used to encourage rhythmic expression. Many recent recordings for young children also encourage creative exploratory movement rather than synchronization with a beat or pattern. Hap Palmer's *Creative Movement and Rhythmic Expression* (Educational Activities, Inc.) provides delightful exploratory experiences with rhythmic movement.

Learning to Hear

Music is an aural art, and the development of listening skills is one of the most important objectives of any music program. What kinds of music attract young children? How can teachers encourage attentive listening?

Alford (1971) reported that young children show a greater degree of response to music which is predominantly rhythmic or melodic rather than that which is harmonic or dissonant. McDonald and Schuckert (1968) found that when children were allowed to choose between a jazz selection and a classical selection, jazz was the preferred choice. However, some children showed increased interest in the classical selection over a period of exposure time.

Studies by Fullard (1967), Greer, Dorow, and Hanser (1973), and Allen (1959) revealed very young children's ability to learn to identify orchestral instruments by matching pictures of the instruments with their sound when played. Instruments identified by three-, four-, and five-year-old children included violin, clarinet, cello, flute, viola, French horn, bassoon, oboe, and trumpet. Young children appear to be discriminating in selecting an appropriate timbre, also, when choosing percussive instruments for rhythmic activities (Shuter 1968). Such information suggests a guideline for planning listening experiences:

Music listening experiences may be included as an important part of an early childhood music curriculum. Discrimination tasks, including identification of individual or families of instruments may be appropriate and may increase interest in listening to many different kinds of music.

The Bowmar albums, including *The Young Listener*; records developed for identification of instruments; and selected albums from the Folkways recordings of music from other cultures are valuable sources.

Learning to Learn

A final guideline is formulated from studies in which music was used as an aid to cognitive development in other curriculum areas:

Music and movement may be useful in motivating and helping children to

Dorothy McDonald

118

acquire verbal concepts, oral communication, and aural discrimination skills.

Because music is a pleasurable and non-threatening experience for most children, it can sometimes be used to help children with special needs feel comfortable while learning. Seybold (1971), a speech therapist, reported that a remedial program which included singing conversations, and singing games which required primary color identification and provided experiences with verbal concepts such as "up and down," yielded significant posttest gains in language development test scores for normal, but speech-delayed, children. Greenberg (1972) and Pruitt and Steele (1971) developed programs for children in Head Start classrooms, and have cited significant gains, not only in music concept formation, but also in cognitive skills such as right-left discrimination, color identification, counting, and body image.

In similar fashion, a teacher may use familiar, favorite songs to enhance developmental skills. The use of substitute words in many familiar songs can provide reinforcement for skills such as color identification ("Mary Wore a Red Dress," for example).

What can be said can also be sung. A teacher can initiate singing conversations using tonal chants (perhaps the familiar descending minor third, "sol-mi") to encourage children to formulate thoughts into phrases and sentences. Music may help these kinds of experiences become enjoyable and successful games.

Music for the young child should be planned for more than tension release or leisure-time entertainment. Developing sensitivity to one's world—perceptual, cognitive, and emotional—is an important goal for the education of young children. For "if we awaken the artist . . . at a tender age, when [the child] is so receptive to all beauty, then [the child's] later life will be incomparably more fulfilled and enriched" (Michel 1973, p. 19).

References

Alford, D. L. "Emergence and Development of Music Responses in Preschool Twins and Singletons: A Comparative Study." *Journal of Research in Music Education* 19, no. 2 (Summer 1971): 222-227.

Allen, E. B. "A Study of Perception of Instrumental Tone Color by Children of Nursery School Age." Master's thesis, University of Kansas, 1959.

Boardman, E. L. "An Investigation of the Effect of Preschool Training on the Development of Vocal Accuracy in Young Children." *Council for Research in Music Education Bulletin* 11 (Fall 1967): 46-49.

Christianson, H. *Bodily Movement of Young Children in Relation to Rhythm in Music*. New York: Columbia University, 1938.

Cooper, R. M. "Music and the Two-Year-Olds." *Music Journal* 31, no. 1 (January 1973):13.

Drexler, E. N. "A Study of the Development of the Ability to Carry a Melody at the Preschool Level." *Child Development* 9 (March-December 1938): 319-332.

Duerkson, G. L. *Teaching Instrumental Music*. Washington, D.C.: Music Educators National Conference, 1972.

Fullard, W. G., Jr. "Operant Training of Aural Musical Discriminations with Preschool Children." *Journal of Research in Music Education* 15, no. 3 (Fall 1967): 201-209.

Greenberg, M. "A Preliminary Report of the Effectiveness of a Music Curriculum with Preschool Head Start Children." *Council for Research in Music Education Bulletin* 29 (Summer 1972): 13-16.

Greer, R. D.; Dorow, L.; and Hanser, S. "Music Discrimination Training and the Music Selection Behavior of Nursery and Primary Level Children." *Council for Research in Music Education Bulletin* 35 (Winter 1973): 30-43.

Hermanson, L. W. "An Investigation of the Effects of Timbre on Simultaneous Vocal Pitch Acuity of Young Children." *Dissertation Abstracts International* 32, no. 7 (January 1972): 3558-A.

Jersild, A. T., and Bienstock, S. F. "A Study of the Development of Children's Ability to Sing." *Journal of Educational Psychology* 25, no. 7 (October 1934): 481-503.

Jersild, A. T., and Bienstock, S. F. *Development of Rhythm in Young Children*. New York: Columbia University, 1935.

Kirkpatrick, W. C. "Relationships Between the Singing Ability of Prekindergarten Children and Their Home Musical Environment." *Dissertation Abstracts* 23, no. 3 (September 1962): 886.

McDonald, M. "Transitional Tunes and Musical Development." *The Psychoanalytic Study of the Child* 25 (1970): 503-520.

McDonald, R. L., and Schuckert, R. F. "An Attempt to Modify the Musical Preferences of Preschool Children." *Journal of Research in Music Education* 16, no. 1 (Spring 1968): 39-44.

Michel, P. "The Optimum Development of Musical Abilities in the First Years of Life." *Psychology of Music* 1, no. 2 (June 1973): 14-20.

Noy, P. "The Development of Musical Ability." *The Psychoanalytic Study of the Child* 23 (1968): 332-347.

Ostwald, P. F. "Musical Behavior in Early Childhood." *Developmental Medicine and Child Neurology* 15, no. 1 (February 1973): 367-375.

Pruitt, H., and Steele, A. L. "Music by Head Start Teachers for the Educationally Disadvantaged." *American Music Teacher* 20, no. 6 (June-July 1971): 29-30, 37.

Romanek, M. L. "A Self-Instructional Program for Musical Concept Development in Preschool Children." *Journal of Research in Music Education* 22, no. 2 (Summer 1974): 129-135.

Scheihing, G. "A Study of the Spontaneous Rhythmic Activities of Preschool Children." In *Music Therapy 1951*, edited by E. G. Gilliland, pp. 188-189. Lawrence, Kans.: Allen Press, 1952.

Sergeant, D., and Roche, S. "Perceptual Shifts in the Auditory Information Processing of Young Children." *Psychology of Music* 1, no. 2 (June 1973): 39-48.

Seybold, C. D. "The Value and Use of Music Activities in the Treatment of Speech-Delayed Children." *Journal of Music Therapy* 8 (Fall 1971): 102-110.

Shuter, R. *The Psychology of Musical Ability*. London: Methuen and Co., 1968.

Simons, G. M. "Comparisons of Incipient Music Responses among Very Young Twins and Singletons." *Journal of Research in Music Education* 12, no. 3 (Fall 1964): 212-226.

Smith, R. B. "The Effect of Group Vocal Training on the Singing Ability of Nursery School Children." *Journal of Research in Music Education* 11, no. 2 (Fall 1963): 137-141.

Smith, R. B. *Music in the Child's Education*. New York: Ronald Press, 1970.

Williams, H. M. "Techniques of Measurement in the Developmental Psychology of Music." In *Studies in Child Welfare: The Measurement of Musical Development*, edited by G. D. Stoddard, pp. 11-31. Iowa City, Iowa: University of Iowa, 1932.

Yendovitskaya, T. V. "Development of Sensation and Perception." In *The Psychology of Preschool Children*, edited by A. V. Zaporozhets and D. B. Elkonin, translated by J. Shybut and S. Simon, pp. 1-64. Cambridge, Mass.: MIT Press, 1971.

Young, W. T. "An Investigation of the Singing Abilities of Kindergarten and First Grade Children in East Texas." Bethesda, Md.: ERIC Document Reproduction Service, ED 069 431, 1971.

Dorothy McDonald has further expanded these ideas in her book *Music in Our Lives: The Early Years*. See p. 238 for ordering information.

Sylvia F. Burns

Children's Art:
A Vehicle for Learning

In the aftermath of popular interest in young children's learning abilities, numerous programs and curriculum materials have been designed with the goal of helping children achieve success in school. Little attention, however, has been directed toward providing for learning through creative art experiences. It appears that art, while recognized as a vehicle for the development of a child's imagination and self-expression, often is not accorded adequate consideration for its cognitive, social, affective, and motor learning potential. For the most part, early childhood art activities seem to fall into two categories: (1) Craft-type productions initiated by the teacher for the purpose of making something, and (2) hit-or-miss exposure to different media. Both of these approaches reflect poor understanding of art as a rich resource for multiple learning opportunities.

In the first type of art program, activities are highly-structured, teacher-directed performances allowing for little or no creative statement from the participants and little real learning other than perhaps that of following directions. The procedure is dull, lifeless, and fraught with frustration for those children who either cannot put the rules into operation or perform the necessary manipulations. Or, if they try to break the lock-step method being proposed and their end product differs too much from the teacher-made model (as it usually does), feelings of failure and worthlessness may fill the classroom. Such feelings often are abated by concerned teachers who then retrouch or redo the child's work so that he or she will have an "acceptable" finished product to take home. This product orientation also may be found in activities which involve more teacher participation than child participation, leaving room for little personal or intellectual interest.

In direct opposition to this rigid approach is the laissez-faire theory of art. With little planning other than supplying materials, teachers turn children loose "to create." Adult interaction may be visible in the form of invitations for participation but generally, the activities merely become brief encounters with various art media and offer little continuity either in experience or learning for the children.

Neither of these approaches serves children well. The first cannot be rec-

Sylvia F. Burns, Ed.D., is presently a staff member of the Department of Education at Queens College, New York. Formerly, she taught at State University at Farmingdale and was Director of the Herricks Nursery School & Kindergarten in Nassau County, New York.

ognized as creative art at all for it simply indoctrinates learners into direction following. The second method relieves the teacher of responsibility for an awareness of the kinds of learning that may be taking place. However, many teachers are concerned with offering young children good experiences in the creative arts. They focus on providing youngsters with opportunities for the development of creative expression through active involvement with various media. There is acknowledgment that children perform explorations with color, shape, and space as first steps in their artistic development. As they gain some familiarity with different media, they are expected to go on to work more creatively and more individually. That teachers encourage such explorations is evident in the fact that art work in the use of clay, paint, crayons, and collage has long been a staple activity in early childhood programs. These experiences generally have taken place during that part of the curriculum known as free play and as such have been afforded minor consideration beyond their creative value. However, widespread acceptance of art as an appropriate play activity should not preclude the fact that these same activities do have important educative meanings.

A closer look at visual arts in the early childhood curriculum reveals numerous rich opportunities for children to acquire knowledge. But, if they are to derive these benefits, their teachers first must appreciate contacts with art media as a vital source for learning and recognize the kinds of knowledge that children can be helped to acquire. This acceptance can be a guiding force in planning for variety and continuity of experiences which will encourage both creative expression and intellectual development.

Basic learnings

At a very fundamental level, children who are exposed to art media such as paints or crayons or clay learn about themselves. They find out that they can create something by using the materials. When the fruits of their labors generate positive responses from adults, children begin to acquire a sense of their own worth and to see themselves as persons who "can do." When the teacher's appreciation of a child's efforts is not tinged with qualitative judgments, the child senses honest recognition of himself or herself as a person of value in his or her own right. Growing self-concept has

been enhanced by the adult's behavior. Children learn more from a simple statement such as, "I see you've been working on that for a long time," than from critical evaluations of their productions or from the proverbial "I like that" offered by some teachers.

Some of the most valuable learnings to be acquired from contact with art media are those perceptual skills such as size, shape, and distance, that are fundamental to beginning reading and writing. Before children can differentiate between such abstractions as letters and numbers, they need many different opportunities to develop perceptually through a variety of experiences with less complex concepts. The many colors of paint and crayons, the variety of shapes that can be drawn, painted, cut and pasted, all contribute to perceptual development.

Teachers need to be cognizant of the fact that visual discrimination in children can be encouraged with opportunities to learn about attributes of size, shape, and color in a variety of media. Likewise, perceptions of sameness and difference can be fostered through contact with these simple stimuli. Differentiations among the many gradations of a single color is yet another factor that refines the child's visual skill while serving as an important antecedent learning to reading the printed word. Similarly, handling paint brushes, crayons, or chalk of varying lengths and widths generates a tactile perception of size while contributing to the development of writing skills.

As children participate in activities involving these tools, their small muscles are continuously being developed. They learn to control the implements to meet their personal needs and pur-

123

poses as they move their arms and hands to form desired shapes. Growth in perceptual-motor coordination enables one to achieve mastery of elements in the environment and may be observed as drawings and paintings become more representational and/or detailed. Here, teachers may note the outward manifestations of other new understandings. When young learners begin to seek and absorb meaning from the world around them, when they recall images of experiences and things and strive to symbolize them, art activities become a vehicle for each individual's expression of ideas and feelings about his world.

Thinking skills

Many art activities have unlimited potential for the development of thinking skills in young children. Take paper, for example. As they work with paper—color it, paint it, cut into it, tear it—children learn about its properties. Some kinds tear easily and cleanly, others tear in a ragged manner, while yet a third kind needs to be cut with scissors. Applying finger paint to manila paper gives one effect, applying tempera results in a different response, and water in a third. Children learn that paper itself reacts to many kinds of handling. Such direct contact builds up a variety of understandings which then allows the learner to form generalizations about paper. These firsthand experiences are the roots of perceptual and mental activities which are important prerequisites to more complex thinking and learning.

As the young child works with a medium, his/her thinking is stimulated by the need to make decisions. What color paint should be tried out next?

What happens to the clay if it is pounded some more? If the child pushes the clay together and rolls it, will it resemble the piece as it started out? How can a round styrofoam ball be attached to the wooden base of his stabile? Involvement in what they are doing and the freedom to explore the material and make their own decisions about it contribute to children's capacity to think for themselves and to carry out a task.

It is well to remember that self-determined tasks abound in the visual arts. As the material is set before a child, he or she is faced with some immediate intellectual activity involving basic problem-solving skills. First, the child becomes aware of the medium. She or he then integrates this awareness into present knowledge. If the subject is easel painting, a child probably is familiar with the method, yet a number of decisions must now be made such as which color to use first and where to put the first stroke. The child is organizing his or her thoughts as he or she undertakes the task. On another level, the problem of composition arises as the child organizes the several elements of an idea and plans the picture. The entire act of painting is a thinking process which is practiced over and over each time the easel is approached.

Painting

Painting, of course, takes on different forms. At times, the teacher may decide to have the activity take place on the table using sponges or string or cotton swabs. Children's cognition is fostered through such variety, for they learn about the many different ways in which paint can be applied. This is the underlying element that should be considered by teachers when offering a variety of painting activities, not the use of sponges or string because they are different from a brush. The cognitive learnings that come from personal engagement with paint in various activities are lasting when understood from the mental processes point-of-view, and thus, all activities should be offered a number of times. It is the teacher's responsibility to decide when the children, or a particular child, seem ready to try out the medium in new ways, but the goal is not variety per se, it is the learning derived from the changed approach.

Clay

Wet, water-based clay is another valuable medium for the development of perceptual-motor skills in young children. Initially, the learner's tactile awareness of the clay stimulates interest. As the child smoothes it, rolls it around, or squeezes it through his or her fingers, he or she is becoming sensitized to its unique pliability. Gradually, the clay is perceived as something which responds to commands. Each touch creates a difference in form or a new impression and a new challenge as the young worker strives to give shape to an idea. Here, too, recall of encounters with people, places, and things comes to the forefront of the child's thinking as she or he replicates images in a three-dimensional medium.

Mastery of this three-dimensional perception has been found to be an important initial step for reading, inasmuch as perceptual development moves from the concrete to the abstract, or two-dimensional. In addition to reading, work with clay provides for

the development of concepts of mass and form which are fundamental to mathematical learnings in the future, while the modeling process itself follows the course of a child's small motor development. Pounding with the fist or rolling the clay with the palm of the hand usually precedes using the fingers for more detailed work.

Collage

One activity all children love is collage. As a learning medium, collage is more than just a collection of things to be pasted together on a background of cloth or cardboard or paper. The experience of collage contributes to children's learning when specific materials are selected and combined. For example, a collage may be composed of things that are red or yellow or shiny or round. One time the focus may be texture, another time color or pattern. Children's awareness of these attributes may be stimulated through their participation in acquiring items for use in the activity, thereby contributing to the development of their classification skills. While combinations of material for collage are infinite, judicious use is important. Too many different items may be confusing for the average young child and the resultant activity becomes mere accumulation of pieces carelessly pasted together. It is a good idea to separate items according to a specific attribute rather than have young children select materials from one box containing vast unassorted numbers of things.

Figure-ground perception can be developed as children paste circles or squares on top of rectangles, or seek items that are striped or checkered to paste on solid backgrounds. Numerous

combinations in various stages of complexity may be derived by interested teachers.

Here, too, the way in which the items are pasted onto the background deserves consideration. While many teachers subscribe to the notion that fingers should be used in pasting, small sticks or cotton swabs are recommended as best for collage. The intellectual synthesis of the visual and tactile elements of materials used in this art form ought not be hampered by fingers coated with paste, for clear impressions are important when children are learning to perceive and articulate similarities and differences. Many exciting collage experiences have been known to deteriorate as the children became engrossed in painting their fingers with the pasting medium and lost interest in the choosing and organizing aspects of the activity.

Language

Children's language development is one specific area that can be fostered through the visual arts. They need encouragement to voice their learnings—"It looks like," "It feels like," "It is dripping, dripping all the way down to the bottom of the page," etc. If the learning environment is accepting and free, the child will verbalize actions and insights as he or she works. The teacher, however, can elicit language by means of careful guidance. "You pulled it apart." "You used very long strokes." "That is a very clear blue." "Yes, the clay is sticky today." As the teacher gives voice to the child's work and points out specific, understandable elements, the learner is helped to focus on these particulars and to see them in the context of the whole while at the same time becoming familiar with language to describe actions. The child's work takes on a new dimension when language is added to it, and this learning becomes meaningful because it is identifiable and related to himself or herself.

Language learning becomes obvious as the child begins to use words to describe actions. Often, several repetitive situations must occur before the language is adopted into the child's working vocabulary. When this does take place, the teacher should recognize the learning and plan for its continuity. The adult's choice of language should draw upon the child's past knowledge when making comparisons, describing the activities, or offering encouragement. In this way, the child is given a point of reference for new words and understanding them becomes easier. A child thus may acquire more than one term for an item or process and is able to expand his or her vocabulary while learning new concepts and techniques. Too, the children should be encouraged to state their needs as they seek the appropriate tools for their task. "I need a large brush." "Where can I find a wider brush." "Thicker red paint won't run." "More paste, please."

Language and concept development often are interwoven at this age. Take the word "sticky" for example. Does it connote the same thoughts when used with clay as it does when applied to tape or glue? How else can the child be helped to develop the concept of stickiness and to internalize it, and still differentiate among the realities if not through firsthand experiences?

Math and science

Frequently, the teacher's language

will establish root learnings in mathematics or science. Early counting experiences are spontaneously invited when adult and child talk over a painting in terms of "You used one, two . . . six colors in your picture." Or, the identification of prenumber concepts such as next to, around, between, heavier, lighter, provides children with tangible understandings as they simultaneously explore art media. Form and balance are apparent in collage and clay modeling as well as concepts of aesthetics, but all too often, the work is accepted by adults on the basis of appearance alone.

Mathematics itself is concerned with relationships. Inherent in many art activities are similar relationships . . . of one medium to another, of size to shape, of color to color, of the child's actions upon the material. While the learners themselves may be intent upon simply exploring the properties

of whatever it is they are using, the additional learnings should be comprehensible to the teacher so that she or he can bring them forth when the situation seems appropriate. In this manner the teacher is providing for the development of foundational cognitions from which other understandings will emanate. Estimating how much clay is needed for a project or pouring paint into containers (measurement) are simple learnings that can be culled from the media by knowing teachers.

Scientific learnings such as cause and effect and spatial relationships abound in art work as do the skills of comparing and classifying. It is the integration of these concepts with the use of a variety of media that forms an appropriate learning environment, an environment that is dependent upon the teacher's knowledge of what to look for as well as the preparation of activities with

128

specific goals in mind. The following list merely hints at some of the available learnings.

Crayons — Initial color perceptions, use of small muscles, perceptual-motor development, space and shape relationships, pictorial representation of the child's world. Counting, matching, grouping of colors, whole-part relationships, use of crayons for rubbings (paint over with thinned tempera—scientific learning that some things do not mix).

Paint — More complex medium than crayons involving another approach to perceptual learning. A constantly changing medium good for scientific learnings: looks different wet than when dry, opaqueness can be covered over (What is underneath the visible color?). Variations in texture, fluidity, different textured effects depending upon brushes used. Can be mixed to change color, dripped into another color. Can be used on materials other than paper (Is the result the same?). Excellent vocabulary builder.

Paper Collage — Size relationships, shape discrimination, whole-part concepts, arrangement (design). A two-dimensional experience for reading. Problem solving (choosing from offered materials). Beginning math (classifying, counting shapes).

Three-Dimensional Collage — Separating and putting together of items. Bringing together shapes and elements in the world (important for beginning reading). Sorting, comparing, seeing similarities in items, classifying items of same shape and/or material. Use of items in new ways (seeing alternatives). Problem solving (how to fasten).

Clay — Sensory-tactile perceptions via shaping, rolling, pulling, pounding. Representation of personal ideas and perceptions of things in the world. Concepts of mass, change, relationship of parts to whole, fractions (whole, half, quarter). Math (many, few, larger, smaller, more), may also be used for addition and subtraction.

Finger Paint — Compare consistency. Motor development, change of form. Development of control (not confined to small area). Visual-motor coordination, figure-ground perception. Vocabulary builder.

Creating an environment

When preparing for art activities in the classroom, care should be taken to insure that there is sufficient time for intimate exploration of the media by the children. Freedom of technique, while mandatory, often needs encouragement. Such encouragement is offered through time and repetition as well as setting up the activity in such a way as to invite participation. The teacher's role should be supportive, but not pressured. The child must first

129

become interested in trying, then be allowed to formulate a personal working style and problems. What questions will the medium pose? How will they be handled? The major contribution that a knowing teacher can offer is to focus the child's attention on a specific area of the task—color, paste, the process of cutting, or the texture of the material. A single-focus approach often is less confining, for it allows a port of entry for the newcomer to the activity. As the activity is repeated during the week or over the year, the child will find her or his own means of communication with the medium and become more engrossed.

It is more important for the adult in charge to focus on the learning possibilities inherent in the activities than to pressure for style or perfection of a finished product. While art is a viable medium for the development of many of the learnings already discussed and others not touched upon, it is, at its root, a vehicle for creative expression and personal enjoyment. Therefore, the teacher should expend considerable energy toward providing materials and atmosphere. This communicates to the learner that the activity has value.

If children are to be encouraged to experience art media to their fullest capacity, it is important for teachers to have a working knowledge of each medium to be used in the classroom. When teachers know, through their own contact with the materials, just what the possibilities for usage may be, they will be better prepared to encourage children's participation. Also, insight into the child's progress through exploring and manipulating to controlling different materials will be gained if teachers periodically go through the process. Understanding and appreciation of the range of possibilities to be found in working with a specific medium enables adults to identify with children's working problems and thus to offer constructive suggestions. In addition, knowledge that comes from such personal contact is helpful in deciding on procedures such as when to introduce certain materials or how long an activity should be allowed to continue for the first, or successive times.

For the average classroom teacher who does not have an extensive personal background in art, contact with different media allows for the exploration of one's own feelings concerning particular materials. Many adults, for instance, permit clay to be used in the classroom but do not have any idea of its feeling in the hand, nor of its workability. The frustrations of clay that is too soft or too hard or too crumbly for optimum molding needs to be personally understood as much as the joy of success at the completion of a self-imposed project. The impact of a positive sensory communication between self and media is one that cannot really be surmised, it needs to be experienced. In-service courses or workshops should be arranged to provide these opportunities, but even personal exploration during a lunch period will contribute to the teacher's understanding and enhance the art program that is offered to children. The problems that often arise in planning and following through an art experience generally stem from the adult's lack of identification with what is taking place.

Knowing what to look for, setting specific goals for learning, and supporting the personal involvement of the children as they explore and create are prime functions of the teacher during these art periods. Knowing the specific learning possibilities allows the adult to make the activity more interesting, important, and challenging while sowing the seeds of knowledge, for creative art is an exciting as well as versatile vehicle for learning. 🖊

References

Barkan, M. "The Values of the Arts in Experience and Education." *Art . . . For Children's Growing.* Washington, DC: Association for Childhood Education International, 1955.

Greenberg, P. *Art in Early Childhood.* New York: Early Childhood Education Council of Nassau-Suffolk, 1965.

Lark-Horovitz, B.; Lewis, H. P.; and Luca, M. *Understanding Children's Art for Better Teaching.* Columbus, OH: Charles E. Merrill, 1967.

Linderman, E. W., and Herberholz, D. W. *Developing Artistic and Perceptual Awareness.* Dubuque, IA: William C. Brown Co., 1964.

Lord, L. *Collage and Construction.* Worcester, MA: Davis Publications, 1958.

Montgomery, C. *Art for Teachers of Children.* Columbus, OH: Charles E. Merill, 1968.

Jean Durgin Harlan

From Curiosity to Concepts:
From Concepts to Curiosity
Science Experiences in the Preschool

The four-foot skyscraper lists precariously as one more embellishing block chimney is added to the top. Then, CRASH, the laws of gravity prevail! The nearby teacher remains admirably composed and makes no comment. She is confident that her four-year-old block builders have thus added one more bit of practical knowledge to their growing store of science understanding.

But have they done this? Is there evidence that accurate data has been abstracted from this familiar calamity? The builders might convince us that such was the case if they launched a discussion of probable causes for the structural failure. They might do so if they began to rebuild an improved version of the skyscraper that would compensate for the pull of gravity to achieve balance.

Sometimes these things happen, but do they inevitably happen? How many experiences are needed before children are able to apply the learning? Do we know, or do we just hope that children will spontaneously come to learn about the predictable elements in their physical world through their play experiences?

There is broad professional consensus that an intrinsic learning motivation called curiosity can be relied upon to lead children from repeated first-hand experiences to the discovery of cause and effect concepts. This belief seems to imply that the young child's curiosity is an ever-flowing fount. But if we observe children's day-by-day action in a preschool setting we may question this assumption. There we might see that children's free use of familiar materials can become stereotyped. Many children follow strong preferences for favored playthings and for cherished play styles.

133

Relatively few children in the group may display a persistent capacity to see fresh possibilities in familiar materials. Apparently, then, routinely available play equipment does not stimulate curiosity in all children in a constant way.

While the term curiosity is variously defined, there is agreement that curiosity can be called forth by novel events to help children discover concept-building information. Research evidence also indicates that limited situations can be set up to require unguided discovery learning through trial and error. But, as Gagné points out, "Discovery without guidance makes the learning of concepts a terribly slow process" (Gagné 1966).

Perhaps we ought to take less for granted the role that spontaneous curiosity plays in the learning process. The postulates about curiosity might need to be expanded to include the adult guidance role. Thus, curiosity, sustained by adult sanctions and provisions, leads the child toward concept building discoveries. Concepts, once attained, open new pathways for sustained curiosity to pursue.

To guide science discovery learning in the preschool two teacher functions appear to be needed: (1) nurturing children's curiosity and (2) providing active learning experiences that extend and clarify common events in the lives of young children.

The teacher has a continuous role to play in reviving children's curiosity that may have been dulled by familiar-

Jean Durgin Harlan, M.S., is an instructor of child development in the School of Home Economics at Ohio University, Athens, Ohio. She is also Head Teacher of a four-year-old group at the Nursery Child Care Center, Ohio University.

ity with materials, or unwittingly devalued by unconcerned adults. When the teacher's own sense of wonder is vividly expressed and acted upon, curiosity behavior is modeled for the children. According to noted science educator Glenn Blough, "There are no records of children being inspired by teachers who themselves are not inspired" (1971).

Planning Early Science Experiences

Unfortunately, providing relevant science learning experiences can be a stumbling block for many preschool teachers. This hesitation can be understood when one searches for guidelines to develop a framework of preschool science experience, for this is relatively uncharted territory. Preschool teachers who want to enrich their children's understanding of their world through purposeful science experiences may find these planning steps useful.

1. *Choosing appropriate concepts to explore with children.*

   The deep interest some children express in their environment can provide direction for areas to explore. Hasty entries in the teacher's notebook can lead to good follow-up experiences. ". . . Carrie, Sarah, Ernie: earthworm and caterpillar fanciers. . . . Matt wants to know *for sure* what keeps the stars up. . . . Aaron brought in his planet book. . . . Tom asked how the music gets out of the guitar."

   However, child-instigated projects alone rarely cover all the science concepts that young children can develop and gain from. Suggestions about concepts having broad appeal for children can be found in various texts written for preschool educators. Science textbooks for primary grades suggest concepts that also have meaning for preschool children. The teacher's editions provide good background information for adults and many of the experiments can be adapted for preschool use. (Avoid outdated textbooks, or ones that treat science solely as a subject to be read about.)

2. *Developing Concepts.*

Because concepts are built slowly, many simple, tangible facts need to be established before children can relate them to a central abstraction.

Providing an assortment of disconnected "science happenings" in a random way may not serve this purpose. A single experience of observing a stalk of celery in a glass of dyed water doesn't do much to develop firm ideas about capillary action or plant growth needs.

A desultory exposure to a variety of isolated activities is insufficient to help four- and five-year-old children tie together important ideas that can have meaning in their lives. It would be a better use of time and materials to consider a few broad concepts in as many concrete instances as can be devised.

3. *Adapting older children's experiments to preschool needs.*

Experiments geared for primary grade children may need to be altered to suit the learning modes of younger children who have a hard time waiting for turns to use materials. They are eager to touch and handle, for they still use their hands to "see" in the sensorimotor way.

Therefore, experiments should be those that make use of abundantly available materials or common objects that can be brought from home. Then several children can actively participate at one time.

Materials used in science explorations must meet the criteria for safety and developmental appropriateness for young children.

When written records are part of the grade-school experience, abacus tallies or other tangible units of measure like paper-clip chains make meaningful substitutes for young children.

Since there seems to be a high correlation between the degree of young children's interest in a project and the amount of resulting mess, self-help cleanup procedures should be incorporated into the science plans.

4. *Presenting early science experiences.*

Materials to be explored should be presented in a problem-solving or discovery fashion. This allows children to try materials in their own way to see what happens. Francis Hawkins movingly described this approach in *The Logic of Action*. The teacher's guidance role should be relaxed and indirect, with the intent of stimulating the child's thinking. "What do you think might happen if . . .?" The discovery approach precludes telling the children what outcomes to expect or demonstrating the one right way to experiment. The teacher supplies correct labels when they are needed. Interest grows when the teacher and the children "find out" together.

5. *Reinforcing concepts.*

Many forms of broadening early

Photos by John I. Harlan

science concepts are possible in the preschool setting. The most natural reinforcement of learnings consists of continuing to identify the explored concepts through use of scientific vocabulary as they are encountered in everyday occurrences. "See how the sponge **absorbs** the spilled water." "The floor is smooth and your socks are smooth. Your feet slip when there isn't much **friction.**"

Reinforcement can be achieved structurally when related concepts are presented sequentially. The understandings from one group of experiences can lead directly or transfer indirectly to those that follow.

Stories that use science ideas as a frame of reference can be read to the children. The ideas needn't be specifically alluded to in the text, but might be pointed out by the teacher as the story is being read.

Simple jingles can be improvised and sung to familiar tunes. Art projects, field trips, creative movement, puppet stories, cooking experiences, math and language games, and dramatic play can all be laced around the central conceptual core. The range of possible extensions can be a pleasant challenge to the teacher's inventiveness.

The most important reinforcement can be the interest and support of parents. Keep them informed about ongoing science projects through newsletters or parent meetings. Encourage them to let their children continue experimenting with safe, common materials at home.

Applying the Steps

These are some ways to apply the planning steps to introduce the concept of gravitational pull, for example.

1. This topic might be instigated by a child's problem with balancing a block structure or for older children a teeter-totter. Background information for teachers is well presented in *Gravity* by Bertha Parker.

2. What concrete experiences could help young children understand the invisible force of gravity? Children usually conceive of pulling in terms of a visible force tugging at a visible object. This is not the case with a child who has had many experiences with the invisible force of magnetism. A child who has felt the compelling tug of unlike poles and the push of like poles of magnets held in his own hands can put credence in an unseen pull strong enough to hold people and houses onto the earth's surface. (The distinctions between magnetism and gravity must be carefully maintained. The similarity lies only in the invisibility of a pulling force.) Experiencing the effects of magnetism lays a tangible, small-scale foundation for children's acceptance of the vast and constant invisible pull of gravity.

Other explorations could involve the children in experimenting with the ef-

fect of gravity on achieving balance. With some adult help children can make balances from scrap lumber, a yardstick, paper cups, and pipe cleaners. Another type of balance can be made from a paper towel tube. Commercial balances could be used. Supply

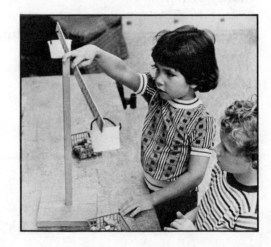

the children with stones, washers, bottle caps, or other common materials to balance and compare.

Encourage children to try out new ways of balancing themselves or moving on a balance beam. Weigh the children to find out how much gravity pulls on them. (Our class together weighs nearly 500 pounds on the post office loading dock scale!) Try to visit a store where a balance scale is used to weigh purchases.

Make a simple roly-poly toy with a weighted, rounded bottom that refuses to tip over. Try to locate one of the balancing inflatable toys for the children to play with. Let them make a similar balance toy with tinker toys. Experiment with balancing an apple on a fingertip with and without two forks inserted in the apple, handles angled downward like a tightrope walker's pole. (If children notice that the heavy parts are low, or that they weigh the same, that's fine. However, the center of gravity explanation is more than most young children can deal with.)

Some of these activities are described in books found on the science shelves of a children's library:

Gravity by Bertha Parker
Gravity All Around by Pineard Levine
The True Book of Science Experiments by Illa Podendorf
Adventures With a Cardboard Tube by Harry Milgrom

3. To extend the children's understandings of earth's gravitational pull, read a direct discussion of gravity written for young children:

Gravity At Work and Play by Sune Engelbrektson

Uphill and Downhill by Julius Schwartz

Gravity concepts can be related to these stories for children:

The Day We Saw the Sun Come Up by Alice Goudey

Little Bear by Else Minarik
    Chapter 3, "Little Bear Goes to the Moon"

As dramatic play stimulus, provide children with coils of soft wire like the one Little Bear wore on his pretend trip to the moon. Space helmets can be devised from many other materials as well. Let the children use crayons, tempera paint, old spools, and aluminum foil discards to transform a cardboard furniture carton into a space ship.

After singing "Jack and Jill Went Up the Hill," ask the children why Jack fell down instead of up the hill. Suggest creative movement activities relating to lifting objects of differing weights: the heaviest stone in the world . . . the lightest bit of milkweed fluff. Suggest moving like astronauts walking on the moon where the gravity pull is weak . . . moving like heavy dinosaurs, like light mice . . . pretend to walk on a swaying tightrope, carefully balancing. You will think of other ideas that will add meaning to the abstract concept of gravitational pull as you try these suggestions.

How can the worth of these activities be evaluated? Their effectiveness can be verified informally as children reflect their new understanding in their discussions at play and as they apply learnings to solve problems arising during the school day. Parent comments about the child's new interest in aspects of the physical world are another source of evaluation.

There is, however, no precise way to measure the surge of pride in accomplishment and the sense of mastery a child feels when he has gained understanding of a useful idea. It is hard to rate the degree of triumph registered on the face of a child who has successfully launched his own paper glider, or perfectly balanced a ruler on a block fulcrum for a few breathless moments.

The importance of working toward science concepts in the preschool years is most strongly evidenced in the signs of quickened curiosity in the children. These signs increase as children gradually become confident that wondering, trying out, and discussing help them find out why things happen. Children who have explored together to reach new understandings come to believe in themselves as learners and in curiosity as a valid tool for learning. ⟨7⟩

References

Blough, G. O. "Some Observations and Reflec-
tions about Science Teaching in the Elementary School." *Science and Children*, December 1971.

Blough, G. O., and Schwartz, J. *Elementary School Science and How To Teach It.* New York: Holt, Rinehart and Winston, 1974.

Englebrektson, S. *Gravity At Work and Play.* New York: Holt, Rinehart and Winston, A Young Owl Book, 1963.

Gagné, R. M. "Varieties of Learning and the Concept of Discovery." *Learning by Discovery; A Critical Appraisal,* edited by L. S. Schulman and E. R. Keislar. Chicago: Rand McNally, 1966.

Goudey, A. *The Day We Saw the Sun Come Up.* New York: Charles Scribner's Sons, 1961.

Hawkins, F. P. *The Logic of Action.* Newton, Mass.: Elementary Science Study, 1969.

Minarik, E. *Little Bear.* New York: Harper and Row, 1957.

Milgrom, H. *Adventures With a Cardboard Tube.* New York: E. P. Dutton & Co., 1972.

Parker, B. *Gravity.* Evanston, Ill.: Row, Peterson, and Company, 1957.

Pine, T. S., and Levine, J. *Gravity All Around.* New York: Whittlsey House, McGraw-Hill, 1963.

Pondendorf, I. *The True Book of Science Experiments.* Chicago: Children's Press, 1972.

Schwartz, J. *Uphill and Downhill.* New York: McGraw-Hill, 1965.

Todd, V., and Heffernan, H. *The Years Before School: Guiding Preschool Children.* New York: Macmillan Co., 1970.

Judith Bender

Large Hollow Blocks
Relationship of Quantity to Block Building Behaviors

It is as if the child were forever tasting and never eating; always having his palate tickled upon the emotional side, but never getting the organic satisfaction that comes only with digestion of food and transformation of it into working power. (Dewey 1902, p. 21)

John Dewey wrote the above as he considered the ". . . continuous initiation, continuous starting of activities that do not arrive . . ." (p. 21). Three quarters of a century later I observe young children interacting with classroom materials—good materials, challenging materials, well-designed, packed with *possibilities* for the growth of minds, muscles, curiosity, and adventure. But why are so many young children teased by this passing review of delicacies, yet not really getting their teeth into the nourishment?

Several important factors probably are related to this temptation/starvation syndrome.

1. Adults must be familiar with the *potential of classroom materials* in order to recognize their multiple dimensions for children's learning. Licensing requirements or administrative personnel have often mandated materials without translating the values or the possibilities for use to the teacher. Teacher training experiences, however, often encourage students to memorize and theorize but do not provide firsthand interaction with materials through which students of all ages learn.

2. A second factor is *continuity of experience*. Materials must be available over an extended period of time, so that children can *grow* through repeated and deeper experiences, so that an intense involvement is generated between the child and the activity. Once having tempted we must feed the child! Too frequently we simply offer children "Today's Special." Today you may use the workbench. Today we will make a collage. Today we will have water play. But what about tomorrow? The tools are put away. The collage has gone home. The water table has been sent to the room down the hall. Materials were put away for another time, another day, next week, next month, next spring. The child has deliciously tasted again and again; but, where is the feeling of accomplishment, of power?

3. The temptation/starvation syndrome is also related to the necessity for an *adequate amount of materials* with which to work. Too often as children work in groups the supply is too meager. When tempted, an appetite begs for a sense of satisfaction. Quantities of certain materials are closely related to what Dewey referred to as "working power."

Temptation/Starvation and Large Hollow Blocks

Nowhere is the temptation/starvation syndrome more evident than in the classroom use (or lack of use) of large construction blocks, often referred to as *large hollow blocks*. There is not only a scarcity of professional literature relating directly to large block building (as opposed to unit blocks where there is both plentiful information

Judith Bender, M.Ed., is a Child Development Specialist with the Anne Arundel County, Maryland, Health Department. She is a former teacher of both young children and adults.

and a long established respect for sufficient specified quantity), but there is also little emphasis in teacher training regarding the values and use of these blocks in early childhood education. Many early childhood programs reflect this neglect. Large blocks, so dynamically utilized as a basic social studies learning material under the influence of Dewey, have today become misunderstood or nearly extinct.

Activities other than paper drill work are crucial to such skills as internalizing knowledge about the world, solving problems, helping others, and developing interdependence, initiative, and imagination. The large building blocks are specifically designed to enhance all these aspects of children's learning.

Large block construction is one tool through which children can build a base environment for playing out their understanding of the world. Through these materials children form and reform the settings from which relevant role play

emerges. These blocks should be continually accessible as new experiences develop so that as children gain ideas and learnings, they can test them through their interaction with each other. This play is the essence of social studies; the accumulation of facts derived from pictures, books, trips, or observations is much more meaningful when these learnings can be rehearsed and made a part of self. The drama changes and new ideas are provided by real life experiences, but the block construction provides a continuous means through which to develop and understand these new ideas and incorporate them with those that were already familiar.

The provision of an adequate quantity of blocks and accompanying building boards is closely related to their potential for children's learning. If children are creating continually evolving and changing environments for learning, then it is important that they have enough building materials and related props to work with. When the

Children can cooperate to find solutions to construction problems.

Diana Morrow

141

supply of blocks and accessories runs out, the play disintegrates. My observations of hundreds of early childhood programs have revealed two inconsistencies: Behavior in relation to large building blocks as described in the literature has not been the kind of behavior observed; and differences exist between the quantity of large building blocks recommended and the quantity available in most programs.

Observing Block Building: 20 Blocks Versus 70 Blocks

I became especially interested in the ways that children use large building blocks in relation to the quantity of blocks available. Six four-year-old boys who had regularly attended the same child care center for at least eight months were observed. The children were already friends and cobuilders and were in their own relaxed, familiar environment using familiar materials. A series of half-hour observations were conducted as the children used 20 blocks, and again as an additional 50 blocks were added for a total of 70 blocks. The nine behaviors I chose to observe fell into three broad categories: problem-solving behavior in relation to social relations, behavior in relation to imaginative play, and behavior in relation to structural operations. (Detailed description of categories in Table 1.)

Discussion of Observations

Evidence of peer cooperation to achieve goals. With 20 blocks, only one or two children did most of the construction, and there were soon no blocks left with which to build. The other children observed periodically left the scene, or occasionally returned to the structure to walk on it, jump from it, climb over it, etc. There was little sustained interest. When the children had 70 blocks, all six were active participants in the building process and in the ensuing dramatic play or physical activity. Sus-

tained interest resulted in a longer attention span.

There was little cooperative conversation as children used the 20 blocks, and when children did relate to one another the language was primarily directive in nature (e.g., "don't," "get off," "go away," "jump off"). As children used the 70 blocks, the vocabulary centered mostly around the role play (e.g., "Here are some fishing poles," "I'll go get an ax," "This is for the mosquitoes"). There was much conversation about extended ideas (e.g., boats, piers, gas, rainstorm, crab trap). This is the kind of language upon which teachers can build further experiences, for this is how a teacher can learn of children's conceptions,

---

Table 1

Problem-solving behavior in relation to social relations

Evidence of peer cooperation to achieve goals

Disputes settled without teacher involvement

Structures developed to attain privacy

Behavior in relation to imaginative play

Structures developed as vehicle for dramatic play

Structures used as vehicle for dramatic play

Additions of related materials to extend ideas

Behavior in relation to structural operations

Structural changes made during play

Structures used for the express purpose of physical activity

Solutions discovered for techniques of construction (bridging, enclosures, openings, stairs)

---

misconceptions, and interests. The 70-block situation created opportunities for cooperative as well as parallel and solitary levels of play. In the 20-block situation, mostly parallel play was observed with each child talking to himself or herself.

Disputes settled without teacher involvement. The teacher settled many disputes when children were playing with 20 blocks, but there were no observed disputes with 70 blocks. Disputes arose with the 20 blocks primarily when (1) too few blocks had to be shared among six children, (2) there were not enough goal-oriented activities once the blocks had been used, (3) children demolished structures and blocks were merely strewn on the floor, resulting in random behavior which often led to aggressive action.

Structures developed to obtain privacy. A child may seek privacy for himself or herself through a block structure. Two children may seek privacy as they strengthen a friendship, or an entire group of builders may use the large blocks to establish their own turf, thereby promoting a feeling of group cohesiveness. With 70 blocks, individual children were observed building their own enclosures apart from the rest of the builders, and getting inside the enclosures with a few articles (e.g., doll, pots and pans, blanket, toy radio). Their motivation may have been privacy as well as a use of blocks to attain solitary play. Seventy blocks also allowed enough so that the children who wished to could solve the problem of privacy or solitary play, while the larger group could continue cooperative play. The 20-block situation did not allow for creation of personal privacy without depriving everyone else of blocks. Although several attempts were made by a single child through the use of a simple four-block enclosure, these blocks were quickly requested and confiscated by other builders.

Structure developed as vehicle for dramatic play. In the 20-block situation and the 70-block situation, an equal number of observations were made of children purposely

constructing a specific idea as evidenced by their discussions (e.g., "This is going to be a car"). Possibly there were no additional incidents of this as children used the increased number of blocks because the group worked consistently on one idea for a longer period of time.

Structure used as vehicle for dramatic play. There were many more observed incidents of a structure in use in relation to dramatic play, either during or following the actual building process, with 70 blocks than with the 20 blocks. The final structures using the additional blocks may be more conducive to imaginative play and the extension of ideas that keep play alive and changing. Also, the larger number of units suggest shapes, angles, enclosures, heights, etc., which appeared to stimulate new ideas for play in relation to suggestive visual clues.

Addition of related materials to extend ideas. Because there was no structure in use as a base for dramatic play with 20 blocks, added materials served no real purpose in relation to the blocks and were therefore not acquired or were used in unrelated, in this case often destructive, ways. The builders using the 70 blocks needed related materials and found opportunities and ways to use them that were symbolic of both real life and imaginary situations.

Structural changes made during play. The increased number of blocks led to an increased number of times children changed the form of the structure to meet a new idea. The challenge of discovering changing forms, shapes, and directions seemed greater when there were more manipulative units. One idea often led to another ("Turn this into the boat ramp," "Take that down and put the beds there").

Structures used for the express purpose of physical activity. As the group interacted with 20 blocks their primary activity consisted of using the blocks to achieve purely physical feats (as a structure to walk across or jump from, or as stepping-stones). Such activities were repeated over and over. One walk-across activity lasted ten minutes. When the additional blocks were added

143

much of this behavior was interspersed in the dramatic play. It seemed to be a carryover from previous styles of play, the full potential of the increased possibilities not yet fully utilized. With some of the 70 blocks, a few children constructed the same simple patterns for physical activity that they had created with the 20 blocks. Additional experience with the 70 blocks may have led to new forms.

Solutions discovered for techniques of construction. The larger quantity of blocks seemed to encourage and make possible a variety of construction techniques. Several of these techniques would appear within a single structure using 70 blocks. The construction pattern with the 20 blocks consisted of one small structure of perhaps ten blocks placed in two simple layers (from which children would jump or walk across) plus additional blocks strewn singly on the floor and used as "stepping-stones."

Summary. More children were able to become actively involved in both the process and the followup play when 70 blocks were used. Therefore, each child received the benefits of more opportunity for the positive block building behaviors. A total of only 19 incidents of positive block building behaviors were observed as children used the 20 large hollow blocks, contrasted with

83 positive behaviors when the same children used the set of 70 blocks. Early childhood programs should therefore consider offering an adequate quantity of large hollow blocks if children are to gain from the experience.

I highly recommend more extensive research that would include such factors as larger and varied population samples, varying amounts of blocks, and attention to other observable areas of behavior in addition to those mentioned, such as leadership, reciprocity, vocabulary usage, etc.

Recommended Quantity and Dimensions of Large Hollow Blocks

The quantity of blocks is related to their use as a learning material. The dimensions of the larger blocks should be exact multiples of those of the smaller blocks. The following recommendations reflect several different suggestions for construction of one set of large hollow blocks. These blocks are meant to be conceived of as a set containing a minimum number of units.

Berson (1959) stated that there must be sufficient quantity to make cooperation inevitable and for children to build structures

Block structures can serve as vehicles for dramatic play. Related materials can be symbolic of both real life and imaginary situations.

Diana Morrow

large enough to move about in. She recommended the following:

1 set: 80 blocks cut in—

	squares:	11″ × 11″ × 5½″
	rectangles:	22″ × 11″ × 5½″
	rectangles:	5½″ × 11″ × 5½″

(p. 91)

"The only disadvantage of hollow blocks is that one set is hardly enough to feed the imagination and enterprise in a group. Expensive as they are, their durability and challenge are good reasons for the presence of two sets in different parts of the room" (Berson 1959, p. 97). Christianson et al. (1961) reflect that:

Hollow box blocks are of major importance at each age level in nursery school and should be available for both indoor and outdoor play. They may be stacked in one corner of the playroom near the doors or stored on a dolly which may be moved whenever desired and rolled into a closet or outdoor shed overnight. Blocks of proportional sizes may be purchased or made. (p. 97)

Leeper et al. (1974) recommended a minimum quantity of 60 blocks for one set.

1 dozen   24″ × 12″ × 6″
3 dozen   12″ × 12″ × 6″
1 dozen   24″ × 6″ × 6″ with some
                 triangles

(p. 345)

The largest quantity should be blocks with the biggest dimensions, to assure sturdy structures. Building boards are also valuable for providing opportunities for roofing, ramping, benching, and an extension of both construction and play ideas.

An Economical Decision

While blocks can be constructed from wooden fruit or vegetable boxes, cardboard cartons, milk, soft drink, or other carriers, purchase or construction of an adequate number of sturdy wooden large construction blocks can be justified.

- They are a one-time expenditure. They last.
- They need little upkeep because they do not wear out. If repair is ever needed, children can help to see that they are

Large hollow blocks provide children with the opportunity for deep involvement and continuity of experience that promote extended and developing learnings.

Diana Morrow

kept in good condition. A sandpaper block can be kept by the block shelf for quick attention to rough spots.

- They provide no waste, no ends, no pieces to throw away.

- They are used every day for long periods of time; they are not a once-in-a-while activity.

- They can substitute for more expensive large muscle apparatus since they encourage climbing; lifting; balancing; motor strength and coordination; jumping; crawling into, over, or under.

- They can substitute for expensive play screens sold for puppet stages or stores since children can make their own.

- They serve as instant furniture—chairs, tables, doll beds, steps, etc.

- They can be combined with numerous other activities to add new directions to play—with unit blocks as a base for building; with music activities as areas to dance around, on, or over; as stage sets for coal mine, library, boat, flower store; with art media as individual work surfaces when covered with plastic.

- They can be used both indoors and outdoors.

Recognition to Resolution

Large hollow blocks, so popular with children, provide children with the opportunity for deep involvement and continuity of experience that promote extended and developing learnings. The quantity of blocks available is certainly related to the quality of children's experiences with them.

It is important to assure that initiation of children's activities leads not to dead end or treadmill experiences, but to transformation into the "working power" which Dewey describes. Take a closer look at the quality of children's behaviors as they use materials. Explore the learning potential of the *large hollow block*.

References

Berson, M. P. *Kindergarten: Your Child's First Big Step.* New York: E. P. Dutton, 1959.

Christianson, H. W.; Rogers, M. M.; and Ludlum, B. A. *The Nursery School: Adventure in Living and Learning.* Boston: Houghton Mifflin, 1961.

Dewey, J. *The Child and the Curriculum.* Chicago: University of Chicago Press, 1902.

Leeper, S. H.; Dales, R. J.; Skipper, D. S.; Witherspoon, R. L. *Good Schools for Young Children.* 3rd ed. New York: Macmillan, 1974.

Arline Kahn Julius

Focus on Movement: Practice and Theory

I ask a group of four-year-old children to:

Say "hello" with a finger . . .
Say "hello" with a hand . . .
. . . with an elbow . . . an arm . . .
their head, feet . . . and finally, their
whole body.

Gradually the children involve themselves in various greeting postures and gestures. We all know children love to move. Movement is constant in life. "Movement is characteristic of all matter. It's the nature of the universe. Stillness . . . is illusory; a function of time as in the movement of rocks, or of the limits of our perceptions, as in the atoms. Only a vacuum is still. Movement is all around us and beating and pulsing within us" (Agresti 1977, p. 1). But what has all this to do with education?

When I was a nursery school teacher, I used to collect movement ideas like the one above. But they were gimmicks. I could not extend them or generate new ones. Without understanding the meaning behind suggestions, one is apt to use them once or twice and then forget about them. It may be helpful, therefore, to relate child development theory to practical ideas for move-

Arline Kahn Julius, Ed.D., is Assistant Professor, Early Childhood Education, Bernard M. Baruch College of the City University of New York. She has taught nursery school, Head Start, kindergarten, and fourth grade.

ment activities, incorporating methods from theater games and improvisations (Spolin 1963).

Movement: A Basis for Development

What is the justification for using movement education as basic for thinking, communication, socialization, self-confidence, and for specific concepts and skills? How are these characteristics developed? What are some examples and practical ideas for developing them?

Sensorimotor Origins of Language and Imagery

There is evidence that humans made use of gestural language before the development of speech (Hewes 1973). Studies of wild chimpanzees indicate use of a primitive gesture language (Goodall 1968). Evidence that chimpanzees and gorillas can learn sign language gives further credence to the belief that language has had an evolutionary history of signs and movements (Linden 1974). Gesture (including body language) and vocal intonation may be considered psychologically more significant than actual words in social communication (Sapir 1967).

Babies' earliest learning in sensorimotor in origin—up to the age of two, the primary way babies learn is through their own actions. In learning to move and to adapt to objects, they find out the nature of things and adjust their actions accordingly. Finally, children can think about these actions without actually engaging in them.

Let me give one example from Piaget's descriptions of his daughter (Piaget 1952), which illustrates the action or movement base of thinking. Jacqueline (age one year, four months) is trying to grasp a chain that has been hidden in a small matchbox. The box is partly open, but the slit is not large enough for grasping the chain. After numerous unsuccessful attempts, she looks intently at the slit in the box, then opens and shuts her *mouth*, wider and wider—an attempt at representation that is expressed as a motor action: an imitation of the act of "opening."

The imagery, prior to language, that results from the internalization of these actions is the beginning of abstract thought. Thus, action or movement, natural to children, is the raw material for intellectual development.

Movement as Means of Expression

Movement is necessary for expressing feelings, moods, and emotions. Language alone is inadequate, so we say: "I'm speechless!" "I'm walking on air," "I had a sinking feeling" (Russell 1975, p. 3), or "I was really moved by that." Children's movements are less controlled than those of adults. They may actually shake with anger, shiver in fear, or jump for joy. What we can do in movement education is help refine these actions, channel the emotions

Alan Pearlman

What is another way you can move around the room without walking?

148

constructively, and increase the variation of expression appropriately. In addition, we want to increase the *range* of possible expressions, extend it to gentleness, tenderness, forcefulness (Brearley 1969).

Let me throw something to you. Catch it! It's a ball . . . now it's a ping pong ball.

Now it's a soap bubble.

Now it's a falling leaf. (Is it green or is it a fragile autumn leaf?)

You are able to modify your reactions accordingly. However, a four-year-old child cannot yet express all of the appropriate variations in movement.

In *The Three Bears*, the *quality* of movement that Goldilocks makes when sitting in a chair that is too small needs practice and control (Brearley 1969). Careful observation of the nature of objects and the result of our actions on them is necessary. Expressive movement develops from large gestures to a more detailed form. Dramatic activities, such as acting out stories or role playing in the doll corner, offer opportunities to develop the appropriate quality of expression and increase the range of expressed feelings.

Sit up proudly.

Make your face look aggressive.

Look timid.

Sit as a very old person does or as if you are tired.

These actions help us to empathize with mood and character—activities that are also relevant for the next topic.

Egocentricity and Movement

Young children are unaware of the feelings of others, find it difficult to put themselves in another's position, and assume that others think as they do. Objects and persons are seen from their own point of view.

Piaget's description of a child's conception of space is illustrative of this inability to imagine a point of view other than one's own (Piaget and Inhelder 1956). Children were asked to indicate scenic views from different perspectives. In one task they were to choose pictures that represented a mountain view as seen by variously positioned dolls. The children kept choosing the view that *they* could see, rather than the dolls' viewpoints.* Children's drawings illustrate this same characteristic. Young children juxtapose objects, relating them to themselves rather than to a base line or horizon (Lowenfeld and Brittain 1970).

In order to differentiate oneself from others and from objects, we must become, first of all, aware of the extent and limits of our own bodies. We do this first through motor actions, not just by "seeing" (Flavell 1963).

For individual children, awareness of self and one's relationship to other objects may best be learned by muscular and kinesthetic sensations, movement and touching, rather than by using the eyes. These individuals have been labeled *haptic* in contrast to those who are *visual*. Although everyone has some haptic tendencies, about one in four learns mainly through this sense; these children use their "touch-space" as the basis for creativeness (Lowenfeld and Birttain 1970, p. 242). For example, after performing a body movement, a child can draw the event. However, unless this action occurs, the drawing, if attempted at all, remains primitive and stereotyped. Although all children can benefit from this kind of stimulation, haptic children are frustrated and inhibited if most teaching is done through visual means. Other sense impressions are needed.

Focus at this point on feeling with your own body. You are probably contained by a chair, but not all of you are angled on it. Some of you may be rounded, some angular. Feel with your body parts. Feel the chair with your arms, feel the seat with your thighs, your feet in your shoes (Spolin 1963). We don't feel everything with the palms of our hands.

---

*This study has been challenged on the basis that the tasks were too difficult for four- and five-year-old children (Borke 1975). The fact remains, however, that the children chose pictures that indicated their own perspective, rather than any random wrong view.

Relax all of your body. Now just move your head . . . add a shoulder . . . one arm . . . an elbow. Sequential movement enables you to become conscious of how to move all the parts and stimulate awareness of them. Can you move the smallest part? Two small parts? Make a circle with your mouth; with your eyes.

Put some sticky tape on any part you want to shake. Think about that part. Take it off and put it someplace else. Shake that part (Andrews 1954; Canner 1968; Diamond 1968).

We also need to learn the relationship of our bodies to others, to things around us. *Where is your body in space? How do you view your space? Stretch and see how high your space is. How could you make yourself go higher? Lower?*

If you ask children to move about in the room, they will probably run into each other. It takes practice with groups in order to anticipate how other people will move. One must put oneself in another's place and change one's egocentric perspective to do this. Awareness of the self as part of a larger environment is a prerequisite.

Older children can be asked to move in pairs, perhaps touching fingertips. Now without touching. Make the same movement as your partner, now the opposite. Try different ways of coming together, moving apart—forward quickly, backward slowly. Come together as if you agree with each other, as if you disagree. (Gray and Percival 1962; Spolin 1963).

These movements involve planning, sequencing, imagery, and most important, anticipation of the actions of others. Socialization skills are generated.

Self-Confidence and Skill Testing

Self-confidence comes when you can test your own skill and do things independently. Sutton-Smith (n.d.) theorizes that girls do not develop as much confidence as boys in our society because they are not encouraged to test their motor skills in the same way as boys.

In a classic study (McGraw 1939), one twin was trained in swimming and roller skating before the age of two. The other twin caught up later, but the trained child always remained better coordinated, surefooted, and less fearful. Interestingly, too the trained twin had a richer fantasy life. This latter finding indicates a confirmation of the linkage between motor development and imagery.

Self-confidence comes, too, with a nofailure situation. There can be no wrong answers when a teacher gives general instructions for movement. The limits are set, but every child can be unique within these boundaries.

What is another way you can move around the room without walking?

How can you move while sitting?

How would you move if you were in a very tiny box? In a great big box? Pushing a heavy box? (Andrews 1954)

These are no-lose suggestions. Everyone feels good. In addition, these are problem-solving situations.

Movement as Integrating Other Learning Activities

Movement may be regarded as an integrating factor for all of our senses. We hear, see, and feel movement. We listen to movements: footsteps—bare footsteps, the puppy's footsteps. We recognize friends by their footsteps. We can "see" the music when the conductor communicates to the orchestra (Russell 1975).

*Pretend to **feel** a bowl of sticky dough: pull it; scrape it off your fingers. Show the action for this. You are translating texture into movements.*

Body awareness and movement of body parts have been suggested as one means of learning a reading vocabulary (Chenfeld 1976). Children learned the word for the body part they moved and wrote a sentence on the function of this part. Children also made shapes with their bodies, stood on shapes taped to the floor, and formed shapes with groups of two or three.

What pattern is made as you move on the floor? Suppose you were in the snow or on the sand. There is chalk on your feet (Andrews

1954). *Can you make letters or numbers?* Could this be a way to learn the differences between *p, d,* and *q:* using one's own body for the left-right and up-down directions (Frostig and Home 1964).

What better way to learn concepts such as large and small, narrow and wide, quick and slow, forceful and light, straight and twisted? Concepts such as up, over, upside down, out and in, are enriched by movement. *First, second,* and *third,* are words that are part of movement sequencing.

Can we really understand the meaning of certain words without having *felt* the movement of them: *wiggling, soaring, surging, flying, swaying, circling, penetrating, growing* (Russell 1975, p. 10).

Then there is spatial reasoning. Through actions on things, children discover height, depth, length, distance.

Categorization skills: *Move slowly near the floor in a twisted line. Move quickly near the*

floor in a twisted line. Children can learn to note the similarities in the actions and contrast them to the differences.

Social studies and science: *How did Columbus act when he asked the Queen for the ships? How does it feel to be sailing on the water?*

Action, rather than telling or rote memorization, gives meaning to concepts. "Movement has the power to totally involve the child . . . it is the most basic and strongest means we have to receive knowledge" (Joel 1972, p. 21).

Two Approaches to Movement

One approach to movement education is based on the Laban system. Laban's theory (1943) was introduced and developed in British schools in the 1940s. Although influential on modern dance, the American

There are no right solutions; there are many possible solutions.   Alan Pearlman

151

version became popular only in the 1960s. The system starts with a purely physical approach; that is, one that explores the use of all the parts of the body without appeals to the imagination.

Laban (1943) analyzed movement qualities into three basic elements: time, space, and weight. These elements are varied by the use of *contrasts*: slow-fast, forward-backward (or up-down, left-right), and heavy-light. These concepts are arranged in terms of high, low, or medium levels; sudden or gradual stops or flow; and straight and angled or twisted and curved ways of locomotion. Theoretically, one feels these movements without the necessity of imagining them first. Imagery can be used later, after basic movements are learned.

The child learns how to move, where to move, and what parts of the body to move. The means of locomotion can be variations of natural reactions: walking, running, hopping, skipping, galloping, jumping, leaping, or any ways children can invent.

"See if you can turn around slowly as you move low down near the floor" (Gray and Percival 1962, p. 82).

"Walk as heavily as you can, pressing your feet into the floor slowly and heavily" (Gray and Percival 1962, p. 85).

In contrast to the physical approach, the dramatic approach makes use of *pretending* or being something or someone else, as in the following suggestions (Blackie, Bullough, and Nash 1972).

"You are candles which someone lights . . . and you burn down" (p. 17).

"You are a mechanical toy which can be wound up and which stops when the clockwork runs down" (p. 18).

Less specific suggestions (Diamond 1968):

Pretend you are holding a balloon in the wind.

Pretend the floor is newly painted; or pretend it's hot, or icy, or slanted, or covered with peanut butter.

According to Laban (1943), children should not be asked to use their imaginations until they have mastered control of

their bodies. Suggestions for drama should come later because a repertoire of movements is needed before using additional thinking processes. Children may also be less imitative with a movement background. A suggestion such as "Let's all be airplanes," at an early stage, is more likely to lead to stereotyped actions.

There is no need for rigid rules. A teacher can use different kinds of suggestions if they seem helpful. In any event, drama proponents may well argue that children will use their imaginations regardless of instructions (Blackie, Bullough, and Nash 1972).

The Role of the Teacher

The teacher's role involves attitudes as well as understanding of the subject matter. Your attitude must be a flexible one that will permit exploration and experimentation. This doesn't mean, however, that you just tell the children to take off their shoes and dance. Guidance toward clear objectives occurs through observations, suggestions, comments, acceptance of ideas, and appropriate questions. Although your focus is specific, opportunity for discovery occurs by the presentation of problem-solving situations in the form of suggestions and key questions (Gilliom 1970). *How many ways can you move your feet while you keep your hands on the floor? How quietly can you move?* Attention is drawn to the answers to the tasks, with observation and discussion following (Russell 1975).

Opportunities for a wide range of practical experiences and activities to work together with other children and explore one's own capacities with a feeling of accomplishment and success can be provided by the teacher.

The need for a flexible attitude is highlighted in the following story related by a dance teacher (Borah 1967). She had brought balloons into class to illustrate light, airy movements. To her surprise, instead of floating around, the children started to blow *themselves* up like balloons—bursting cheeks, round fat heavy breaths. The result was movement, but movement of an unexpected kind. The children started from within themselves, not with the adult's conception of balloons.

For most flexibility, use your voice to adapt to the children's actions rather than restricting the children to the set rhythm of piano or records. Voice quality can vary with the ideas and moods you wish to project and can be supported by percussion instruments such as drums or bells. Music can be added after the children have developed a background of movements (Russell 1975).

Appropriate verbalization is needed at times to help translate action into abstract thought. Language brings the names of body parts and movements to a conscious level. A range of vocabulary can be used to describe movement qualities and action words at the very moment they have most significance.

Start movement exploration gradually. Children need to know their body parts and how to move them in order to have a repertoire with which the teacher can work. A second grade teacher had been developing movement possibilities for several months while motivating reading about penguins. The class had seen films on penguins, discussed the life of penguins, observed the anatomy of penguins, drawn penguins, etc. One day, another teacher peeked into the room and noticed the whole class moving penguinlike to music. Intrigued, she borrowed the record and after a brief introduction, tried to involve her own class. The result was extremely disappointing.

Use all your space, if the space is not too overwhelming. Make the most of what is available to you. Children should not just face the teacher. You do not want them to be dependent on you. They are not "performing." The teacher moves, too.

A movement comes from within the body. "Adult movements imposed on a child may appear to get quicker results but will look as artificial as powder and lipstick on a five-year-old" (Gray and Percival 1962, p. 71). Don't demonstrate "how to." Whole classes have lumbered around holding their arms out like an elephant's trunk. *How does an elephant really walk? Notice the difference in leg movements compared to how a dog walks* (p. 41). Careful observation is needed.

Try to involve the whole class, but be supportive of those who are more inhibited. Getting started may be difficult. You could start while the children are playing musical instruments, suggesting a movement for part of their body. Forming a circle gives security and allows for a natural feeling of unity. Try gathering the shy ones close to you at first. Getting down on the floor also helps as an aid to grouping (Canner 1968).

There should be a signal established prior to beginning that tells the children to stop when needed, whether it is "freeze" or "curtain" or just a pause in the music.

You can begin the movement activity with a familiar experience using ordinary actions like running or walking. *Show how you walked to school this morning. Were you in a hurry? Were you with someone? How many ways can people walk?* (Andrews 1954).

You may start with the children's own bodies, their area of most concern. Explore while they are sitting. *How can you move your arm . . . your head?*

Children's drawings suggest movement. Use a file of pictures: a rocket taking off, a horse rearing. Try touching objects and textures: prickly, spiky, pointy, smooth. Listen to the clock and translate the sound. Clap or stamp to the syllables in names. Experiment with sounds. Do a laughing dance (Canner 1968). Watch the shadows. Try poetry or drama. Movement experiences for older children may involve group work and a sequence.

You could choose a theme. Try the contrasts with Laban's elements: time, space, and weight. Repeat the actions, then change by stressing another element. Decide what part of the body is to be moved

and how and where in space. Give choices.
Even here there is room for autonomy: You
may lead with your elbow or with your
nose.

If you have children demonstrate their
movement sequence, have *several* demonstrate. In this way, you do not give the
impression of "one right way." There are
no *right* solutions; there are many possible
solutions. Note who you ask, and eventually involve every child.

And then, at the end:
With a finger . . .
With a hand . . .
. . . with an elbow . . . an arm
. . . their head, feet . . . and
finally, their whole body . . .
Ask the children to
Say "Goodbye."

References

Agresti, M. "The Dance of Life: Dance as Wor-
ship." Paper presented at North Shore Uni-
tarian Universalist Society, May 1977,
Plandome, N.Y.

Andrews, G. *Creative Rhythmic Movement for
Children*. Englewood Cliffs, N.J.: Prentice-
Hall, 1954.

Blackie, P.; Bullough, B.; and Nash, D. *Informal
Schools in Britain: Drama*. New York: Citation,
1972.

Borah, A. L., Dance Teacher, American Ballet
Theater: Personal communication, 1967.

Borke, H. "Piaget's Mountains Revisted:
Changes in the Egocentric Landscape." In
Child Development: Contemporary Perspectives,
ed. S. Cohen and T. Comiskey. Itasca, Ill.:
Peacock Publishers, 1977.

Brearley, M. *The Teaching of Young Children*. New
York: Schocken, 1969.

Canner, N. . . . *and a time to dance*. Boston: Bea-
con, 1968.

Chenfeld, M. B. "Moving Moments for Wiggly
Kids." *Phi Delta Kappan* 58 (1976): 261-264.

Diamond, V. A., Music Consultant, Hofstra
University Laboratory Preschool: Personal
communication, 1968.

Flavell, J. H. *The Developmental Psychology of Jean
Piaget*. Princeton, N.J.: Van Nostrand, 1963.

Frostig, M., and Home, D. *The Frostig Program
for the Development of Visual Perception*. Palo
Alto, Calif.: Consulting Psychologist Press,
1964.

Gilliom, B. C. *Basic Movement Education for Children: Rationale and Teaching Units*. Reading,
Mass.: Addison-Wesley, 1970.

Goodall, J. "A Preliminary Report on Expressive
Movements and Communication in the
Gombe Stream Chimpanzees." In *Primates:
Studies in Adaptation and Variability*, ed. P. Jay.
New York: Holt, Rinehart & Winston, 1968.

Gray, V., and Percival, R. *Music, Movement and
Mime for Children*. London: Oxford University
Press, 1962.

Hewes, G. W. "Primate Communication, and
the Gestural Origin of Language." *Current
Anthropology*, 14, nos. 1-2 (1973): 5-11.

Joel, L. "The Impact of Impact." *Dance Scope*, 6
(1972): 6-25.

Laban, R. *Modern Educational Dance*. London:
MacDonald & Evans, 1943.

Linden, E. *Apes, Men, and Language*. New York:
Saturday Review Press/Dutton, 1974.

Lowenfeld, V., and Brittain, W. L. *Creative and
Mental Growth*. 5th ed. New York: Macmillan,
1970.

McGraw, M. "Later Development of Children
Specially Trained in Infancy." *Child Development* 10 (1939): 1-19.

Piaget, J. *The Origins of Intelligence in Children*.
New York: International Unviersity Press,
1952.

Piaget, J., and Inhelder, B. *The Child's Conception
of Space*. London: Routledge and Kegan Paul,
1956.

Russell, J. *Creative Movement and Dance for Children*. London: MacDonald & Evans, 1975.

Sapir, E. "Communication." In *The Psychology
of Language, Thought, and Instruction Readings*,
ed. J. DeCecco. New York: Holt, Rinehart &
Winston, 1967.

Spolin, V. *Improvisation for the Theater*. Evanston, Il.: Northwestern University Press, 1963.

Sutton-Smith, B. "Play as Variability Training."
New York: Teachers College, Columbia University, n.d. Mimeographed.

Patricia J. Eggleston and Mary Knox Weir

Water Play for Preschoolers

Squishing toes in the mud and walking in the rain are probably two fond memories shared by all of us. We often forget these pleasureable experiences and deny them to young children. Without thinking very hard, many of us can give a long list of reasons why water play is not acceptable—such as "children get more colds," "they get wet," "it's messy," "too many changes of clothing are needed," "extra people are necessary," "parents won't like it," "not enough space." Even though these arguments can be refuted, many are still wary about water play. Hopefully this article will diminish some misconceptions about water play by providing a framework for understanding its value and by showing the ease with which it can be incorporated into a program.

All of us can begin to understand the value of water play by thinking of how we, as adults, react to water. How many of you relax by taking a hot bath or shower or are soothed by walking near streams in the woods or sitting by fountains in the park? Further understanding comes from watching children use water in a variety of ways and for a number of different reasons. Tense, angry children often relax as they play with water. The nonthreatening nature of it helps create an environment in which they feel safe and comfortable. It cannot hurt them nor can they physically hurt others with it. For the hesitant, quiet child who is often concerned about cleanliness and neatness, it provides a place to be messy and safe.

Throughout history people have socialized at the sources of their water supply. Socializing in all of its forms occurs for children, too, when water play is provided. Talking, sharing, laughing, touching are some of the good, exciting experiences shared by them as they play. As in other types of social play the topic of conversation does not necessarily center around the activity but can be a time for sharing other experiences.

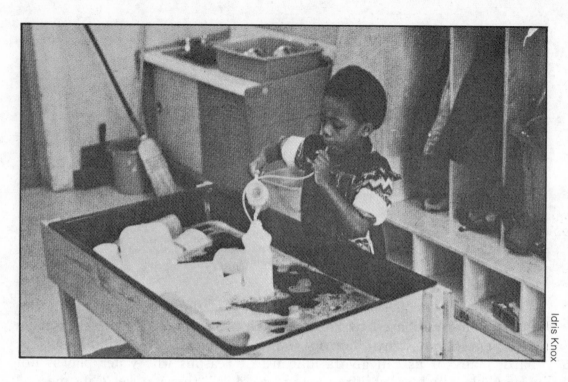

Idris Knox

In recent years most of the experiences offered to young children have had to be rationalized for the intellectual content even though we feel that the social and emotional reasons for activities are equally important. As we have stated, water play does provide opportunity for social and emotional growth, and it also provides opportunity for intellectual stimulation. Water, a substance quite different from solids, has exciting properties that children can explore. It, for instance, does not easily stay in one place. Chil-

dren are often seen experimenting with this property when, after spilling their juice or milk, they move it around with their fingers. Water then provides another framework in which one can carry on such activities as measuring, comparing, corresponding. How many times have you watched young children practice pouring a quart of water into a cup over and over until they finally realized it will not fit.

Combining water with other media adds another dimension to its properties. Water disappears into a sponge, making the sponge soft and squeezy. Some objects disappear in water such as sugar or salt; others disintegrate such as some kinds of paper products. When used on concrete or wood, water changes the color and texture of these materials—a light grey, dull sidewalk becomes shiny and dark grey from water. Dirt when combined with water forms a substance with which we

Mary Knox Weir is currently Assistant Professor in Child Development and Family Relations, School of Human Resources and Family Studies at the University of Illinois, Champaign. Mrs. Weir has spent 25 years teaching in day care and nursery settings.

Patricia J. Eggleston, Ph.D., is Assistant Professor in Early Childhood Education at Indiana University, Bloomington, Indiana. She has previously taught preschool, day care, and Head Start.

are all familiar. Mud has fine properties of its own to be explored!

Many of us are aware of the value of water play activities but find ourselves uncomfortable when we try to present it. How is it possible to provide rich and meaningful water play that is enjoyable for both children and adults? A good beginning for successful water play is preparation. One of the major worries is that children, when involved, become the sponges. Adequate protection includes full-length waterproof aprons (easily and inexpensively made from oil cloth), boots or plastic bags over the shoes, sleeves pushed over the elbows, and extra changes of clothing available.

Other major worries are spillage and damage to the room. However, if the floor is first covered with plastic, then with several layers of newspaper, and a partially filled 20- to 25-gallon washtub is provided for the water play activities, the floor is protected and the possibility of damage to school furniture is eliminated. If a water table is used, the children can stand on rag rugs or mats in order to protect the floor and the children's shoes. The tub, by its size, limits the number of children who can use it at any one time, thus there is less crowding, splashing, and conflict over materials.

Preparation also means providing for cleanup. Sponges, mops, paper towels, and storage space for the equipment are essential. Children can now assume a major share of the responsibility for cleanup.

When these steps are taken to make water play comfortable for children and staff, a variety of activities which involve water are possible. Some of the activities which children have enjoyed make use of these materials: (1) straight water; (2) water and soap: bubbles, washing, finger painting; (3) water and color: baggies, cupcake tins; (4) water and other substances.

STRAIGHT WATER PLAY

Materials Needed

1. Enough water in the tub or water table—at least 4 inches.

2. Measuring cups, funnels, squeeze bottles, measuring spoons, ladles, sieves, sponges.

3. Some of the containers ought to hold the same volume but be of different shape and size.

4. A storage shelf or bin close by so the water does not become overfilled with the materials to be used.

The Activity

Water play is an activity that can be presented every day for the entire work/play free choice period. In most good programs this means that water will be available for an hour or so. Using the materials listed, and not just a hodge-podge will enable children to develop a basic understanding about measurement. Be sure not to overload the tub with materials. A good rule of thumb is: Can you still see the water?

WATER AND SOAP

A. Bubbles

Materials Needed

1. A mild nondetergent soap.

2. Individual containers.

3. Plastic straws.

4. Food coloring.

5. For larger bubbles than straws will provide, try adding glycerin and a coat hanger bent into a circle shape. This means, of course, a larger, shallow container such as a cake tin or dishpan must be provided.

6. Towels for drying.

7. Hanging racks or clotheslines, clothespins (regular size).

Donna J. Harris

The Activity

Dolls, doll clothes, nonpainted wooden blocks, furniture, dishes, walls, easels, paint jars can all have a turn at the washing table. Care needs to be taken that some of these articles are not left to soak and are dried immediately after washing, for instance, the blocks. Some items in the room such as painted rubber families and/or community helper dolls cannot be washed because the paint will wash off.

159

B. Soap Painting

Materials Needed

1. A mild nondetergent soap powder.
2. Egg beaters or whisks.
3. Food coloring or powdered paint in salt shakers.
4. Mixing bowls.
5. Cafeteria-style trays or table tops covered with plastic or oil cloth or linoleum unless table top is non-porous and stain resistant.
6. Pail of rinse water.
7. Towels for drying off.
8. Brushes.

The Activity

Many children who fear the traditional finger painting find soap painting a socially acceptable way of getting messy.

When water is mixed with soap, a different feel and texture is experienced than when water is mixed with other substances. If children are permitted to do their own mixing, they will have a better understanding of this process.

The process of mixing and manipulating the soap and water is more important than the product.

The amount of water used provides different possibilities for soap painting by varying the consistency of the soap: very thin for painting with brushes, medium for finger painting, thick for soap sculpturing.

WATER AND COLOR

Muffin Tins

Materials Needed

1. Muffin tins or plastic ice cube trays.
2. Food coloring in the squeeze bottle or powdered tempera in small bowls.
3. Plastic eye droppers.
4. Small containers of water.

The Activity

If color mixing is restricted at the easel this activity is an excellent alternative for color experimentation.

Using tempera paint offers the child a wider variety of color choices; however, food coloring is simpler, less messy, and has a different texture. Both color activities are important.

WATER PLUS

Materials That Can Be Used

1. Dirt	3. Cornmeal	5. Sugar	7. Cocoa
2. Sand	4. Flour	6. Salt	

The Activities

Water mixed with these materials provides a variety of textures. The amount of water used will determine the kind of activity. As in soap and water the range is from thin to thick.

Some food disappears in water (salt, sugar), other food will not mix easily with water (cocoa, flour).

All activities listed above can be considered as inside as well as outside activities. Because of limited space, the number of water play activities mentioned only begins to exhaust the endless variety of combinations.

Carol Seefeldt

"Is Today Tomorrow?"
History for Young Children

"Is today tomorrow?" asked Alethea as she bounded into the kindergarten room. For Alethea's teacher had told her over and over the day before, in answer to her eager and continuous questions, that "tomorrow is the day we will go to the zoo."

Young children who have little concept of time, and even less understanding of the events of the past, have generally been given limited exposure to the concepts of history. Yet, as early as 1921 Margaret McMillan wrote that preschool children can start the study of history "as long as it is approached from a point of view suggested to the teacher, not by learned professors, but by the bright eyed children themselves. . . ."[1] Children are highly interested in the past. Who has not heard a young child beg for "just one more story about the olden days when you were little?" Furthermore, many of the concepts associated with the study of history are familiar to young children, and other concepts can be easily managed and enjoyed by them when presented in meaningful, active ways.

The study of history has been defined as a time oriented study that refers to what we do know about the past. History deals with the concepts of change, the continuity of human life, and includes knowledge gained from a critical and systematic investigation of the past.[2] Using this definition, the concepts of time, change, the continuity of human life, and the past can be identified as appropriate to introduce to young children.

---

[1]Margaret McMillan, *The Nursery School* (New York: J.M. Dent & Sons, 1921), p.215.
[2]Peter R. Senn, *Social Science and Its Methods* (Boston: Holbrook Press, 1971), p.74.

The Concept of Time

An understanding of time is necessary for the study of history.

What notion of TIME has our Tommy got? As he flattens his small palms and nose on the bathroom window and gazes out dreamily at the terrace and the mulberry tree? Does yesterday exist for him, save as something very distant, vague and separate as were, a little while ago, his own toes and feet?[3]

Research would seem to indicate that young children, as Tommy in Margaret McMillan's London nursery school of the early 1900s, have very few concepts of time.[4] And yet even the youngest baby, crying from hunger or discomfort, experiences time as he waits for someone to care for him. These daily experiences of being hungry and fed, being cared for, gradually develop in the child the differences between day and night, morning and afternoon.

In the preschool, routines, the things that happen in a predictable order, an order the children can count on and depend on, help the children to develop an understanding of time. "I don't know what time it is," said three-year-old Sarah in a child care center, "but I know my daddy will come and get me because he always comes to take me home after my nap." Flexible as they might be, the regular routines of washing before lunch, playing outside after nap, or reading a story before going home convey ideas about time to the children.

Young children, even though they cannot tell time by the clock, are intrigued with measures of time. As they become familiar with the things that measure time, children are experiencing concepts of duration, the sequence of events, and temporal order.

Children can use:

... a stop watch to see how long it takes them to .. put the blocks away .. hang up their coats .. hop across the room.

... an hour glass to turn over and watch the sand trickle into the bottom glass or use the hour glass to see if they can .. wash the tables .. pick up the scraps .. get ready to go home before the sand empties into the other half of the glass.

... a cooking timer that buzzes when set to remind them to .. take the cookies from the oven .. to come in from play .. or to get up from rest.

... an old alarm clock to play with .. to turn the hands .. to take apart .. to set the alarm.

Learning about history, dealing with the events of the past also requires that children develop a sense of the passage of time. "What did you do today?" the teacher of the two-year-old asks as she helps her into her coat before going home. "What did we have for lunch yesterday?" "What did we do last week?" "What did you like best about the year in kindergarten?" are all questions that help children to recall the passage of time.

---

[3]McMillan, *The Nursery School*, p.235.
[4]*Ibid.*, p.238.

Carol Seefeldt is Assistant Professor of Education at the University of Maryland. She has worked in the public schools of Milwaukee, St. Louis, and Granite City, Illinois and directed a private kindergarten program in Tampa, Florida. She taught at the University of South Florida, Florida State University, directed an eight week leadership training program for Head Start, and served as Regional Training Officer for Florida's Head Start Program.

Richard Farkas

The Concept of Change

With the passage of time comes change. History, in many respects, is the study of change. The record of man's existence is a record of change. Some changes represent progress, others do not. Nevertheless, change is a part of living and being able to adapt to change is critical. Change is not valued for bringing something new and different or innovative, nor is it feared for the differences it brings. Rather the value of accepting the inevitability of change, and methods for adapting to change are taught to the children.

Change surrounds the children. Whether a child care center, kindergarten, or primary classroom, things are constantly changing. Children's observations can be focused on the changes that occur in the pets, seeds bulbs, and plants in the classroom. The children themselves change. They grow, learn new skills, lose teeth, get their hair cut, and make new friends. Children can discover all of the ways they have changed. They might:

... find out how much they weighed at birth, go outside and fill a plastic bag with enough sand to equal their birth weight. A bathroom scale is usually adequate to weigh the bags of sand. Actually holding 6 pounds of sand in their hands, children gain some understanding of exactly how much they have changed since their birth.

... taste a bit of strained baby food, perhaps string beans, and then taste the string beans they now eat. Why did they need the strained food when they were babies? What can they eat now that they could not eat then? How have they changed?

... examine items of clothing they wore when they were much younger. Many children may be able to bring in some item, a bonnet, baby shoes, christening dress, or old diaper, to compare with the clothing they now wear.

... begin a history book of their year in the preschool. Snap shots, taken throughout the year, pieces of work the children have completed, records of weight and height, some of the interesting things they might have said can be recorded in the history book. At the end of the year each child will have a booklet of her own life, a booklet that will give her a meaningful understanding of change.

The Concept of the Continuity of Human Life

Although life is continually changing, there is a continuity to human experiences. Exploring the children's family history provides a sense of the continuity of human experiences. Not every family will be able to give their children a complete family history, yet each family has something unique and of worth to give their children from the past. McMillan, who taught children of working class families wrote:

What is it to belong to an old family? Just this. It is belonging to people who are worth thinking about and being remembered for a long time, at least by their own children. At the bottom of all this is a dim consciousness that life is not a trivial thing, not a mere

scurrying across a stage and ending in utter darkness, but a play with some kind of relating and meaning to the acts.[5]

For many parents who are faced with the struggles of day to day living, the questions their children ask about the past may seem rude, prying, or strange. Teachers might help these parents to see the value of talking to their children about their own past as they interest the children in their family's history.

Every parent, no matter what they remember of their past, can talk to their children about the games they liked to play, the things they liked to do, how they used to do their hair, catch a cricket, fold sheets, or play in puddles.

The Concept of the Past

Children are intensely interested in the past, both the immediate past and the very long ago. Helping children to understand and explore the past does not mean that a true historic sense of time can be developed. In helping children to gain a concept of the past, Wann stated that "Adults must shuttle back and forth with children from the past to the present as they react to the ever present urge to understand what has gone before. This dipping into the past without concern for a logical development of chronology from the past to the present does not violate basic principles of learning."[6]

Even though the past is untouchable and far away, experiences with the

[5]*Ibid.*, p.239.
[6]Kenneth D. Wann, Miriam Selchen Dorn, and Elizabeht Ann Liddle, *Fostering Intellectual Development in Young Children* (New York: Bureau of Publications, Teachers College, Columbia University, 1962), p.53.

past are possible for young children. Many resources are available to help young children understand the past.

. . . people as resources

Their own parents, grandparents, the school staff, the neighbors, are all resources for helping children to understand the past, The grandfather who can tell about hitching up his horse to go to church, a grandmother who shows the children how she used to wash clothes on a scrub board, or the mother who tells the children about listening to the radio before the advent of television all give the children a vicarious sense of the past.

. . . objects as resources

Tools, kitchen utensils, rolling pins, old wooden cookie cutters, kettles, eggbeaters, are all excellent resources. As the children wonder over the marvels of a coal oil lamp or a hand eggbeater, they can compare these objects from the past to the ones in use today.

Other antiques, those that can not be handled by the children, can still be shared in the classroom. Children seem to understand that something very old is very valuable.

Nearly every community has some type of museum to preserve the traces of the past. The local library, fire station, or church may house relics for

Richard Farkas

the children to observe. If only large museums are available in the community, the teacher could select one room for the children to visit or just one section of the museum for a field trip. Older homes, buildings, mansions that have been renovated and restored can also be visited by the children.

Toys and models that depict things from the past are enjoyed. Cars, boats, and planes that are modeled after those no longer in use, give the children an opportunity to make comparisons between the things they know and use today and things from the past. With any object from the past teachers initiate discussions to help extend and clarify children's concepts. "Why do you think the train was made this way?" "Who do you think used this?" "How do you know it was used a long time ago?" "How is it just like the ones we use today?" are questions that might stimulate children's thinking.

The Methods of the Historian

Preschool children are not being prepared to become historians, but there is much in the historic method that can be of value to them. The historian uses the methods of science in order to interpret and understand the past. Historians, as scientists, formulate problems, gather information and data, observe the data, analyze, infer, and reach conclusions based on their data. These processes, the same ones that are involved in problem solving and the scientific method, can be developed in young children.

. . . identifying a problem

Children must be able to identify their own problems, at least they

should perceive the problem as their own. When a problem is determined by the teacher and presented to the children for solving, it may be an exercise for the children rather than a problem to solve. Problems that arise in the classroom, school, home, or immediate community have elements of being "real" to the children.

. . . gathering information

In order to solve a problem, information must be gathered. Historians gather traces of the past as they attempt to solve problems. Children might examine traces of the past — books, relics, objects — or they might interview older people to obtain information.

. . . observing data

After the information has been collected, careful observation takes place. Children's skills in learning to observe are fostered continually as they are asked to describe what they see, feel, taste, touch, and hear throughout the day.

. . . analyzing information

Once gathered and observed, information is analyzed and inferences are made. Children, as historians, based on their observations of the traces of the past, make inferences as to what life was like, how people lived, what they did, and what they believed in a long time ago.

. . . drawing conclusions

In problem solving, children may, because their data is incomplete or their inferences are less than accurate, draw conclusions that are also incomplete and inaccurate. Rather than correcting the children's conclusions, the teacher concerned about the process of problem solving, and not a correct answer, accepts the children's judgments. Activities that will clarify the children's conclusions could be planned for the future.

The Role of Play

Just as the teacher structures and plans experiences and activities designed to foster children's understanding of history and build concepts of time, change, continuity of human life, and the past, she provides opportunities for children to play.

Fostering children's play, props suggestive of some period in the past that is of interest to the children, can be added to the dramatic play area. A sunbonnet, cowboy hat, long dress, old lunch bucket, tools, boots might stimulate children's play. Historic films, stories, slides are shared to give children additional information as a base for their play. Large blocks of time and as much space as possible, both indoors and out, are set aside for play.

Together, a program rich with play and experiences planned to foster concepts associated with the study of history can develop the preschool child's understanding of history. This understanding will not be complete or final, it may even be vague, on the order of a precept rather than a concept, and yet however incomplete, this understanding will form the foundation on which all future learnings will be built.

Ruth F. Bogdanoff and Elaine T. Dolch

Old Games for Young Children:

A Link to Our Heritage

Group games and gamelike activities are an integral part of human social interaction. Infants begin to explore their surroundings by devising gamelike activities. They grasp and release objects. Soon they learn to drop them on the floor. If the objects are picked up and handed back to babies, the game has begun. Very young children quickly learn to play "Peek-a-Boo" or "Where's the Baby?" These games become "Hide and Seek" when older children play them.

The traditional games upon which we will focus are those which have been played for hundreds of years. Affairs of honor and ownership were often decided on game fields; for example, certain Native American nations played lacrosse to resolve territorial hunting, fishing, and farming rights. Today, as in centuries past, athletes compete in games of skill and grace in a multitude of settings from city sidewalks and open fields to international arenas.

In our constant search for innovative and appropriate ways to help young children learn about themsleves, others, and the world about them, we plan activities that have gamelike characteristics. Sometimes we instigate games that we remember from our own childhoods. Most of these have roots in our rich cultural heritages. We hope you will choose games that appeal to you and that seem to be right for the children with whom you work and play.

"Little Sally Walker." "Doggie, Doggie, Where's Your Bone?" Do you know how to play those games? Do you know in what way they are alike? Each has been played for generations in all parts of the United States. These games or their variations have been played for centuries from Scandinavia to Africa and from England to China. Although the origins of folk games are difficult to document, researchers have found references to "Ring Around the Rosie" in Great Britain, southern France, and Germany. "Oats, Peas, Beans" and "London Bridge" are other games that were played in diverse forms in ancient times in African countries and all through western Europe. In the United States these games are played by many ethnic groups with their own variations. The themes and actions tend to be universal while the variations reflect the lifestyles and cultural mores of the people who play them.

In the past, adults played similar games at various kinds of celebrations, festivals, and parties. Sometimes they were played at the end of the day's work as families

Ruth F. Bogdanoff, M.A., Instructor, Early Childhood Education, Department of Child Development and Family Studies, Purdue University, West Lafayette, Indiana, and former nursery school, kindergarten, and first grade teacher.

Elaine T. Dolch, M.S., Assistant Professor, Department of Child Development and Family Studies, Purdue University, and former nursery school teacher and child development specialist.

gathered on the town square or village green. Other group games were part of religious rituals. Frequently political happenings, current events, or caricatures of famous people were the inspirations for these activities. Many evolved from traditions associated with various professions such as farming, food preparation, and soldiering. Other games were concerned with courtship and marriage. Chance, physical strength, and strategy became elements typical of more complex games to be played by adults and older children.

When families gathered, everyone from the youngest to the oldest member was there to participate or watch. Young children learned game rules, rituals, and traditions as they observed and played with adults. As work-play polarizations increased, adults played fewer and fewer folk games. Children then taught the games to other children. Because games today are taught by children, not parents, children learn to play the games of the neighborhood and adapt them according to their understanding and experience. Thus children in different locales may play games that have originated in other cultures, but in each locale the games have their own ethnic flavor.

Our culture currently emphasizes organization, strict age grouping, and often supervised, contrived togetherness. Many twentieth century children are catapulted from one adult-directed or supervised activity to another. The rich traditions of playing games could soon be lost unless adults provide opportunities for the young to learn to play them. The renewed interest in the preservation of our multiethnic origins is but one good reason for us to consider games that might serve some of our goals in early childhood education. Within the wide varieties of activities that might be classified as games, children can be offered experiences that are not only fun, but that also strengthen all aspects of growth and development.

Games from a Piagetian Viewpoint

Piaget (1962) and DeVries and Kamii (1975) underline the value of game-playing to support the development of thought processes and moral judgment that emerge during the concrete operational period. This stage, between the ages of seven and twelve, follows the sensorimotor period of

Children may enjoy playing games with the group at first, then decide to watch for awhile.

Ruth F. Bogdanoff

infancy and the preoperational period of the preschool and kindergarten years during which children have integrated language with perceptions and actions into their thought processes. While children in the concrete operational stage are still bound in thinking to concrete experiences, they can now manipulate ideas and actions mentally without using physical materials.

For example, ten-year-old Sara can choose and buy an appropriate gift for mother, though she may need to plan several months in advance to earn the money. Unless an appropriate gift were suggested by an adult, Eric, a preschool child, would only be able to choose something for his mother from within his immediate field of choice at the time of selection. He could not take into account pertinent factors, such as money needed, whether the gift was too large to carry or too awkward to hide, and so forth.

Children who are thinking at the concrete operational level, as Sara is, have a different qualitative thought process than those at the preoperational level, as Eric is. They are developing characteristics of operational thought, i.e., transformation, decentration, and reversibility, while egocentrism is diminishing. These thought processes enable concrete operational level children to reason, use logic, and generalize from past experience. If we look at the nature of the games described by Piaget (1965) and then at the characteristics that differentiate the preoperational level from the concrete operational level, it will be apparent why games facilitate intellectual and moral development during that period and why those same games are not appropriate for the preoperational child.

Kinds of Games

The games to which Piaget refers require cooperation and coordination or collaboration on the part of the players while they are engaged in a contest of powers prescribed within a framework of rules. The rules limit the action and ensure a winner and a loser (Sutton-Smith 1971). In "Hide and Seek," for example, the players through cooperation organize themselves into hiders and a seeker, with a home-safe base. The hiders oppose the seeker by trying not to be seen until they can run home free. Rules that limit the how, when, and where one hides, and that determine when one may run home free and penalties for the losers are accepted by all the players.

Thought Processes Required

From a developmental point of view, games such as "Hide and Seek," which require the players to keep the overall movement of the game in mind while planning strategy for competition, are not likely to be successful for children at the nursery school and kindergarten level. Children who are functioning at the preoperational level lack the thought processes of transformation, decentration, and reversibility. Furthermore, they still retain a strong egocentric viewpoint. They understand the actions of games as a series with each situation unrelated to the other, except that the situations occur together in time.

Transformations. Players must be able to understand that the situation in which they find themselves may be caused by a preceding action. As when Sara planned not only the gift, but how she would get the necessary money, so eight-year-old Federico, as he plays "Hide and Seek," must realize that his *run* to home base related the hiding situation to his arrival home safely on base. At the concrete operational stage, he can plan this transforming part of the situation. However, if Federico were younger and thus thinking preoperationally, he might see his role as one of hiding, then of touching base to be safe, overlooking the run to home as part of the process of the game. Then, if he should be caught as he runs to base, he might think it unfair because in his mind he *is* at home base because he wants to be there. He does not

171

see the necessary process of running home as part of the sequence of the game.

Decentration. Decentration, another thought process of the concrete operational stage, is essential to understanding the object of the game. Action taken in winning/losing games must be congruent with the goal of the game. Children at the preoperational level cannot decenter sufficiently to see the game as a whole and the relationship of all its actions to the goal. Therefore, they have no basis to select action appropriate to the outcome of the game. For example, if Kai hides at the preoperational level he may be thinking so hard about keeping hidden (he is centering on hiding) that he does not try to run home. Or, he may center on the whereabouts of "It" and leave his hiding spot to find "It." When children do not comprehend the overall goal of the game and their roles in relation to others, they have difficulty in keeping the game moving toward the goal.

Making Use of Past Experience Through Reversible Thought. Reversibility is the ability to think of an action and then reverse that action to the original situation. Children can learn to generalize from past mistakes and choose successful game actions as they gain experience. In the preoperational stage, Kai tends to hide in the same spot each time even though he is easily caught there. He uses the same strategy to run home unless a better way is demonstrated to him. The child, Rosa, in the concrete operational period can reason that because she used a particular hiding spot and was caught, she can cancel that thought and try another hiding space. She can generalize from one experience to another because reversible thinking is more flexible.

Diminished Egocentrism. The choice of successful game action also requires that the egocentrism of the young child must have waned sufficiently so that the players can see the opponent's point of view as well as their own. At the concrete operational level, children can usually manage this, some earlier than others. Sara was able to put herself into mother's position to consider what she could use as a gift. Federico (at the concrete operational level) avoids "It" because he can guess what "It" will do, where "It" will look, or how fast "It" can run before he acts or delays action accordingly. Furthermore, with egocentrism diminished, the player can accept the rules as objective limits and does not feel failure as a personal penalty affecting self-concept.

Egocentrism is still strong with preoperational children. They tend to think only of their own role in the game. Kai finds it hard to wait during games to get into the action. If he is hiding and feels the wait is too long, he may come out of his hiding spot and say, "Here I am!" If he is caught, he will not understand why and may feel it is an unexpected disappointment that he may attribute to the other players' hostility toward him or to his own incapability. He may even reject or ignore the idea that he is a loser and continue playing as though he were not caught. The preoperational child is still too egocentric to accept a winner or loser as the game's outcome.

Lack of development of thought processes in the preoperational child (i.e., transformations, decentration, ability to make use of past experience through the use of reversible thought), combined with the usual childhood egocentrism, is an obstacle to playing the kinds of games to which Piaget refers. The young child is incapable of choosing actions from several intangible alternatives that are appropriate to the game as a whole and that determine who wins or loses. Games such as "Hide and Seek" belong in the curriculum for children in the concrete operational period of the school years.

Should games be played in preschool? If so, what kind? We think playing carefully chosen and appropriately taught games offers advantages for young children. Table

1 outlines the progression of complexity, as children advance through preoperational to concrete operational periods.

Characteristics of Games Appropriate for Children at the Preoperational Level

Cooperation or Collaboration

Games of all types develop social awareness. All games require cooperation or collaboration to some extent. Chauncey (1969) and Kessen (1975) indicate that group singing and dancing games are taught to Russian and Chinese children two to six years of age. Some of these games are traditional, some are revised, but all are used to further group consciousness and consideration of peers. We may differ with the Russians and Chinese in our viewpoint of social and political values, but as world population grows, it may be well to enhance group awareness in our children. For many years early childhood educators have been primarily concerned with preserving the individuality of each child. The time may have arrived to balance this focus on individuality with concern for the group.

The games discussed here will emphasize cooperation. These games have been most widely played in this country. Teachers may wish to adapt these games or use adaptations of other games from the heritage of the children in their programs.

Role Alternation or Role Reversal

The goal orientation of competitive action/counteraction can be replaced by role alternation or role reversal to give function to the players. For example, in the "Farmer in the Dell," the player assumes one role identity (one of the chorus) and then another (the farmer's spouse, etc.) in sequence. This is role alternation. In games like "Punchinello" where the player is a follower and then a leader (Punchinello) and then a follower again, the players reverse roles although they do not act against each other (Sutton-Smith 1971). Participating in more than one role requires children to modify their actions to fit those of others. This becomes a preliminary decentering opportunity for those approaching the concrete operational level where they are ready to make this change. According to Sutton-Smith, "In sum, there is abundant evidence, in these pastimes of the four- to seven-year-olds, of social actions and counteractions, paving the way for the true role reversibility of games proper" (p. 303).

Ritualized Sequence of Action

Some games use a ritualized sequence of play to structure the action, rather than

"All fall down" (together). In first game playing experiences, youngest children, because of their egocentrism, need to participate in unison as in "Ring Around the Rosie." Ruth F. Bogdanoff

Table 1. Developmental

Level	Child's Thought Development	Game Requirements	Suggested Games	
I	**Preoperational**	Pattern or sequence game Two-step sequence	Ring Around the Rosie Roll the Ball (small group) Hokey Pokey (modified) Humpty Dumpty and other nursery rhymes This is the way the _____ walks (tune of Mulberry Bush)	
	Very limited verbal understanding	No verbal instruction necessary to teach game		
	Strong egocentrism	Continuous participation by all No waiting necessary Two to four children		
	Little group awareness, child involved primarily with adults	Game depends on adult action No role alternation required		
II	**Preoperational**	Basic pattern game Not more than three steps in sequence	Punchinello (circle style) Did You Ever See a Lassie? Hide the Clock Little Sally Walker Paw Paw Patch Variation of Mulberry Bush (with child's choice of action)	
	Verbal understanding not dependable	No verbal instruction required		
	Egocentrism still strong	Continuous participation Five to eight children		
	Awareness of other children's presence but most interest in adult's expectation of child's behavior.	Role alternation with help of the leader only		
III	**Preoperational**	Basic pattern game Four to five steps in sequence Limited choice of action within framework of game	Looby Loo Doggie, Doggie, Where's Your Bone? Musical Chairs (modified) Are You My Kitten? Duck, Duck, Goose (modified)	
	Coordination of language with action nearly complete	Some verbal instruction supported by demonstration		
	Egocentrism less strong in game situation	Wait short periods for turn with group action interspersed		

rules to guide the action. Rather than ending when a winner is determined, the sequence game, sometimes called a pattern game, terminates after everyone has had a turn or after the sequence of movement or activity is complete, as in "Mulberry Bush." Preschool children easily remember the sequence of the action through which they move. The predetermined sequence minimizes the need for choices for children who are so young and egocentric that they are unable to make a viable choice that will keep the game moving toward its goal. Yet such a sequence allows room for choices based on children's ideas that do not affect the flow of the game to its outcome. For instance, "Sally Walker" chooses her own successor. "Punchinello" determines his own actions as well as his successor. Games that use role alternation or role reversal as a sequence of action are appropriate for the preoperational child although the youngest ones may need help from adults in making a choice.

Guidelines for Choosing Games

Level	Child's Thought Development	Game Requirements	Suggested Games
III cont.	Good awareness of all players but limited understanding of their roles in game	Six to ten players One-to-one interaction possible	Mulberry Bush
	Primary interest in own role	Role alternation between players may now be part of game	
IV	**Late preoperational**		A Tisket-a-Tasket
	More objective understanding of role in action of game	Players required to make some choices of action	Squirrel in the Trees
	Good verbal understanding	May use verbal cues as well as action	Charlie over the Water
	Egocentrism diminishing	Turn taking can be part of game	Find My Child London Bridge
	Enjoys coordination with group Will subject own interests to group effort	Understand and enjoy role alternation and some role reversal Eight to twelve children	Knock, Knock
V	**Concrete operational**		Word games (G-H-O-S-T)
	Reversible thought and lessened egocentrism Understand rules as objective framework for action	Decisions of strategy determine outcome of game	Tag (modified) Hide and Seek Kick the Can
	New interest in competition within coordinated effort	Competition may be used Team action may substitute for personal involvement	Competitive races and relays Follow the Leader
	Uses language easily for thought	Verbal element can be definitive part of game	Darts Horseshoes Pease Porridge Hot Simon Says

Late Preoperational Stage Exceptions

In the late preoperational stage (between five and seven years), as children enter a phase transitioning into operational thought, the use of some games with a minor element of competition may be appropriate. Games in which a child who is caught may become "It" without losing the game work well if the adult is cognizant of the game-playing experience of the group and minimizes this competitive part of the game-playing situation for players who do not yet understand it (Level IV). Children are likely to become increasingly aware of other players' actions because of a singling out process which affords a chance to use intelligence adaptively. Some children are ready for this competitive experience earlier than others. With or without the element of competition, all of these games offer active use of thought processes essential to children's development as they must adapt to the moves of other players and make simple choices.

Further Advantages of Group Game Playing for Preschoolers

Sensory Discrimination

Games based predominantly on a sequence of action and role alternation offer many advantages for children throughout the preoperational period. Games also provide experiences in different kinds of sensory discrimination such as *visual* discrimination where the child must attend to visual cues as in "Find My Child" or in hiding games; *auditory* discrimination as in "Hide the Clock"; and *tactile* discrimination where the child must be alert to the cue to action as in "Duck, Duck, Goose." Alertness to sensory cues is required in many games.

Verbal Skills

Language and verbal skills are encouraged through the responses to challenges as in "Find My Child." As players describe definitive characteristics of the "child" who is "lost," each verbally expresses concepts. When actions are coordinated with words, e.g., "Mulberry Bush" or "Looby Loo," skill in clarifying word meaning through actions is the focus of the game. The difficulty of the game should be based on children's ability to comprehend verbal instructions, their ability to use language meaningfully, and their understanding of cues given as in pantomimes.

Motor Coordination and Self-Concept

Coordination of gross and fine motor movement to those of other players as they move in and out, under and over, and around and through, give experience in directionality. Such understandings of self in space can only develop through experience and are critical both for game skill later and the basic understanding of space and time. Games should be chosen which will use skills children have developed and extend their growth.

"Put your one foot in" can be substituted for "Put your left foot in" when children are too young to grasp the right/left concept that is traditionally part of the "Hokey-Pokey."   Ruth F. Bogdanoff

Concept Formation

Concepts of color and number are also included in games. "I see something yellow" facilitates color concepts, and games such as "Knock, Knock" encourage one-to-one correspondence. Of course, all singing and dance games encourage rhythm and timing as well as familiarity with simple melodies.

Teacher's Role

Many areas of function and understanding are introduced and reinforced as children acquire game skills from the simplest to the most sophisticated levels. Games should be chosen to match the children's abilities, interests, and cultural backgrounds as well as the program's curriculum goals. Traditional words and actions of games will often be adapted to fit particular needs and interests of the teacher and children. For example, "Little Sally Walker" may become "Little Barry Barlow" or the name of one of the children in the group. The "Farmer in the Dell" may choose a husband or a spouse instead of a wife. Children's everyday experiences and creative ideas will determine the action in games like "Paw Paw Patch" or "Mulberry Bush." "Duck, Duck, Goose" may become "Triangle, Triangle, Circle" to emphasize pertinent concepts. Opportunities for improvisations of folk games are endless.

Suggestions for Introducing and Playing Games

- Relate the game to a familiar activity, routine, characterization, or finger play.

- Demonstrate the details of playing the game.

- Avoid complicated verbal instructions— sing or chant words to help the children become familiar with music and rhyme.

- Coordinate words with actions—actions give meaning to words and make them easier to remember.

Teacher-supported innovations stimulate problem solving and creative thinking. Encouraging children to take initiatives of action within the framework of game sequences is valuable experience in preparing children to meet greater challenges where the choices are between alternative actions that evoke penalties.

The rich potential of stimulating growth and development through the playing of games is realized when young children participate and cooperate spontaneously, not because they have been coerced into being part of the group. It is essential, too, that the teacher become an enthusiastic, involved participant!

References

Avedon, E. M., and Sutton-Smith, B. *The Study of Games*. New York: Wiley, 1971.

Bartlett, V. *The Past of Pastimes*. New York: Anchor, 1969.

Chauncey, H., ed. *Soviet Preschool Education*. New York: Holt, Rinehart, & Winston, 1969.

Culin, S. *Games of the Orient: Korea, China and Japan*. Rutland, Vt.: Tuttle, 1958.

DeVries, R., and Kamii, C. *Why Group Games? A Piagetian Perspective*. Urbana, Ill.: ERIC Clearinghouse on Early Childhood Education, 1975.

Gomme, A. B. *The Traditional Games of England, Scotland and Ireland*. New York: Dover, 1964.

Harbin, E. O. *Games of Many Nations*. Nashville, Tenn.: Abingdon, 1954.

Hendricks, J. *The Whole Child*. St. Louis, Mo.: Mosby, 1975.

Kamii, C., and DeVries, R. *Piaget, Children, and Number*. Washington, D.C.: National Association for the Education of Young Children, 1976.

Kessen, W. *Childhood in China*. New Haven, Conn.: Yale University Press, 1975.

Newell, W. W. *Games and Songs of American Children*. New York: Dover, 1963.

Opie, I., and Opie, P. *Children's Games in Street and Playground*. New York: Oxford, 1969.

Piaget, J. *The Moral Judgment of the Child*. New York: Free Press, 1965.

Piaget, J. *Play, Dreams and Imitation in Childhood*. New York: Norton, 1962.

Spence, L. *Myth and Ritual in Dance, Games and Rhyme*. New York: Watts, 1947.

Sutton-Smith, B. "A Syntax for Play and Games." In *Child's Play*, ed. R. Herron and B. Sutton-Smith. New York: Wiley, 1971.

V. Helping Children Cope

While teachers are not expected to be therapists, social workers, or family counselors, they must recognize and meet young children's affective needs and support and encourage their social and emotional growth.

Young children need understanding adults to help them cope with fears, crises, and unexpected events, particularly those that they cannot begin to understand because of the complexity, abstractness, or sheer magnitude. Children also need guidance in learning to cope with the everyday problems in their lives.

Every child has fears. Some are more realistic than others, but all fears are real to the child who has them. Hyson's article can assist teachers in helping children cope with fears and other perplexities as well. Her down-to-earth approach works.

Death as a topic of discussion is not as taboo as it was a decade or two ago, but that does not make the topic any easier for children to understand or for adults to competently and sensibly discuss with young children. Furman explores children's views of death and offers concrete suggestions for teachers.

Teachers must help children cope with all kinds of feelings, including uncontrolled exuberance, aggression, and hostility. Some children may need professional understanding and guidance.

Children must develop the skills for coping with their world and the people in it. This section recognizes that children need adult support and guidance while learning those skills.

Marion Carey Hyson

Lobster on the Sidewalk
Understanding and Helping Children with Fears

One day when Jeff was almost three, he and his mother met a neighbor outside their apartment building. The neighbor, just back from shopping, was carrying a large brown bag.

"Come here, Jeff," the neighbor called. "Let me show you what I bought." She reached into the bag and placed a live lobster on the sidewalk. As it moved slowly toward Jeff, waving its claws in the sunlight, he screamed with panic. The apologetic neighbor rushed the lobster to its waiting pot.

At Jeff's day care center several weeks later, Jeff sat on the floor while his teacher showed the group a new book about the sea. While turning the pages, she came to a delicate illustration of a lobster. Jeff's eyes widened. He jumped up and tried to close the book.

"Jeff!" the teacher said. "There's nothing to be afraid of!"

"There's nothing to be afraid of!" Generations of teachers and parents have said it, and generations of children have just as firmly rejected it. A lobster, a friendly babysitter, a new hairdo, a vacuum cleaner—such "harmless" things can cause reactions ranging from mild worry to outright panic. Where do these fears come from, how do they develop, and what can be done to help children overcome them?

The Origins of Fear

Fear is not confined to children. We are all afraid of something, but our fears come in many sizes and many degrees of

realism. When you think about it, a totally fearless person would be foolhardy . . . or dead. Some fears are clearly sensible and protective. No one scoffs at a person who is cautious about crossing the street, who backs away from the edge of a cliff, or who shrinks from the pain of surgery.

Sometimes an imaginary-sounding fear turns out to have a basis in fact. Children are often unable to reveal traumatic experiences, so adults tend to dismiss their concerns as imaginary. But there are far too many children who have to worry about very real and disturbing events:

Marion Carey Hyson, Ph.D., is a kindergarten teacher at Charlestown Play House, Phoenixville, Pennsylvania. She is a former nursery school, high school, and college teacher. Her doctoral research dealt with the development of coping strategies by young children.

being bitten by rats, being abandoned, being abused.

Other fears are less directly tied to present dangers. Some people theorize that many of our most basic human fears—of sudden, looming movements, of loud noises, of being alone or enclosed—are left-over survival reactions from our early ancestors (Bowlby 1973). Even today such reactions may occasionally save us from harm.

Other fears are less easily explained because they do not seem to have a reasonable cause. Why should anyone be afraid of a lobster on the sidewalk, or a worm, or a Halloween costume? Such reactions are easier to understand if we recognize the role of cognitive processes in producing fearful responses. We fear not what will harm us, but what we *think* will harm us. We interpret an event in the light of our past experiences, our present understanding, and the total situation, and on that basis we *infer* that the event is either harmless or dangerous. The same stimulus—that lobster on the sidewalk—might cause reactions ranging from amusement to interest to fright in people of different age or with differing experiences.

If what we fear is partly determined by our interpretation of events, it is understandable that children have more "irrational" fears than adults (Maurer 1965; Bauer 1976). But irrationality is in the eye of the beholder. Piaget and others have demonstrated that, in many respects, children's thinking operates differently than adult thinking. Both its content and structure are constantly changing as the child assimilates new experiences and accommodates thinking to those experiences. An event that seems innocuous to an adult may quite logically appear menacing to the young preoperational child. Thus, not only do children exhibit more fears than adults, but the *content* of these fears changes as the child develops.

The following sketches of some children and their fears may illustrate the cognitive processes and emotional needs that influence developmental changes related to fears.

Louis and the babysitter. Seven-month-old Louis sat in his high chair, banging a spoon against the tray. Suddenly his happy expression changed to one of sober alertness and then to fear and distress. He turned his head and began to wail. Marge, his babysitter, was confused. What had she done to upset Louis?

Fear of strangers is one of the first fears parents and caregivers notice in infants. Before seven or eight months, Louis often showed distress when he was hungry, wet, or tired, but it could not be said he showed fear. What's happening now?

The child's changing *interpretation* of the situation influences the appearance of fearful behavior during the first year of life (see Lewis and Rosenblum 1974). In the second half of that year, changes occur in infants' awareness of the unfamiliar (Kagan 1974; Shaffer 1974). Louis has recently acquired a memory or mental representation of his mother and other familiar people. Once he has such a standard to draw upon, he becomes aware of Marge's status as an unfamiliar person who does not match this mental image or schema. Sometimes, especially if the mother is holding the child in well-known surroundings, this kind of unfamiliarity causes the baby to become more interested (Sroufe 1974). But if the newness—the discrepancy between the familiar and the unfamiliar—is too great, or if other aspects of the situation contribute to wariness, the baby may "evaluate" the situation as threatening rather than interesting.

Paco and the haircut. Mrs. Velez, a teacher at 18-month-old Paco's day care center, had always worn her black hair long and loose. One Monday morning she appeared with a new, much shorter hairdo. Paco stared at her, burst into tears when she spoke to him, and refused to come near her for the rest of the day.

As children enter their second and third year, their fearful reactions increase and extend beyond the fear of strangers. While there are many individual differences in the kinds of things toddlers may find fearful, Paco's reaction to his teacher's haircut illustrates the fear of transformations or changes in familiar things.

Understanding how children interpret such transformations helps explain their distressed reaction. Objects and people have an identity that is maintained despite surface changes. A table is a table whether it is viewed from above or underneath, and Mrs. Velez is Mrs. Velez whether her hair is long or short—a self-evident truth to an adult, but difficult for young children like Paco to grasp. He can not be sure that his teacher is really the same person with a new haircut. The same thinking process influences toddlers' fears of other transformations—Halloween masks, wigs, new glasses, a doll with a missing arm, a slowly collapsing balloon.

Amanda and the vacuum cleaner. Two-year-old Amanda runs to hide in her crib whenever her mother vacuums, and now she will not go near the machine even when it is turned off. Her mother has tried to explain how it works, but nothing seems to help.

Our technological society depends on inanimate objects that perform obediently at human command. But toddlers see these lifeless gadgets as less docile than they really are. Young children attribute their own feelings and motives to everything around them, including inanimate objects like vacuum cleaners (Piaget 1929). To Amanda the vacuum cleaner is a noisy, all-devouring creature that will consume her like a piece of household debris. The toilet, chiming clocks, fire engines, water hoses, and escalators also appear threatening to some young children as a result of their egocentric and animistic interpretation of the object's function (see Fraiberg 1959).

Peter and the monster. Four-year-old Peter was having a hard time napping at school. After one tearful session, he confided to his teacher that he was afraid that a monster was hiding in the closet and would come out if he closed his eyes.

Unlike Paco and Amanda's concrete fears, the fears of older preschoolers often appear in response to imaginary dangers—monsters, ghosts, bad dreams, Frankenstein. The influence of television provides only a partial explanation, since younger and older children may be exposed to the same material and react differently.

The appearance of these imaginary fears is again related to children's intellectual development. Peter can symbolize or mentally represent what he has never seen (Piaget 1951). This ability enormously extends his potential for learning. But in these years during which children are just beginning the "conquest of the symbol" (Elkind 1974), the dividing line between symbol and referent, between fantasy and reality, is thin indeed.

Songs, stories, television—or the child's own imagination—may produce inventions that blur the distinction between "real" and "just pretend." Often these creations are strikingly wild and fierce. Peter had been having a hard time with his own aggressive feelings; his angry outbursts scared him more than they scared his classmates. Like many four-year-olds, he is both fascinated by and fearful of aggression. No wonder his imaginary world is populated by untamed monsters.

Shawn and the tornado. Shawn is eight. She has never told anyone, but she is afraid of tornadoes. Every time she sees dark clouds on the horizon, she expects to see a funnel snake down and roar toward her house.

At Shawn's age, more realistic fears begin to take the place of the monsters and ghosts of a few years before. Natural disasters such as tornadoes, floods, and fires, or concerns about injury and illness, worry the schoolage child (Maurer 1965; Bauer 1976), who has begun to differentiate more clearly between what is pretend and what is real. Still, the dangers Shawn and her contemporaries fear are unlikely to occur. She does not yet think in terms of the probability of an event; if a tornado happened somewhere else, she feels it could happen to her. Again, her developing cognitive abilities will gradually help her make a less egocentric and more accurate assessment of potential dangers.

* * *

These examples suggest a pattern in the developmental sequence of children's fears. Fear begins in infancy with unfamiliar versions of concrete objects or persons. In the later preschool years imaginary, symbolic fears appear. In the school years children's attention shifts to more concrete, realistic concerns. These changes seem to be tied to important changes in the cognitive processes through which children interpret and evaluate the significance of a potentially threatening event, as well as to changes in the social and emotional issues that dominate children's needs.

Individual Fear Patterns

The trends just described provide an overview of general developmental changes in children's fears, but each child has an individual pattern.

Some children are, from their earliest months, more aware of and sensitive to visual novelty. This tendency may, especially in boys, predict later fearfulness (Bronson 1970). Paco, who was so upset by his teacher's haircut, is always the first to notice a new toy or a chair out of place.

Individual experiences and concerns may influence the intensity and the content of fears. Shawn's home was damaged by a windstorm several years ago.

Once a fear is established, it may persist because of the emotional rewards or "secondary gains" a child receives. Peter's monster worries, while genuine, also provide him with his teacher's undivided attention and concern.

Jeff's reaction to that lobster illustrates both developmental and individual patterns of fear. Although an adult would realize the lobster meant no harm, Jeff's interpretation was quite different. Jeff had no mental slot for this unfamiliar creature—the lobster was unassimilable to his limited experience. Using his own motives as an egocentric standard by which to judge the lobster, Jeff sized up its forward movement and waving claws as signs of hostile intentions. Since Jeff had been a biter, he was inclined to see others as possible biters, too. Later, at his day care center, Jeff reacted to the picture—the symbol—as if it were real. The picture *was*

Specific information that allows children to anticipate and predict what will happen in a scary situation will give them an increased feeling of control over their lives.

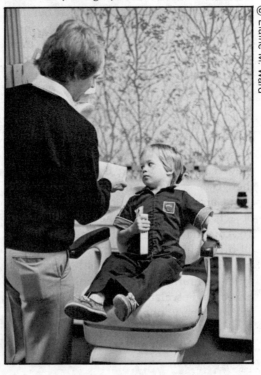

© Elaine M. Ward

the lobster. It is likely, too, that Jeff received a few "secondary gains" from the whole episode in the form of extra lap time from mother and teacher.

Recognizing Fear

Although most young children have fears, it is not always easy to recognize when a child is afraid. While an infant will usually cry loudly when frightened, older children's reactions are more varied. One child who is afraid of dogs may scream and run away from an approaching dog; another may stand frozen in panic. It isn't hard to tell that these children are afraid, but other signs are more difficult to detect. The child who shows an exaggerated fascination with dogs, constantly asking about them and looking for them, may be as worried as the others. Or the child who shows no reaction in a situation where fear would be expected may be deeply fearful under that unconcerned exterior. It takes careful observation and sensitivity to children to recognize when fear is being expressed.

Helping with Fears

Knowing the kinds of fears to expect in children, and understanding the reasons for those fears, what can adults do to help?

One thing to do is to wait. Children's fears, even those intense enough to be classified as phobias, usually disappear without any special treatment (Miller et al. 1972). Jerry's fear of the toilet, for instance, will very likely disappear as he gets older. He will acquire information and experience—after hundreds of visits to the bathroom where he never is flushed away. His animistic beliefs about toilets will gradually change to a recognition that toilets differ from people in a number of significant ways. The desire to hold on to his bodily products (and therefore the fear of the instrument that whisks them out of

sight) will become less powerful. As the reasons for his fear disappear, so will the fear itself.

In the meantime, sensitive adults may be able to help children cope with their fears by using the following techniques:

- Talk about fears. Although reassurances and rational explanations will not always help, children who can put their worst fears into words (or maybe into drawing pictures) may be better able to manage them. Sometimes a good book can pave the way to a helpful discussion.

- Provide opportunities for dramatic play. One of the many functions of play in children's development is the chance it gives them to re-create and master scary feelings and experiences. Through play, the child who is afraid of being left with a sitter may become a parent leaving the child-doll at home and then returning; the child who is afraid of the doctor can sometimes be seen gleefully giving shots to all the stuffed animals. Turnabout is indeed fair play.

- If a child is afraid of a specific object, try presenting it in smaller, less threatening forms first. For example, introduce a tiny puppy before a full-grown German shepherd, toy fire engines before a visit to see real ones, a dishpan of water before a swimming pool. Therapists find that this sort of gradual desensitization works well in treating serious phobias (Marks 1969). Teachers can use similar techniques informally.

- Focus on underlying cognitive skills. A child who is afraid of masks, for example, may need many concrete experiences with object permanence (the concept that a person or thing retains its identity even when it is transformed or out of sight). Even older children enjoy peek-a-boo, hide-and-seek, or games in which small objects are hidden and found again. A good way to begin with an especially fearful child is to let the child control the hiding and the finding, putting a cloth over the teacher's face and removing it.

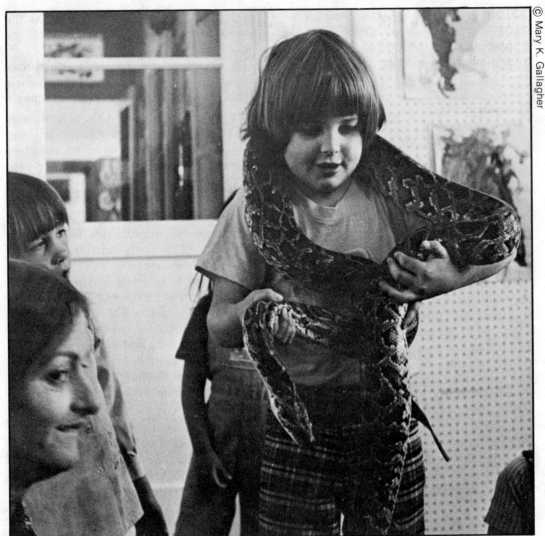

Changes in children's fears seem to be tied to important changes in the cognitive processes through which children interpret and evaluate the significance of a potentially threatening event, as well as to changes in the social and emotional issues that dominate children's needs.

• If a child's fear seems to be centered around a particular conflict or need, it may be more helpful to work on that need than on the fear itself. An understanding teacher can help Peter deal with his own angry feelings through talk, play, or constructive problem solving. Better awareness of and control over his own aggression may reduce Peter's fear of the monster's symbolic aggression. In the process, the monster may go somewhere else to live.

• If the child's fearful behavior seems to be persisting because of the secondary gains that are rewarding it, the child can be helped to achieve those rewards through other channels. By hugging Amanda when she is not afraid (as well as comforting her when she is frightened, of course), her teacher can give Amanda the affection she needs without selectively reinforcing her fearful behavior.

• Broaden the range of a child's coping skills (Murphy and Moriarty 1976). A baby has only one reaction available when frightened—crying. As children grow older, they begin to develop alternative ways of dealing with fear and stress. The more alternatives they have, the better they can cope with their feelings. Adults can help children increase their sense of control over their lives. Vague reassurances ("Don't worry about the doctor, dear") will not help much. Specific information that allows children to anticipate and predict what will happen in a scary situation ("These are the things the doctor will do when she arrives. Here are the kinds of instruments she will use.") will give them an increased feeling of competence (Kanfer, Karoby, and Newman 1975). Knowing and practicing alternative behaviors also reduces a child's sense of panicked helplessness. Teachers can help children practice "What could you do if a big dog came up to you? If it started to thunder? If you got lost?" The point is not to come up with a specific answer, but to help children think of many solutions to problems. Then, when confronted by a potentially threatening event, they have options: They can back away, shout, close their eyes, hold someone's hand, ask questions.

Just as children like Jeff, Paco, and Amanda are active participants in the creation of their own fears, they can be active participants in overcoming them. It is easy to forget that most children *want* to grow up and become competent and effective people. By understanding how children interpret their world, with its opportunities and dangers, adults can help them in this task. ▨

Contact the author, Marion Carey Hyson, 585 Conestoga Rd., Berwyn, PA 19312, for reprint information.

Bibliography

Bauer, D. H. "An Exploratory Study of Developmental Changes in Children's Fears." *Journal of Child Psychology and Psychiatry* 17 (1976): 69-74.

Berecz, J. M. "Phobias of Childhood: Etiology and Treatment." *Psychological Bulletin* 70 (1968): 694-720.

Bowlby, J. *Separation*. Attachment and Loss, vol. 2. New York: Basic Books, 1973.

Bronson, G. W. "Fear of Visual Novelty: Developmental Patterns in Males and Females." *Developmental Psychology* 2 (1970): 33-40.

Bronson, G. W. "Infants' Reactions to Unfamiliar Persons and Novel Objects." *Monographs of the Society for Research in Child Development* 37, no. 3 (1972): serial no. 148.

Dunn, J. *Distress and Comfort*. Cambridge, Mass.: Harvard University Press, 1977.

Elkind, D. *Children and Adolescents: Interpretive Essays on Jean Piaget*. 2nd ed. New York: Oxford University Press, 1974.

Fraiberg, S. *The Magic Years*. New York: Scribner, 1959.

Kagan, J. "Discrepancy, Temperament, and Infant Distress." In *The Origins of Fear*, ed. M. Lewis and L. A. Rosenblum. New York: Wiley, 1974.

Kanfer, F. H.; Karoly, P.; and Newman, A. "Reduction of Children's Fear of the Dark by Competence-Related and Situational Threat-Related Verbal Cues." *Journal of Consulting and Clinical Psychology* 43, no. 2 (1975): 251-258.

Lewis, M., and Rosenblum, L. A., eds. *The Origins of Fear*. New York: Wiley, 1974.

Marks, I. M. *Fears and Phobias*. London: Academic Press, 1969.

Maurer, A. "What Children Fear." *Journal of Genetic Psychology* 106 (1965): 265-277.

Miller, L. C., et al. "Comparison of Reciprocal Inhibition, Psychotherapy, and Waiting List Control for Phobic Children." *Journal of Abnormal Psychology* 79 (1972): 269-279.

Murphy, L. B., and Moriarty, A. E. *Vulnerability, Coping, and Growth*. New Haven, Conn.: Yale University Press, 1976.

Piaget, J. *The Child's Conception of the World*. London: Routledge & Kagan Paul, 1929.

Piaget, J. *Play, Dreams, and Imitation in Childhood*. New York: Norton, 1951.

Shaffer, H. R. "Cognitive Components of the Infant's Response to Strangers." In *The Origins of Fear*, ed. M. Lewis and L. A. Rosenblum. New York: Wiley, 1974.

Sroufe, L. A.; Waters, E.; and Matas, L. "Contextual Determinants of Infant Affective Response." In *The Origins of Fear*, ed. M. Lewis and L. A. Rosenblum. New York: Wiley, 1974.

Wolman, B. *Children's Fears*. New York: Grosset and Dunlap, 1978.

Erna Furman

Helping Children Cope with Death

Perhaps there are some among you who find the topic of death particularly trying because you have recently lost a loved one or because you suffer from old bereavement wounds that are still sore and painful. To those who are hurting and struggling to cope, I extend my sympathies and also my apologies lest this article contain thoughts that might inadvertently make things harder for you.

Many of us go through life for long periods without thinking about death. When it suddenly strikes very close to us, it comes as a shock, not only because it always represents a loss but also because we get the horrible feeling that "this could be me; this could happen to me, to my family, to my children and friends." We have a tendency to deal with this fear by adopting one of two extreme attitudes. We may feel the impact as though the tragedy had really happened to us. We put ourselves in the shoes of the bereaved or of the dying and feel so overwhelmed and anxious that we are unable to extend ourselves appropriately to those who need our help. At the other extreme, we shield ourselves and behave as if "this is not real; this did not happen to me; I don't want to hear, read, or talk about it." This reaction too prevents us from extending a helping hand because it keeps us from coming to terms with our own feelings. Often we waver from one extreme to the other until, hopefully, we reach a kind of middle ground where we are able to feel, "There but for the grace of God go I; it is not me but it could be." When we arrive at this hard-to-reach point we begin to be able to think and feel with others and to help them as well as ourselves.

Many years ago at the Hanna Perkins (therapeutic) Nursery School, we were working without thinking about death. Then within one year, two mothers of young children died, leaving their families as well as therapists, teachers, peers, and friends stunned. We had to cope with the immediate reality and struggle to come to terms with what had happened. But this was only the beginning. In the course of the next few years, we found that, without having sought cases of bereavement, we had in intensive treatment 23 children of all ages who had lost a parent through death. Each analyst who treated a bereaved child and worked with the family found it so difficult and painful that we turned to each other to share and learn together. We hoped that in this way we would be better able to understand and help our patients and, perhaps, formulate some thoughts that might be of general interest and serve to assist others (Furman 1974). I would like to share with you some of the things we learned, trying to pick out what might be particularly helpful to teachers of young children.

Erna Furman, B.A., is a faculty member of the Cleveland Center for Research in Child Development and Assistant Clinical Professor, Department of Psychiatry, Case Western Reserve University Medical School, Cleveland, Ohio.

186

As you know, it does not take the death of a parent to bring children to an encounter with death. Many grandparents, siblings, relatives, and pets die. There are also many daily events which bring children face to face with death, be it a passing funeral procession or a dead worm in the backyard. The worst bereavement is the death of a parent. It is a unique experience distinct from all other losses, such as divorce or separation, and distinct from other experiences with death. Many nursery school teachers may be fortunate enough never to have a pupil whose parent dies, but they are surely called upon to help with some less tragic bereavements and the many daily encounters with death—the ants a child steps on or the dead mouse someone brings for show-and-tell (Hoffman 1974).

The danger of parental bereavement does not lie in the formation of isolated symptoms or difficulties. The main danger is that it may arrest or distort a child's development toward becoming a fully functioning adult.

Our bereaved children came to treatment with many different symptoms. Parental death is unique; it happens to unique people who respond in unique ways. Our patients most often responded in a disturbed, unhealthy fashion, sometimes at the time of the bereavements, sometimes not until many years later. But we were deeply impressed that some children only about two years of age, because of very optimal circumstances, could master their tragic loss. By contrast, we had much older patients who could not master it at all. I do not mean to imply that the two-year-olds master this stress more easily; on the contrary, it is harder. Nor is it short-lived for them; it lasts longer. I am not speaking of the degree of pain and anguish, but the ability to master ultimately. To me that means that these children were upset, struggled and suffered, but were able to mourn their par-

ents and to progress in their development. The danger of parental bereavement does not lie in the formation of isolated symptoms or difficulties. The main danger is that it may arrest or distort a child's development toward becoming a fully functioning adult. Many of the factors involved touch upon the role of the teacher and offer an opportunity to develop in children those qualities which will enable them to master a future bereavement or to help them and their peers to cope with a current loss or minor encounter with death.

Helping Children Understand Death

The first crucial factor is children's ability to understand death in its concrete manifestations, *i.e.*, to understand that death means no life, no eating, no sleeping, no pain, no movement. Those children who at the time of bereavement already had a rather good grasp of the concrete facts of death had a much easier time. We found that children from toddler age on show interest in dead things. They find dead insects or birds. When they can tell that a sibling is different from a teddy bear, that one is animate and the other not, they can also begin to understand what *dead* means. For example, when the toddler plays with a dead fly and notes that it does not move, it helps to confirm the child's observation by using the word *dead* and explaining that the fly will never move again because it is dead. Most young children have not yet been helped to acquire this kind of basic concrete understanding of what *dead* means, how things die, and what we do with the corpse. It is much easier to acquire concrete understanding of death from insects or small animals, since they do not have great emotional significance for the child; this knowledge paves the way for later understanding of death in people.

McDonald (1963) studied the responses of the peers of our two bereaved Hanna Perkins Nursery School pupils. She found that children's first interest focused on what death is. They could not direct themselves to the aspects of loss, empathy, or sympathy for a peer's loss until they could understand concretely what death means. McDonald also noted that each of the children's questions required a special effort of thoughtful awareness and listening by the teachers. Initially, and without knowing it, teachers closed their eyes and ears and implied, without words, that death was not a welcome topic. Once their attitude changed, the children's questions just poured out. It is very difficult for all of us to talk about death, even dead insects. Most of us were not helped in this respect when we were children so we tend not to help children or do not know how to help. With special effort and by struggling to come to terms with questions about death ourselves, it is possible to overcome our difficulty to some extent.

Support for Parents

Parents usually do not mind when teachers talk at school about death as it relates to insects, worms, or even animals. Some teachers have found it helpful to meet with parents to discuss how such incidents are handled. Parents, perhaps even more than teachers, find it very difficult to talk with children about death, fearing that sooner or later the child will say, "Will I die?" "Will you die?" We are frightened of the answers that we would rather not give. However, the eventual next step in children's understanding death is that of relating it to themselves and to those they love and need. A meeting with parents on this subject does sometimes help to bring such questions into the open and offers the teacher an opportunity to help the parents. Whether a teacher wishes to arrange such meetings depends on the teacher's relationship with the parent group and the extent to which both sides are ready to grapple with the subject of death.

When a child asks, "Can this happen to me or to my mommy?" the answer should take into account the child's sense of time.

A parent is hesitant to say, "No, I won't die," because he or she eventually will die. Yet should the parent say, "Yes, I will die," the child understands this to mean tomorrow or next week. We find that a young child can best understand when the parent says, "No, I do not expect to die for a long, long time," stressing the *no,* and adding that he or she expects to enjoy the child as a grown-up and have many years of being a grandparent.

Children before age five or six are incapable of abstract thinking and therefore unable to grasp religious or philosophical explanations. They usually distort them into concrete and often frightening concepts that have little to do with religion.

Parents usually also raise the question of spiritual answers to the question of death. Children before age five or six are incapable of abstract thinking and therefore unable to grasp religious or philosophical explanations. They usually distort them into concrete and often frightening concepts that have little to do with religion. I know some very religious parents who chose not to introduce religious explanations to their

James Baritot

children under the age of five precisely because they knew these concepts would be distorted and might later interfere with the children's attitudes about religion. By contrast, doubting or unbelieving parents quite often use explanations that involve *heaven* and *God*. This happens because they have not thought matters through themselves and want to shield the child from something frightening. In shielding the child they only shield themselves and create confusion in the child. Something that is not really believed by the adult cannot come across as true or reassuring to the child.

In our experience the most understanding parents have given concrete explanations of death and burial. When, in response to what they had heard from others, the children asked, "What about heaven?" or "Does God take people away?" the parents replied, "Many people believe that. Many people believe other things too and as you get older you will learn about them and will understand them better. Right now it is important that you understand how we all know when someone is dead."

The concrete facts of death are usually much less frightening to children than to adults. An anecdote about one of Barnes' (1964) patients illustrates this point. A father had struggled very hard to help his young children understand what *dead* meant and what being in a coffin meant because their mother had died. Some months later their grandfather died. As the father tried to tell his little girl that they would choose a nice box with a soft blanket inside so that grandfather would be very comfortable, the little girl interrupted him and said, "But daddy, if he is really dead then it doesn't matter about his being comfortable in the coffin." For that moment the child certainly had a better grasp than the father.

Bearing Unpleasant Feelings

Another factor which facilitates a child's mastery of bereavement is the ability to bear unpleasant feelings, particularly sadness and anger. Obviously, there is no way to anticipate the kind of feelings that come with a bereavement. Separations are very different from a loss through death, but there are some similarities. Separations, to a small extent, involve the same feelings of longing, sadness, and anger that we find in much greater intensity at a time of bereavement. Young children are able to bear these feelings to an incredible extent if they have been giver appropriate help in developing this strength.

How does one help a child achieve such mastery? Basically there are two ways. One is to expose children only to bearable separations. When separations are too long they become unbearable and therefore not conducive to experiencing feelings. A very few hours of separation are bearable for a baby, perhaps half a day for a toddler, and at most a couple of days for a nursery school child. But it takes more than adjusting the lengths of separation. The second important step is the adults' willingness to help children recognize their feelings, express them appropriately, and cope with them. Before and after the separation this is the parents' task; during the separation the caregiving person can help.

The goal of assisting bereaved persons is not to foreshorten their or our own pain and anguish but to strive toward inner mastery.

It is often thought that children who do not react, do not make a fuss, or even enjoy the parents' absence, are well-adjusted, good children. To me, these children have not built appropriate mental muscles to bear unpleasant feelings. They shut themselves off from such feelings and therefore have no control of them. For nursery school teachers an excellent time to practice with children in building up the mental muscles for knowing and bearing unpleasant feelings is, of course, during entry to nursery school. At that time one can help parents understand that children who have no feelings, who react as though nothing has happened, or who immediately "love" the school, are children who are shut off from their feelings and in danger of stunting their emotional growth. Many mothers who do not welcome the child's unhappy or angry response to separation at the start of school would be very concerned if the child did not react feelingly to the loss of a loved person or readily preferred someone else in that person's stead. Yet how could a child acknowledge very intense feelings without previous help to cope with them in less threatening situations?

Coping with Bereavement

So far we have considered how difficult it is to talk about death even in terms of animals and insects, and how hard to bear loneliness, sadness, and anger in terms of brief separations. We know, of course, how much greater the hardship is when we have to think about and feel fully the total loss of a loved person. There is no easy way to cope with bereavement. There is no shortcut, either for the bereaved or for those who help them. The goal of assisting bereaved persons is not to foreshorten their or our own pain and anguish but to strive toward inner mastery. Even if we achieve it, it does not mean that we have come to terms with death once and for all. In order to be able to help we too have to empathize anew with each bereavement and struggle through it again.

I would like to turn now to what teachers can do, and often have done, when a child in the nursery school suffers the death of a parent, sibling, or close relative. I do not have any easy remedies to offer, and my suggestions are much more easily said than done because pain and anxiety are an essential part of the task.

The teacher's first question often is, "Should I mention the loss to the child?" I have heard time and again about the fear of causing a child hardship by referring to his or her loss. Some years ago I met a boy whose father had died. His teacher had reported that the boy had no feelings about, or reaction to, the death of the father. When I saw this boy, said "Hello" and expressed my natural sympathy, he broke into tears at once. He cried for an hour and I had to see him a second time before he could begin to talk. I asked him later why he had never shown his feelings at school. The boy replied, "You know, that teacher was so mean! He never even bothered to come to me and say 'I am sorry your father died.' I would never show my feelings to that kind of guy." I suspect that this was not a mean teacher but that his reaction of silence built a barrier between the child and himself.

This and similar experiences have convinced me that the teacher has to take the first step by mentioning the loss and expressing sympathy in a way that implies, "This will be with us a long time. I hope you will feel free to come to me, talk with me, or feel with me about it." In practice, some children will come to the teacher much more than others. However often they do or do not come, the teacher needs to empathize with each and every feeling that may arise and help children tolerate them. This means not to falsify feelings, not to hold them back, not even to pour them out in order to be rid of them, but to recognize and contain them.

It is most important that the children understand not only that the parent or sibling is dead, but also what the cause of death was.

At opportune times the teacher can also help by talking with the child about the factual aspects of the bereavement—how the loved one died, where he or she is buried, and changes in the family setting and routine. I think it is equally important for the teacher to report to the parent what the child shows, thinks, or feels about this experience so that the parent can further

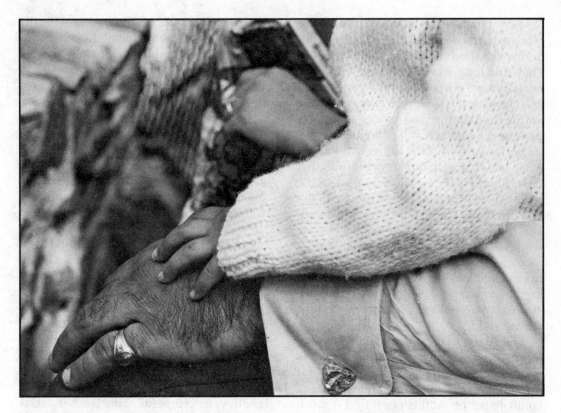

help the child and perhaps be alerted to some aspect which has not yet been expressed at home.

In addition to work with the child, a second area in which the teacher can be helpful is with the parents or surviving parent. Hopefully, before a loss occurs, the teacher will have built the kind of relationship with the parent which will make it possible for him or her to inform the teacher as a friend, a special professional friend who has the parent's and child's welfare at heart. The parent will welcome talking with this teacher and perhaps accept some suggestions—how to tell the child about the death, how to talk it over with the child, whether to take the child to the funeral, what plans to make for the immediate future.

Assisting Parents

Let me now share with you some of the things we have found helpful to parents at such a time. Adults with young children do not die uncomplicated deaths; the deaths are always untimely. This is also true about the death of siblings. It is most important that the child understand not only that the parent or sibling is dead, but also what the cause of death was. When these two things are not understood, when they are distorted or denied, it is impossible for the child even to begin mourning. I do not mean overwhelming the child with frightening details. Hopefully a teacher can help a parent to tell the child enough and in such a manner that the child can achieve a considerable amount of understanding.

Parents always want to know whether they should take the child to the funeral, and what they should say about it. We can only give an answer after we learn more about the specific situation. The child's attendance at the funeral will depend on the type of service, how the parent feels about it, how comfortable the parent is with the rites the family observes, and how able the parent is to extend himself or herself emotionally to the child during the funeral.

Many families are willing to adapt the services to the needs of all the family. Children often find an open casket difficult. They find long services difficult. If the funeral rites are not suitable for a young child or if the parent is unable to care effectively for the child during the services, it is better that the child remain at home with a familiar person and with the full verbal knowledge of what is happening during that time. I had a patient who was sent to the zoo on the day of her father's funeral in the hope that she would not have to be sad. This hope was not fulfilled, and the arrangement produced an almost insurmountable barrier within the child and between child and surviving parent. Mourning has to happen together. Pain and anguish have to be shared. It is not fair to shut out the child.

When it comes to immediate plans for the future, the teacher can sometimes impress upon parents how very important it is for the child to keep the home and remaining family together. Adults often find it much easier to leave the place of distress, to throw away the things that remind them of the deceased. For children the opposite holds true. They need the concrete continuation and help of their surroundings in order to come to terms with what is missing. Sometimes people have asked how parents and children can ever be of support to one another when they have such different needs. When parents understand that their children's greatest need is continued physical and emotional care by the surviving parent, they usually compromise for the sake of the child and find that they benefit as well. Being a good parent brings a measure of self-esteem that cannot be gained in any other way and is especially helpful at a time of bereavement when so many other things seem not worthwhile.

Helping Others in the Group

Along with assisting the bereaved child and parent, the teacher has to extend help to the other children in the nursery school.

This usually starts by discussing with the bereaved parent what to tell the other children and their families. Hopefully the bereaved parent is able to share the truth in simple realistic terms with his or her own child and is willing to have this information passed on. Then the teacher needs to take a few painful hours to call every parent in the nursery group. Each call is long and difficult and should, if possible, include several items: a brief account of what happened to their child's peer, which terms or phrases will be used in the nursery school to discuss the sad event, how the parents can tell their own child and how helpful it would be if the child learned the news first from them, and how to cope with some of the child's questions.

If a bereaved parent is initially unable to allow discussion of the cause of death, the teacher may have to say, for example, "Chris's father died. It is still too hard for Chris's mommy to talk about it, but she will tell us what happened later and I will share it with you." Hopefully, the teacher's relationship with the parent will help to make this delay brief.

Mourning . . . is a process that is not always visible from the outside. . . . Sometimes there are no overt signs of upset and yet the feelings may be there.

The next morning all children will have been told of the death, even if not its cause, by their parents, and the teacher can sit down with them and initiate the first discussion of facts and feelings. The most important point to cover is, "This talk is only a beginning. We will talk about it and feel about it often and for a long time. It will be with us because it is a sad and scary thing."

There are usually three main questions that arise sooner or later: "What is dead?" "Can it happen to me?" and "Can it happen to you?" Until these questions are accepted and coped with, it is generally not possible for the peers or for their parents to extend genuine sympathy to the bereaved. When we are able to assist children in gaining gradual mastery, many months of painful struggle seem indeed worthwhile.

The Mourning Process

If the death is understood, if its cause is understood and the disposal of the body is understood, and if the bereaved child is reasonably sure of his or her own survival and of having bodily and emotional needs met to a sufficient extent, mourning will start of itself. It is a process that is not always visible from the outside because, contrary to what many people think, mourning does not consist of wailing, rages, crying, or complaining. Sometimes there are no overt signs of upset and yet the feelings may be there.

I worked with a mother and child. The little boy lost his father two years previously and experienced some difficulty in the aftermath. The mother told me that she had never cried in front of the child, since she only cries when she is alone in bed. The boy, who supposedly had not reacted at all to his father's death and had certainly never cried or raged, told me in his separate interview that he was not a person who ever cried in front of people. He only cried when he was alone in bed and nobody knew that he cried. He cried night after night but his mother never cried. Although mother and child expressed feelings in the same form, they did not know that the other even had feelings. It was sad to see how hard they had made it for themselves and for each other. However, even if they had not cried at all they might have been able to mourn because mourning is a mental process that consists primarily of two parts: on one hand, a very gradual and painful detachment from the memories of the deceased, and on the other hand almost the opposite, a taking into oneself some traits or qualities of the deceased. How much there is of each part and whether the proportion leads to a healthy adaptive outcome depend on many factors, including the age of the bereaved person, the nature of the bereavement, the preceding relationship, the personality of the deceased. With young children it is particularly important that they take into themselves the healthy rather than the sick attributes of the dead parent and that they detach themselves sufficiently, so that, in time, they will be free to form a parental bond with a new person.

Sometimes parents intuitively understand the ways in which their child's long inner mourning proceeds and sense when the child encounters difficulties. Sometimes it is much harder. It certainly is not a mark of failure to seek professional assistance at such a time. That is yet another area where the teacher can support the surviving parent. The sooner help is given, the better the chances of preventing possible damage to the child's growing personality.

This article is adapted from a talk given in May 1975 at the Seventh Annual Workshop of the Cleveland Center for Research in Child Development for Preschool Educators of North Eastern Ohio.

References

Barnes, M. J. "Reactions to the Death of a Mother." *The Psychoanalytic Study of the Child* 19 (1964): 334-357.

Furman, E. *A Child's Parent Dies*. New Haven, Conn.: Yale University Press, 1974.

Hoffman, Y. "Learning about Death in Preschool." *Review, Spring 1974*. Cleveland: Cleveland Association for the Education of Young Children, 1974, pp. 15-17.

McDonald, M. "Helping Children to Understand Death: An Experience with Death in a Nursery School." *Journal of Nursery Education* 19, no. 1 (1963): 19-25.

Bettye M. Caldwell

Aggression and Hostility in Young Children

How does aggressive behavior develop? What are some effective methods for dealing with such behavior? How can we help young children acquire more prosocial behaviors, such as cooperation and altruism?

I have been active in early childhood education for half a generation now, and during that time I have seen my own professional interests turn almost 180°—from a primary concern with cognitive development (though that was never my only concern in working with young children) to an overriding obsession with how to foster the development of other-oriented, altruistic behavior in young children. This turn-around might not have occurred were it not for my personal style of working, namely, to be right in the thick of the action with teachers and children.

But what is there about my present life that has catalyzed this metamorphosis? For the past five-and-a-half years I have been the director of the Center for Early Development and Education. This is a research project funded during the first five years by the Office of Child Development and sponsored jointly by the University of Arkansas and the Little Rock School District. This year our funds come from the Carnegie Corporation; the Rockefeller Brothers' Fund; Title XX of the Social Security Act; plus financial support from our sponsors, the University of Arkansas at Little Rock and the Little Rock School District. The project originated out of my strong conviction that the experiences a child has during the first five years determine to a great extent later success or failure and the concomitant

The author's work is supported in part by Grant No. SF-500 from the Office of Child Development and by grants from the Carnegie Corporation and the Rockefeller Brothers' Fund; additional support comes from the Little Rock School District and from the University of Arkansas at Little Rock.

conviction that in the case of intervention with low socioeconomic children, there must be continuity between those first five years and later school experience if the early gains are to be maintained. We are housed in a Little Rock public elementary school, and our program of day care, health and family services, and home intervention is directed toward all children ages six months through fifth grade who attend Kramer School. Within that larger context, the particular experience which is most responsible for my own metamorphosis is that of being a public school principal—these three years have had tremendous and far reaching consequences in my way of viewing early childhood education and child development.

Just how has this way of life so significantly altered the way I feel about children and the process of education?

For one thing, I am now convinced that those of us in early childhood education have been unduly arrogant in our attitudes toward elementary education. There was certainly great arrogance (although perhaps unwitting and implicit) on my part in the

Bettye M. Caldwell, Ph.D., is currently Professor of Education and Director, Center for Early Development and Education, University of Arkansas at Little Rock. Previously, she was Research Associate, Department of Pediatrics, Upstate Medical Center, State University of New York, Syracuse; and Professor of Child Development and Education at Syracuse University. Her areas of experience include research in mother-child interaction; work with developmentally retarded children and their parents; design of early enrichment programs; day care; elementary education; and research on home factors associated with favorable development.

thinking that led to the development of the Kramer Project. I was saying in effect, "Those of us who represent early childhood education could take care of America's children if you uncreative people in elementary education just wouldn't mess them up when we have finished with them."

Also I was saying—and there was nothing implicit in this, for I said it openly—"The techniques that we use in early childhood education would help to 'humanize' the schools if you would just watch us and learn from us. *(Why lines, physical punishment, schedules to go to the bathroom, desks in a row?)"* One of the things I have learned is that every one of those seemingly "inhuman" customs had its origins not in the emotional pathology of a distorted teacher but most likely in the gropings of a highly dedicated teacher trying to minimize the careless accidents and deliberate provocations that can be caused by children who have not, during earlier developmental periods, acquired sufficient self-control as to render such seemingly archaic customs unnecessary.

For another thing, I am persuaded by authors such as Toffler (1970) that changes are occurring in our society at an unassimilable rate, and that children are not exempt from the impact of these changes. For example, they are not immune to the impact of the media with its change in acceptable themes. The media demonstrate that "good guys" don't always win, and that quarrels are usually resolved by aggression and cunning. What does "All in the Family" teach about family life? Or about the equality of the sexes? What do children learn from the daily news? They learn that Whites and Blacks are fighting in Boston, but they

195

do not learn that 20,000 children are being bused in Little Rock (where, supposedly, it all started) without incident.

There are many other opportunities for indirect or incidental social learning also—from Watergate, from the words emanating from a thousand songs that demand instant gratification, from such slogans as "do your own thing," from meetings in which adults might not be able to speak because of being shouted down, from direct and indirect forms of racial discrimination that persist in every segment of life, and from international indications that one can only settle disputes by resorting to aggression. While we need to be concerned about aggression and hostility in young children, we need even more to be concerned about these same behaviors in adults, and about the omnipresent indicators that ours is a society that apparently values such behavior.

What Do We Know about Aggression in Young Children

It is always disturbing to have someone say something like, "We really don't know too much about aggression and hostility in young children" —especially when you live with it every day. I am certain that every teacher and every aide is more of an expert on this subject than most of the researchers. But we necessarily have to say that about aggression, especially in young children, for a semantic reason if no other—namely, aggression is usually defined as behavior (verbal or physical) that has injury of a person or object as its *intent*. It can sometimes be very conjectural to try to assign intent to a young child's

behavior. Did the baby who bit another child "intend" to hurt the other child, or was it to soothe aching gums? Did the toddler who pushed another child down in her eagerness to obtain a toy, causing the other child to cry, "intend" to hurt the pushed-down child or merely to get the toy? Does the child who calls his teacher a dirty name intend to defame her or to study her reaction for future reference or to try out words in an attempt to understand their meaning? Obviously, determination of intent is very difficult when we are concerned with very young children. Thus more people now are willing to define behavior as aggressive if it merely has the capacity to hurt or injure or damage, regardless of intent. The word hostility is even more difficult to define with reference to children, but most of us know what we mean by the term—the angry child whose behavior leaves little room for doubt as to its intent.

Although I do not like to labor too long on definitions, I think one more distinction is worth making. This is what Feshbach (1970) has called the difference between instrumental and hostile aggression. Instrumental aggression is the sort which is aimed at the retrieval of an object, territory, or privilege, i.e., that which results when a goal is blocked. Hostile aggression, on the other hand, is oriented to another person, as a person, following some sort of ego threat or a perception that another person has behaved intentionally: "He did it on purpose."

There is some evidence (Hartup 1974) that of these two forms, instrumental aggression is far more common in young children. In fact, the decline in overall aggression with age is largely a function of the decline with age in

Elaine M. Ward

instrumental aggression. In one of the older studies concerned with children's aggression (Dawe 1934), most of the aggression shown by children from about eighteen months to almost six years of age was instigated by disputes over possessions, with the tendency most prevalent among the younger subjects. During these years person-directed, retaliatory, and hostile outbursts increased with age.

Another finding from these skimpy developmental studies of aggression was that the most aggressive children are sometimes the children who also show the greatest amount of prosocial (positive) behavior. This suggests that some children are simply more actively social than others; they engage in more

of all types of interpersonal behavior. In spite of scattered "facts" of this sort, we still know precious little about age changes in aggressive behavior. Even more important, we know very little about time trends in incidence of aggressive behavior.

I think one thing we need to do in order to better understand aggression in young children is to develop some new ways of thinking about it. Because of the semantic problems centering around intent, I think it would be better to look at aggression as another manifestation of self versus other. That is, quite apart from whether the biting baby wanted to hurt his victim, we know that he was concerned with gratification of a self-based need. The child who suddenly took a toy from another might not even have noticed that another child was at that moment playing with it, so focused was she on her own desire to possess and manipulate the toy.

We need to be as concerned about the development in children of a healthy "other" concept as we do about the development of a healthy "self" concept. But how many of us are concerned with this task in our curricula? Not enough, I fear. We desperately need suggestions as to ways to help children develop empathy and concern for others, and our good thinkers need to be giving weight to this need equal to that of the importance of the self-concept.

Practical Suggestions for Those Who Must Cope

Those of us working with children cannot wait until all the data are accumulated and our good thinkers have reached their final conclusions. We are forced to deal with aggression daily and to use whatever bits and pieces of evidence are available to us at the present time—whether or not it is still inconclusive. We must evaluate the data as it comes in and do the best we can to wisely choose our methods of coping with the aggression expressed by the children in our programs. Therefore, I want to discuss some practical guidelines for all of us who must deal with aggression daily. Some of the guidelines are fairly well supported by research findings; others are based more on my personal way of viewing the problem and my attempts at seeking a solution.

Physical punishment of aggression is not the answer. One generalization that

emerges with consistency is that there is a close relationship between high use of severe physical punishment by parents and high incidence of aggression by their children. "Spare the rod and spoil the child" is not borne out by data. However, it is difficult to get causative data. Though the two variables, physical punishment by parents and aggression by children, are closely related, it is still somewhat open to debate whether physical punishment "causes" the higher incidence of aggression. It might be possible to argue that high aggression on the part of the child causes more severe punishment by the parents and not vice versa. At this time we simply cannot say. We do know, however, that they are correlated. Further, it seems logical that the adult who uses physical punishment to deal with physical aggression is communicating: "You are just not big enough to get away with it and I am." The adult also is demonstrating to the child a certain belief in aggression as a viable solution to problems.

Ignoring aggression in children is not the answer. This is something I encouraged students and teachers to do for years. Ample testimony to my approach could be found by counting the number of times children at Kramer have been heard to say, "Mrs. Caldwell won't do nothing to you." I am now convinced that this is the wrong thing to do. Ignoring aggression will not make it disappear. The danger, it seems, in not responding to a child's aggressiveness is that the child may regard the watching adult's failure to deal with the aggressive behavior as adult approval of those actions. Siegel and Kohn (1970) have conducted an experiment which seems to support this interpretation of an adult's permissiveness by children. Working with pairs of preschool age children, they allowed half of the pairs to play with various toys for two sessions in the presence of a permissive (and noncondemning) adult; the other half of the pairs played in a similar setting but with no one else in the room. Most of the children in the adult-present condition exhibited more aggression in the second session than in the first; all of the children in the adult-absent condition decreased in aggression in the second session. The adult's permissiveness apparently was viewed by the children as approval of their aggressive behavior and therefore that behavior increased rather than decreased.

Permitting aggression or hostility to be expressed, and assuming that this will "discharge" the tension, will not work. Much of our current popular psychology, however, continues to promote this viewpoint. An article in a popular magazine recently listed the following consequences which can supposedly result from ignoring anger: taut, angry muscles; malfunctioning internal organs; migraine headaches; hives; pimples; itchy rashes; common colds; problems both mild and serious with the bladder, the stomach, and the bowels; ulcers; colitis; heart attacks; being accident prone; disastrous love affairs; and depression. Advice to openly express your anger and hostility in order to remain healthy and happy has been given for years and is still being given by some. Not only is the expression of anger and hostility supposedly preventive but it is also viewed by some as curative.

Yet this position is questionable in light of recent research findings. Berkowitz (1974) after an extensive review of research conducted on controlling aggression in young children concludes:

> He [the child] should not be encouraged to attack someone to express his hostility in the hope that he will drain some hypothetical energy reservoir. The catharsis notion is an outmoded theoretical conception lacking adequate empirical support which also has potentially dangerous social implications. Violence ultimately produces more violence. (p. 135)

With this principle in mind, there is one hint as to when "punishment" (but not aggressive punishment) should occur. According to a study done by Walters, Parke, and Cane (1965), it is most effective to punish or rebuke a would-be aggressor immediately after the aggressor has initiated the aggressive behavior rather than after the attack is completed or the goal is obtained. In their study, Walters, Parke, and Cane rebuked one half of a group of boys each time they reached for an attractive toy. For the other half of the boys, punishment (again in the form of a verbal reproof) came after the toy had been touched. Later the boys were allowed to play in the room with the desired toy but this time with the punishing agent absent. Those boys who had been rebuked before touching the toy demonstrated a greater ability to resist the temptation when left alone with the forbidden toy.

In order to minimize aggression, we need parent cooperation. One of my colleagues, Richard Elardo, and I conducted a study designed to determine whether or not teachers in day care programs and the parents of the children enrolled held differing values with respect to various areas of

199

children's behavior. According to our research, one of the few important differences between parental values and teachers' values was in the area of aggressive behavior. Parents tended to believe that young children should be aggressive and fight in school, so others will not think they are sissies or cowards.

I have seen evidence of this attitude on the part of parents at our own school. We have had parents pick their son up from school and then drive around the school campus looking for another child who supposedly had insulted their son—in order that when the other boy was located, the son could get out of the car and beat the boy up. Similarly, we had a child whose parents had "dared" him to come home from school without having beaten up the little boy who threw sand in his sister's eyes while they were playing together the previous weekend.

Unfortunately, the school will remain ineffective in its efforts to control aggression in children as long as the parents support and even encourage such behavior in their children. If we are to minimize aggression, the school and the parents must work together.

In order to control aggression, we must strengthen altruism; we must emphasize helpfulness and cooperation as highly valued behaviors. In order to do this, however, we must have a society committed to these values. In 1974 I was a member of a U.S. delegation to the People's Republic of China. Our delegation spent most of its time observing in the Chinese kindergartens, which are for children between the ages of three and seven years. I saw no incidents of aggression on the part of the Chinese children. They did not push, shove, hit, kick, or in any way show hostility toward other students; further, there were no verbal attacks made against one another. The children were helpful and cooperative toward their classmates. At first I was somewhat amazed, but later such behaviors seemed the natural consequence of the societal values. The motto which guides the Chinese is "Serve the people!" and, as far as I could tell, the motto had become a way of life. The highest virtue is service to another person or to the collective, and the worst offense is selfishness.

Our society, I fear, lacks this emphasis on service and concern for other people. We, as a society, value competition and self-advancement. We profess belief in helping others, but usually it is considered secondary to the belief that people must help themselves. If we are to foster altruism in children, our society must esteem this quality. Even if the school and the individual parents agree, little will be achieved until the whole society values helpfulness and cooperation, and other attitudes which are inconsistent with aggression and hostility.

Non-permissiveness in our attitudes toward aggression may be as important as punishment for aggressiveness. We need to learn to communicate the attitude that says, "That sort of behavior is simply not going to be tolerated here." This was one of the major findings of the longitudinal study conducted by Sears, Maccoby, and Levin (1957) on patterns of child-rearing.

Our findings suggest that the way for parents to produce a non-aggressive child is to make abundantly clear that aggression is frowned upon, and to stop aggression when it occurs, but to avoid punishing the child for his aggression. Punishment seems to have complex effects. While undoubtedly it often stops a particular form of aggression, at least momentarily, it appears to generate more hostility in the child and lead to further aggressive outbursts at some other time or place. . . . Thus, the most peaceful home is one in which the mother believes aggression is not desirable and under no circumstances is ever to be expressed toward her, but who relies mainly on nonpunitive forms of control. The homes where the children show angry, aggressive outbursts frequently are likely to be homes in which the mother has a relatively tolerant (or careless!) attitude toward such behavior, or where she administers severe punishment for it, or both. (p. 266)

From my experience, I think the statement above would be just as true if we were to go back through it and every time the authors use the word "home" we were to substitute the word "classroom" and every time they use the word "parents" or "mother" we were to substitute the word "teacher." In our schools, we must communicate to the children a low tolerance of aggression while also using nonpunitive techniques for controlling it. Certainly this will not be an easy task. But all the evidence we have on the subject indicates that this is the most effective means for achieving our goal.

We must help children de-escalate their aggressive behavior. This is for me a relatively new concept which is of importance in helping to minimize aggressive behavior in children. It was born in this practical life I lead —observing the children at their play and observing how it is that most of the aggressive behavior develops. I couldn't begin to count the number of times I have seen a group of children running after each other, playing "monster," or "superman," or any of the other chasing games. Eventually one of the children gets knocked down, or trips, and gets hurt. The child becomes angry and blames a playmate—and the play becomes a fight. The same pattern is typical of play in the sandbox. The children begin innocently making pies, cakes, etc., until someone breaks a cake or pie and the "baker" gets mad and another fight occurs. Whenever these incidents occur and the question "why?" is posed to the children someone will answer, "We were just playing." Think how many times you have heard that explanation. I have come to realize how very often that is correct. Play, which began as positive social interaction, simply escalated too fast and in a manner not anticipated (and often not desired) by the children involved.

Our mistake is that we ususally read intent into the resultant aggressive behavior and reason: "The child should not get away with such behavior; he should be punished." We build intent into their actions, even though it might not have been there with the children (the tripping of a child or the breaking of a mud pie from the children's viewpoint were unintended accidents resulting from too much enthusiasm). If we can avoid being judgmental and simply help the children de-escalate back to the level of play, we will possibly have helped more than if we mete out punishment.

Children need to learn different alternatives to problem situations. It is relatively common for a child to tell me, "I hit him 'cause there wasn't nothin' else to do." Children do have a more limited repertoire of behaviors than adults. But it is up to us to work at

Elaine M. Ward

providing more desirable alternatives for them. Unless we can help a child realize there are a variety of options, some more desirable than others, we cannot expect behavior to change.

We need to be more willing to play with children and to help them learn to play. How many children in your school know all the verses to London Bridge? How many jump rope to the verses we chanted as children? (All their memorization is taken up with commercials.) Or how many of you rationalize that children need to be alone during free play time? The more adults withdraw from children, the more they expose them to peer influence. And the more children interact in the absence of adults (whose be-

havior they could model), the more likely they are to engage in fights and quarrels over property and privileges.

Summary

Our number one objective as teachers should be to facilitate the development of children's behavior that is cooperative and supportive of one another, altruistic and prosocial rather than aggressive. Those of us who work with children know that we must cope with a great deal of aggressive behavior, which is essentially self-centered. Although this is a phenomenon of our age and our culture, it is quite possible that we have been contributing our share to the apparent increase in such behavior. The isolation of our educational endeavors from schools for older children has in the past deprived us of the opportunity to follow the careers of children and obtain the necessary feedback we should have to enable us to adapt our own techniques to the realities of life histories.

For over a generation now we have been taught essentially to let children express their aggression both to "get it out of their system" and to prevent the development of symptoms of emotional dysfunction. As we now look at this practice, it appears to have been misleading. Aggression breeds not contentment and subsequent cooperation; aggression breeds more aggression. Severe punishment for aggression—especially punishment that mirrors the aggressive act itself —apparently does little to decrease the frequency of such behavior.

Nor does ignoring such behavior help; unfortunately, it does not just go away, and there is very little evidence that a child "grows out of it." Apparently children simply grow into more sophisticated manifestations of aggressive behavior, unless the environment in which the child is developing (home, school, community, nation) communicates that such behavior is not valued, and will not be tolerated. If that environment values cooperation and service to others, and if all segments of society support one another in that valuation, apparently children can learn to develop self-control and concern for others.

We, as parents and teachers, need to give some thought to helping children learn to de-escalate their aggressiveness back down to the level of play, where much of the behavior starts.

De-escalating play is different from defusing the hostility which is often theorized as causing aggressiveness. As part of this de-escalation, a plea was made for more, rather than less, involvement of adults with children in their play. The price of liberty is supposed to be eternal vigilance. Vigilance by and extended contact with adults who model nonaggressive behavior is indeed one necessary precondition for the development of children who can cooperate with one another and with adults—and be happy in the process.

References

Berkowitz, L. "Control of Aggression." In *Review of Child Development Research, Vol. III*, edited by B. Caldwell and H. Ricciuti, pp. 95-140. Chicago: University of Chicago Press, 1973.

Dawe, H. C. "An Analysis of Two Hundred Quarrels of Preschool Children." *Child Development,* 1934, pp. 139-157.

Elardo, R., and Caldwell, B. M. "Value Imposition in Early Education: Fact or Fancy." *Child Care Quarterly,* 1973, pp. 6-13.

Feshbach, S. "Aggression." In *Carmichael's Manual of Child Psychology,* edited by P. H. Mussen, pp. 159-259. New York: John Wiley & Sons, 1970.

Hartup, W. W. "Aggression in Childhood: Developmental Perspectives." *American Psychologist,* 1974, pp. 336-341.

Sears, R. R.; Maccoby, E. E.; and Levin, H. *Patterns of Child Rearing.* Evanston, Ill.: Row, Peterson, and Co., 1957.

Siegel, A. E., and Kohn, L. G. "Permissiveness, Permission, and Aggression: The Effects of Adult Presence or Absence on Aggression in Children." In *Child Development and Behavior,* edited by F. Rebelsky and L. Dorman, pp. 234-242. New York: Alfred A. Knopf, 1970.

Toffler, A. *Future Shock.* New York: Random House, 1970.

Walters, R. H.; Parke, R. D.; and Cane, V. A. "Timing of Punishment and the Observation of Consequences to Others as Determinants of Response Inhibition." *Journal of Experimental Child Psychology,* 1965, pp. 10-30.

Charles A. Smith

Puppetry and Problem-Solving Skills

Puppetry can be an especially effective tool for teachers to use in helping young children learn. Young children are fascinated by puppets and readily accept the apparent magic that is responsible for giving them life. Puppets share with fairy tales that timeless enchantment of "Once upon a time. . . ." Because they belong in the realm of fantasy, puppets encourage children to think both imaginatively and creatively, and can foster children's abilities to solve their problems.

During my years as a preschool teacher, puppets were very important personalities for the four-year-old children in my classes. On one occasion, after I put my puppets on and disappeared behind the stage, I introduced a new puppet character never before seen by the children, a rabbit named Briarbutton. One little girl immediately asked Briarbutton if he liked the new clothes she was wearing. The rabbit responded by saying, "Oh, *April*, I like what you have on!" The puppet show then proceeded. But throughout the presentation, April continuously asked those around her, "How did he know my name?" Now April knew that I was behind the stage, and she also would readily admit that I knew who she was. But for April and the other children at this moment it was as though Briarbutton were truly alive, with a mind and personality all his own. April knew that Briarbutton was not alive in the sense that she and real rabbits are alive. But in the magical world of fantasy, where all the restrictions made by reality are suspended, Briarbutton was most definitely "alive."

Teachers can use puppets to gain entry into the child's world. The joy, enthusiasm, and sense of wonder adults experience there with children does not diminish their educational usefulness. On the contrary, adults who are able to relate to this part of the child's life will actually enhance their teaching effectiveness.

There are many different educational approaches to using puppets. Teachers can simply set puppets out and encourage children to create their own "shows" or act out a familiar story. The adult may become involved by commenting on and clarifying what the children do or briefly joining in the play. But young children very often do not have the skill to coordinate their puppet characters to tell a unique story. This form of puppetry may encourage language development but fail to challenge children to think about resolving problems.

Teachers can also use puppets to make educational presentations to children. With this approach, the children play the role of an audience while the adult manipulates the puppets. The show can be either informal and brief or more elaborate with the addition of sound accompaniment and special props. This approach is limited because children are required to be passive spectators. Observational learning may take place, but the lack of involvement by children often prohibits other valuable forms of learning from occurring.

Photos by
Karin Wikstrom

Charles A. Smith, Ph.D., is an Extension Specialist in Human Development in the Department of Quality of Living Programs at Kansas State University, Manhattan. He is a former director of a preschool laboratory and head teacher of four-year-old children.

A more productive approach combines the above two methods, emphasizing both the involvement of children and the planning and skill of adult teachers. This strategy involves an adult *puppeteer* who presents the dramatization from behind the stage and an adult *facilitator* who sits immediately in front of the stage and promotes interaction between the children and the puppets. The *children* can interact with the puppets by commenting on what is happening and by making suggestions. The *puppets* respond by asking for help, disagreeing/agreeing with the children, and making comments about their suggestions.

The adult facilitator plays a critical role in the interactional strategy of puppetry by clarifying what the puppets are trying to communicate and helping the children put their own ideas into words. The facilitator can also be instrumental in securing the involvement of shy children by demonstrating that involvement with the puppet characters is acceptable. Since the puppeteer most often cannot see the children, the facilitator can help by identifying the names of children who are talking and making certain that unacceptable behavior does not interfere with the activity.

Developing Problem-Solving Skills

Sensitivity to Problems

The interactional approach to using puppets is an especially powerful technique for helping children clarify their values and develop social problem-solving skills. Puppet presentations can nurture a *sensitivity to personal and interpersonal problems* by portraying a particular social difficulty that is relevant to young children. Children are not born with an understanding of social interaction; they must *learn* how to identify and resolve the variety of possible problems which can arise over the course of human relationships.

For example, one of the problems we have been concerned about in our child development center is the type of unfavorable judgment that is often made about the worth of other people because of their appearance. Making judgments about others on this basis is often inaccurate and unfair. To present children with this problem, we introduce Seymour, a very unusual, frightening puppet with a large mouth and wild, red hair. When Seymour appears all the other puppets run away; they think he will hurt them because he looks so scary. Seymour and the facilitator let the children know that he won't hurt them or anyone else. He just wants to be friends; he knows he looks different, but he can't help that. Once this introduction is made, the interaction could result in the following exchange:

Seymour Puppet:	"Oh I wish I had a friend!"
Child:	"Seymour, I'll be your friend!"
Facilitator:	"Yes Seymour, Sarah would like to be your friend. She is not scared of you."
Seymour:	"Thank you Sarah. That helps."
Facilitator:	"Oh, Seymour still feels sad. What's the problem?"
Child(ren):	"Briarbutton and Prissy won't play with Seymour. He wants to be friends with them. He's sad."
Seymour:	"Yes, it helps that you are not afraid of me, but I want to have puppet friends too."

The children, with the facilitator's assistance, become involved with Seymour. His sadness touches them. They believe that what they have to say is important to him. They feel close to him and concerned about the misunderstanding. Through this type of dialogue with Seymour, young children become aware of his problem and, thus, more sensitive to the misunderstandings and injustices that can occur because of improper responses to any individual's appearance.

Alternative-Solution Thinking

Another interpersonal cognitive problem-solving skill (Spivack, Platt, and Shure 1976) is *alternative-solution* thinking. This skill involves the ability to identify a number of possible solutions to a particular interpersonal problem. For example, how many solutions could a child think of if her toy gets taken away by another? Grab it back? Threaten the other person? Ask for it? Tell the teacher? Cry? The ability to generate multiple solutions increases the likelihood of selecting an effective strategy to resolve a problem.

In the puppet show about Seymour the interaction might proceed like this:

Facilitator:	"Can you think of anything Seymour could do to get some puppet friends?"
Child:	"He could tell them that he won't hurt them!"
Facilitator:	"Yes, he could do that. Let's think of some more ideas."
Child:	"We could tell the others he is not scary."
Seymour:	"That's a good idea. You could tell them I won't hurt them."
Child:	"Seymour, you could find some other puppets for friends."
Facilitator:	"That's possible. Maybe other puppets won't run away from you Seymour."

Once the children have identified as many solutions as they can think of, then the adult facilitator could offer other possibilities. At some point the resulting list of solutions must be evaluated. This evaluation should be well-timed because quick decisions, even though they may be correct, may discourage other children from verbalizing their own ideas.

Consequential Thinking

A third problem-solving skill involves *consequential* thinking—the ability to identify what might happen when one performs an interpersonal act. For example, the child whose toy was taken by another might think, "If I grab it back or tell her that I will hurt her then she will hit me. If I run to the teacher he will tell me to solve the problem myself. Crying won't help. Maybe if I ask, she will give it to me. If she won't return it then maybe I'll just take it back." Proper evaluation depends on being able to consider the consequences of various potential solutions.

A presentation might focus on consequential thinking by having the puppets try out some of the solutions suggested by the children. The children and the facilitator could then note the consequences. For example, Seymour is unable to convince the other puppets that he won't hurt them because they won't stay around to listen to him. And, though he might someday find potential friends, these puppets are the only possible friends he can have at this time. The children might observe that their efforts to convince the other puppets that Seymour will not really harm them actually results in a lessening of tensions. In this situation the children could learn that they can assume an active role in negotiating conflict.

Awareness of Emotional Consequences

Becoming aware of *emotional* consequences is another important aspect of this problem-solving skill. By observing the interaction and talking with both the facilitator and the puppets, the children could learn that Seymour feels sad when the others run away and that the others feel frightened because Seymour looks so different.

Developing Causal Thinking

Finally, puppet interactions can help children develop *causal thinking*, the ability to relate one event to another over time. Causal thinking reflects an awareness of events that influence our behavior. For ex-

ample, the young child described earlier might conclude that the offender wants her toy because she does not have anything interesting to play with or because she wants revenge. Also, the child who has her toy taken might also realize that the violation will have some effect on her own behavior. Thus, if she decides to grab the toy back, and one of the teachers questions her motives, she might respond, "Well, she took it from me; I was playing with it first!"

In a puppet show involving Seymour, causal thinking could be encouraged by the following type of interaction:

Facilitator:	"Seymour feels lonely. Why do you think he feels that way?"
Child(ren):	"No one wants to play with him. They are afraid."

Young children are fascinated by puppets. Because they belong in the realm of fantasy, puppets encourage children to think imaginatively and creatively.

Facilitator:	"Well, why do you think they are afraid?"
Child(ren):	"'Cause they think he might hurt them . . . but he won't."
Seymour:	"No, I won't hurt them."

Understanding the relationship between interpersonal acts is an important step in avoiding and resolving interpersonal problems. Of course, children make many errors and have many misconceptions about causes. Accuracy is of secondary importance, though. What is important is that children begin to contemplate the possible motives and influences underlying the behavior of others.

Designing and Presenting Puppet Skits

Identifying the Problem

The examples of puppet interactions listed above only begin to convey the range of events that occur during a puppet show. Puppet skits should tell an interesting story which emphasizes interaction among the puppets. Puppets should not be used to lecture children. The brief problem-solving exchanges described earlier are important for giving direction to the story; they should never become so complex as to distract the children from following and enjoying the story.

In addition to Seymour's problem with his appearance, other presentations can be structured around the following types of problems:

- a puppet feels sad but refuses to cry;
- a puppet experiences the death of a pet;
- a puppet and her friend have a disagreement and become enemies;
- a puppet claims he is never afraid because he thinks fear is a sign of weakness;

- a puppet learns how to defend herself against aggression;
- a puppet learns how to express affection.

In our preschool class parents would often ask us to introduce a problem they were concerned about. Sometimes the problem was observed in the class itself. In each case, the goal was to help the children learn developmentally appropriate personal-social skills (Smith 1976).

Development of a Presentation Outline

Once the core problem is identified, the next step is to develop a presentation outline. This outline can be a *script* format that details everything the puppets say and do. The outline can then be taped to the back of the stage. The advantage of a script is that it provides security. The disadvantage is that it is sometimes difficult to follow and often appears rigid or "canned."

Greater freedom can be provided by a *scenario* outline that describes the action that is to take place (see scenario outline). The scenario outline does not have the rigidity of the script but may be more difficult for the puppeteers to follow because it is more open-ended. It might be easier for beginners to write out the entire play and switch to a scenario approach later when they become more certain of themselves.

All puppet presentations should be simple and clear stories of interest to young children. The puppets should not engage in complicated actions or tiresome lectures since adults who use puppets to make self-righteous sermons destroy the magic that gives puppetry its great power. Because of its theatrical traditions, classroom puppetry should be entertaining as well as educational.

Preparation and the Introduction

Just before the presentation of the puppet show, the puppeteer and/or facilitator should set up the puppet stage that can be commercially made, a table on its side, cut out of a cardboard box, a room divider, a clothesline stretched across a room, or a tension rod placed in a doorway with a blanket thrown over it. The stage should not be so high that children will have to strain their necks to see the action or so low that the puppeteer is forced into an uncomfortable position.

Performances should be scheduled at times when children are ready to relax and rest, e.g., when free play is over, just before or after snack or lunch, or just before children are ready to go home. The facilitator and the puppeteer could begin by sitting in front of the stage and briefly introducing the story. In the show "Seymour Finds a

---

Scenario Outline

Seymour Finds a Friend

Purpose   To help children understand that physical appearance is not an effective way to determine another person's worth; to help them understand feelings associated with rejection; to promote effective problem-solving responses to rejection based on appearances.

Puppets: **Seymour**   A puppet who looks scary but actually prefers friendly relationships. Voice is scratchy, unusual sounding.

   Prissy   A softspoken lamb who is easily frightened.

   Herbie   A mouse who is also easily frightened. (This show requires two puppeteers. If a helper cannot be found then the plot should be adjusted to exclude Herbie.)

Props: A blanket.

Plot: *Scene One.* Seymour enters (on left) and introduces himself to the children. He talks about his great interest in making friends with the other puppets. Prissy enters (far right), talks briefly with the children, and begins to move to the left. When Seymour gets her attention, Prissy becomes very frightened and runs away. Seymour reacts with sadness and briefly talks with the children and facilitator about how he feels. He then leaves.

   Scene Two. Herbie appears (far left) and engages children in brief conversation. Seymour enters (on left) and moves toward Herbie. As soon as he sees him, Herbie quickly says something like, "Oh, look at him; he looks scary!" Herbie then runs away. Again, Seymour expresses disappointment and appeals to the children for help. (**Note:** At this point a probem-solving interaction should occur. Seymour could try out some of the children's suggestions. Some may not work. Someone, though, may offer an idea that would work. The remainder of this outline is based on one possible solution.) This solution could begin when Seymour comments that maybe if they didn't see him the other puppets would talk to him. Children comment on this possibility. Seymour then leaves.

   Scene Three. Seymour returns (on left) with blanket and asks the facilitator to cover him. Following this both Prissy and Herbie appear (on right) and comment on that "weird looking thing" they saw earlier. They notice the blanket, move next to it, and begin to talk with Seymour. After a few moments of friendly conversation they both ask Seymour to take the blanket off. Seymour asks if they would run away. They respond by insisting that they would not run away from such a friendly person. When the facilitator removes the blanket, both Prissy and Herbie become afraid and begin to run away. Herbie escapes but the facilitator gently reaches up and stops Prissy from leaving. Prissy gradually loses her fear as the facilitator and children gently insist that Seymour is not harmful and encourage her to stay. As she overcomes her fear, she moves closer to Seymour to get a better look at him. She studies him closely and touches his face and hair. As she does this, she, Seymour, and the children comment about his appearance. Finally, Prissy expresses some relief about Seymour. She thanks the children for helping her understand her mistake. Seymour also expresses his appreciation for their help. The two then agree to go over to Seymour's house to play, and the presentation ends.

Friend," the discussion could focus on things that look scary but are not really harmful. The group could also discuss the wide variation of physical characteristics among people.

The Presentation

During the presentation the puppeteer and facilitator should keep several important points in mind. If they enjoy their involvement, the puppeteer and facilitator will transmit their enthusiasm to their children. They should also take advantage of the theatrical aspects of puppetry. The puppeteer can create special voices for the puppets and produce the types of movements the puppets need to make to convey the range of emotions and attitudes that are a part of the story. The puppeteer should talk more loudly than normal in order to project the sound adequately to the children. Furthermore, both the facilitator and puppeteer should be kind to themselves when they make mistakes. Children are very accepting of little failures, especially if the adults can see the humor in the

situation. One of the common errors I still make is getting my voices mixed up with the puppets. The children think this incongruity is outrageously funny, so I simply chuckle at my own mistake and make adjustments in my voice. The ability to accept and learn from one's mistakes is an important contribution to professional development.

Follow Up

After a puppet show is completed, the puppeteer and facilitator can meet with the children to discuss the preceding events, clarify any difficulties, and reinforce the points introduced. If time permits, a group activity that strengthens the intended effects of the puppet show could immediately follow the presentation. "Seymour Finds a Friend" could be followed by a body-awareness activity like body drawing, where each child lies down on a large sheet of paper, has his or her outline drawn by a partner, and then completes his or her own features with crayons, chalk, and/or paint.

The enthusiasm of the preschool child for informal and brief puppet shows clearly demonstrates their effectiveness as a strategy for encouraging the development of problem-solving techniques.

The enthusiasm preschool children have demonstrated for informal and brief puppet shows clearly indicates that the use of puppets can be an effective strategy for motivating and teaching young children to develop effective problem-solving techniques. Puppets can be used to introduce a variety of issues important to children. Seymour represents any individual who has been touched by racism, sexism, and other forms of ridicule; Mr. Grump is the mean man down the street who seems to have special hostility for children; Mr. Chucklebelly is the type of happy individual who seems to find humor in most any situation; Queen Sarah represents the type of gentle kindness and nurturance which most of us find so healing, while Prissy the Lamb reflects a type of reasonable assertiveness necessary to overcome barriers created by sex-role stereotypes. Thoughtful teachers can create puppet characters based on their own experiences and those of their children.

One does not need to be a professional to begin. Young children do not expect our "homemade" presentations to be as sophisicated as a Sesame Street production. Through diligent work, inexperienced but enthusiatic puppeteers can improve their technique and gradually become more skillful in creating that special magic which touches a child's imagination.

References

Andersen, B. E. *Let's Start a Puppet Theatre*. New York: Van Nostrand Reinhold, 1973.

Batchelder, M. *The Puppet Theatre Handbook*. New York: Harper, 1974.

Bates, E. *Potpourri of Puppetry*. Canyon, Tex.: West Texas State University, 1974.

Hanford, R. T. *The Complete Book of Puppets and Puppeteering*. New York: Drake, 1976.

Lee, M. *Puppet Theatre*. Fair Lawn, N.J.: Essential Books, 1958.

Richter, D. *Fell's Guide to Hand Puppets*. New York: Frederick Fell, 1970.

Smith, C. A. "Peopleteaching: An Approach to Identifying and Enhancing Personal-Social Competencies in Young Children." Presented at the National Association for the Education of Young Children annual conference, Anaheim, Calif., November 1976.

Spivack, J.; Platt, J. J.; and Shure, M. B. *The Problem-Solving Approach to Adjustment*. San Francisco: Jossey-Bass, 1976.

VI. Looking at the Learning Environment

The environment in which we teach has much to do with how we feel and how we act. The room and what is in it can affect our disposition and enhance or inhibit our desire to do our best. Children, also, are affected by the environment. A drab, poorly arranged room can hamper the child's ability to profit from a program that, otherwise, could offer opportunity for tremendous growth.

A setting does not have to be new, sparkling, and well equipped. But it does need to reflect thoughtful planning and careful consideration of children's needs. Setting up and utilizing an environment means more than tacking something colorful, at the child's eye level, on the walls or installing a new piece of equipment outdoors. It encompasses a sensible arrangement of equipment, well planned traffic patterns, clearly identified areas of interest, and the integration of space, materials, and adult roles. Resourceful adults find resourceful ways for providing a growth-enhancing environment both indoors and outdoors, as demonstrated in the first two articles in this section.

No program is complete without an evaluation of the learning environment as well. The final article in this volume discusses the use of the setting for assessing children's development and program effectiveness.

Antoinette B. Suter

A Playground—
Why Not Let the Children Create It?

An interesting playground for three- and four-year-olds requires children, imagination, and a variety of simple, strong, movable pieces of equipment.

"Let's make a house," "You can make it longer," "Look how to make it go down," "Put those two together," "Maybe we can move it on a wagon," "You have to move that block, it's the door," "Now we can put on the roof."

The children are excited, challenged, and intrigued with the endless possibilities presented to them on their playground. When they see it again, it won't be the same—it is the same playground with the same fence around it, the two swings are there, the large flat-bottom boat which is a sandbox and often the center of dramatic play, the jungle-gym, and the large area for digging, all are there—but everything else is different from the way it was yesterday.

A list of our outdoor play equipment is included at the end of this article. The following are taken into consideration when the teachers set up this movable equipment on the playground each day:

- □ the importance of traffic patterns for trikes and wagons;
- □ the need of a child or a small group for quiet play;
- □ present interests of the group;
- □ a recent trip or experience which might spark one kind of play;
- □ the need for the development of large muscles in climbing, crawling, reaching, pushing and pulling, jumping, walking, and balancing;
- □ the physical development and abilities of the particular group;
- □ differences between three- and four-year-olds or with children who have had little experience with large muscle activity.

Antoinette B. Suter, M.Ed., is Teacher-Director of the Methodist Nursery School in Fairfield, Connecticut, and past president of the Connecticut AEYC. Her areas of experience include teacher education and training.

Eight large wooden boxes (well-made and strong) may be the beginning of a house, a fire station, a bakery, an airplane, or a boat. These provide centers for building with large hollow blocks, 5' long 1'' × 5'' boards, ladders, wooden boxes with rope handles, plastic milk crates, and nail kegs. All this equipment is readily available to the children in the playhouse (a 7' × 10' shed) which is on the playground.

Climbers provide challenging opportunities for climbing, and two of them placed near each other with an 8' board between them may provide:

balancing experience

a bridge for dramatic play

a place to fish from.

Another board slanting down from any of several rungs on a climber provides an excellent slide of varying difficulties.

Most equipment for a good playground should not be limited to one use, so there is no slide on our playground. Telephone spools, again moved to be a part of a walking, climbing, sliding, crawling, or jumping setup, provide different heights and experiences in using one's body. Important understandings of spatial concepts can be gained by:

- going backwards across a board
- pulling yourself on your tummy
- sitting sideways
- walking
- humping across
- sliding down, on back or side or tummy, head first or feet first.

The way in which such equipment is used is limited only by the child's imagination and safety precautions. It can all be changed or added to by the children, possibly putting small boards one after another like a long sidewalk, or making stairs with blocks and tires. When settings are the same every day, they become dull and creativity simply does not happen. The varied placement of the boxes, the climbers, and the long boards gives children new ways to look at the same equipment.

One homemade piece of equipment consists of a box with a seat, a round wooden steering wheel, and dials, buttons, and arrows mounted on the dashboard. A movable piece of doweling serves as a gearshift lever. This equipment can be a very important part of a

fire engine	bus	train
car	rocket	camper
airplane	garbage truck	boat, etc.

Photos by
Antoinette B. Suter

215

Behind it one can put a large box, milk crate, or blocks for passengers or cargo in dramatic play.

Simple props which enhance, stimulate, and enable children to play out experiences and trips add immeasurably to the play, to creativity, and to social learnings. This is an important way in which children begin to understand their environment.

Fishing poles, with rubber sinkers, baskets, and paddles often lead to

the building of a boat

pretending to swim in the water

a bridge to fish from

a stove to cook the fish in.

Small pieces of hose, bicycle pumps, ladders, fire hats, telephones, trikes, often lead to

building a fire station with beds in it (out of small boards and large wooden boxes)

a place for firemen to eat "food" (from the sandbox), houses with roofs to climb on.

Climbers can be turned over on their sides, becoming zoo cages for wild animals who must have food and be trained.

In addition there are trikes and wagons which can be safely used on an adjoining asphalt parking lot. Dump trucks, steam shovels, and trenching tools provide opportunities for building roads, digging holes, and mending streets in and around the digging hole.

We know that children are very active, happy, and learning on our playground. Teachers are constantly involved in a supportive, interested way, often

- helping a child, through questions, find a solution to a building problem;
- helping a child find a safer way to climb to the top of a house;
- encouraging or verbally supporting a young child who is just learning to climb;
- giving a hand to a child who is hesitant about crossing an elevated board or going up an inclined one.

Teachers need to be very aware—are there areas or activities which a particular child has avoided? Does the child ever climb? Walk, crawl, or jump from above the ground? Pump on a swing? Ride a trike? Having observed the children carefully, teachers need to understand why a child cannot or does not participate in a given activity. He or she can then help the child gain that skill with patience and lots of encouragement. Mastering a physical skill certainly does increase a child's self-

216

confidence. We find that parents picking up their children at the end of school are always urged to come see

> how high they climbed;
> the building they helped to make;
> the way they fixed the ladders;
> how they put the chimney on;
> how they made the see-saw balance.

On many days all of the large blocks, ladders, small boards, other small boxes and milk crates, large long boards, and climbers, are used. The process and creativity involved in the way they are used is very exciting to see. The playground is especially set up for three groups of children: 16 three-year-olds meeting two mornings a week; 18 four-year-olds meeting three mornings a week; and 18 four-year olds meeting four afternoons a week. The children have a playground that is theirs to change, try out new things, or move almost everything, and they love it! Yes, they do have to share, and often need one more block or that last barrel. The children either use something else or join forces with a friend.

Playing with someone who has a different idea about how to put on a roof, make a tent, or put out a fire does necessitate listening. We help the children from the beginning of the year to talk and listen to each other by modeling the words to say and staying close to add support, but not interfering. It does work! Children can and do communicate their ideas, feelings, and desires with little help from us after a short time. We want them to be independent and to be able to play comfortably and freely without the aid of adults.

Our playground is an exciting place and a very important part of our curriculum. More of us should work to provide materials, equipment, and maintenance so we can give the playground back to the children!

Outdoor Play Equipment

Wooden Boxes: Different sizes, sanded, with two coats of paint so they can be left outdoors. Built of #2 white pine, using 1½" #10 brass screws, in sizes 1' × 3' × 2'; 2' × 2' × 2'; 1' × 2' × 2'.

Cardboard Boxes: Any size, available at stores selling large appliances. To make a shape box, cut holes in various shapes just large enough for a child to crawl through.

Boards: 1. Long, strong boards for slides, walking, climbing, crawling, balancing, etc.—7' or 8' long, 10" wide, made of 2" × 10 " pine.
    2. For building, 5' lengths of 1 " × 6".

Ladders: 4' long; 12" wide uprights of 2" × 2"; rungs are 1" × 2" boards spaced 8" apart.

Barrels: Wooden nail kegs occasionally can be found at lumber yards. Fiber barrels of all sizes are great fun for rolling over, climbing through, fitting into another, etc. Cheap and remarkably durable.

Blocks: Large, wooden, hollow—all sizes.

Telephone Cable Spools: Can be used for rolling, building, as a table, etc.

Milk Crates: Ask for an old one and paint it.

Small Wooden Boxes: Any and all sizes—make holes in ends for rope handles. Children or materials can be pulled in them.

Homemade Car, Airplane, Rocket, or Train: Any wooden frame or box which a child can straddle—attach steering wheel and numbered dials, switches, etc., from old stoves and washing machines.

Rubber Tires

Logs

Climbers: Made of exterior grade ¾" plywood and doweling; a good height is 45", rungs 8" apart, 30" across the bottom. Durable and with endless uses, both standing up and turned on side.

David E. Day and Robert Sheehan

Elements of a Better Preschool

There is a common feeling among teachers, parents and other interested laymen that preschool child care settings should be educational, developmental, and creative.[1] They are thought of as places where children should be able to spend part of their day developing their human potential and enjoying interaction with other children and adults.

We have discovered through extensive observations that all too often preschool programs are something less than we would expect them to be.[2] Furthermore, one type of program does not consistently prove to be better nor worse than other types of preschools. We found that excellent preschools could be based as easily on the stated philosophy of Montessori, the English Infant School, or a more structured behaviorist position.

There were three dominant factors that seemed to relate to the quality of all preschools we have observed. These are: (1) the organization and utilization of physical space; (2) the child's access to materials and the ways in which they are used; and (3) the amount and type of adult-child interaction.

It is very clear that day care/nursery education is going to grow rapidly in the next few years. It is just as clear that we need to look carefully at how we design and practice preschool child care and education. We would like to share the results of our experiences in the hope that it may be of help in achieving a higher level of quality of preschools. Each of the three factors will be discussed in some detail.

---

[1] Preschool child care settings include group day care, nursery schools, Head Start, and combinations of these types of programs.

[2] The data for this paper were based on both formal and informal observations. The formal aspect involved over 80 hours of directed observation in 14 early childhood centers. Examples include integrated day public school groups for five- to seven-year-olds, semi-cooperative day care centers, a Montessori preschool, and Head Start programs. The data gathering was regulated by a carefully designed observation guide. An interview schedule was used with the director or lead teacher. Informal data consisted of Day's near decade of experience in early childhood education — developing preschool programs, training staff, and conducting research.

Physical Setting and Utilization of Space

There is a strong similarity between most nursery schools, Head Start programs, and day care centers we have visited. Although objectives may differ, in most cases the environment offered to the children has the same design. Most programs are arranged in the traditional "learning area" style consisting of blocks, language and reading materials with a rug, records, pictures, and books, the ever present housekeeping corner with a child-size stove, refrigerator and dishes and pans, an art section with one or two easels, and a science area with a few small animals, and an aquarium. We found this most everywhere and it has been present in Europe and America for fifty years or more.[3]

We should like to stress the point that this rather traditional selection of major learning areas does not connote any negative implications regarding programs. The presence or absence of the sand table, for example, does not by itself seem to appreciably affect the quality of what takes place. Rather what is important is the way in which the staff makes provisions for the full use of any area, while at the same time making sure that it does not interfere with the use of adjacent learning areas.

We observed that teachers who believed that their role was to assist the child in making use of all learning areas were spending their time in making this happen. These teachers may have been in the block area helping children develop classification skills or building elaborate towers. They did not, for example, believe that certain areas, such as the block corner, were off limits to adults. Nor did they view adult contact as interference. Rather, these staff members believed that a child's work and play in all of the preschool was too important to be ignored. They viewed their participation with the children as a healthy way of promoting diverse and productive use of all the facilities.

The move to open-space settings in American education has found its way to the preschool. Very often entire programs are housed in a large room or hall with the learning areas separated by waist-high bookcases

---

[3] Michael Auleta, *Foundations of Early Childhood Education: Readings* (New York: Random House, 1969).

David E. Day is an Associate Professor at the University of Massachusetts, Amherst. Dr. Day's work in preschools includes directing an experimental prekindergarten program, consultation with Head Start, and studies of preschool children's language behavior.

Robert Sheehan is enrolled in a Ph.D. program in Early Childhood Education at Georgia State University in Atlanta. He has done research with Dr. Day designing and completing preschool studies. His experience also includes having been a member of a day care staff.

Dr. Day and Mr. Sheehan are currently engaged in a study of the physical environments and licensing of day care centers.

and small dividers. Our research has convinced us that alternatives to this type of setting can and should be found. We would propose that pre-school workers consider the following benefits of having children's centers designed with a combination of large and small private areas. The behavior of both staff and children seems to be significantly improved if all children are not obliged to be in the same room all of the day. Three important effects of separated physical space were identified in our study. First, in the closed space setting, the sound from any one activity stays within that room; the result is often much less distraction by noise or physical activity. We saw children pounding nails in one room while others were being read to in an adjacent room.

Second, in the closed space setting, there can be truly quiet areas. Over and over again we observed very normal children who sought privacy when in a quiet mood; a place where they would not be disturbed by the activities of the center. This seems to be particularly important for a number of preschool age children. Where the private space was available, we found teachers who seemed to be sensitive to this need for getting away and supported children's move to being alone when it appeared necessary.

The separation of physical space also provides for isolating sick chil-

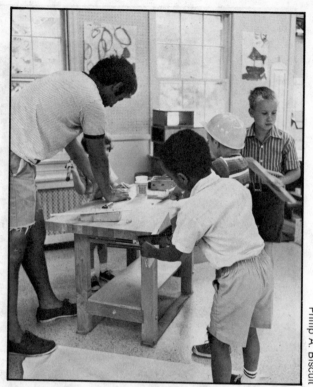

dren without having to send them home, which often is impossible. In day care centers with numbers of children staying late into the afternoon, the closed space setting also allows quiet areas for naps. In each center we visited, staff told us of the impossibility of coordinating the nap time. All children do not want to or need to nap at the same time and for the same duration. Those programs that had separate rooms were fortunate indeed, for they seemed to be less constrained by the range of rest and sleep needs of children. On the other hand, where only one room existed for the entire center we found staff struggling to keep children quiet, thereby frustrating themselves and the children.

The third reason why closed space setting should be considered is that it encourages the arrangement of small group activities. We saw many groups of three or four children working undisturbed, while different larger group activities were taking place in other rooms of the center.

Our favorable predisposition to separate rooms was reinforced on several visits. One in particular can serve to illustrate the three benefits just outlined. This center was housed in three moderately sized rooms connected by a wide hallway, which was used as a fourth room. Each room seemed to have an identifiable personality that was taken on by the children as they moved from room to room. In the "work" room, a child could be sawing wood, pounding nails, or shouting his enthusiasm to a playmate. As he moved across the hall to the "table games" room, he would become introspective and quiet. Here he might listen to a record he selected, play lotto with a teacher or another child, or watch the fish in the aquarium.

The third room seemed to be the place where rather messy art activities took place and where snacks were available. Children in this room were very cooperative and communicative with each other. The hall was used primarily for those few total group activities directed by the staff.

In this center, children could be alone, or very much engaged with others. Walking from one room to another seemed to be all that was necessary to effect this transformation. This alternative to open space made it possible for the staff to make conscious provisions for a child's changing moods and needs.

The Use and Availability of Materials

The materials which the various programs provided fall into two major categories, those which are easily accessible to the children and those materials which were kept in storage areas away from the children. Some programs were using materials in unique ways and making them readily available to the children at all times. Most programs had blocks, house-keeping equipment, picture books, and large motor materials accessible to the children. The more exciting, and from our perspective the higher quality programs, arranged it so that when the children chose to they

Ruth McGrath

could also use construction paper, paste, pipe cleaners, play dough, sponge pieces, leggos, puzzles, and other small manipulative materials. For example, in these programs paint and paper were at the easel; so too were brushes of different sizes. To many preschool workers these observations may bring a "ho-hum" or "so what" response. They would say that good nursery schools have made these provisions all along and we would agree. We should like to note, however, that these practices are not as widespread as we may commonly think.

It is important to note, too, that a child's being able to see what was available was characteristic of preschools where special attention was given to the presentation of materials. The materials were arranged one next to each other, rather than one on top of the other. There was not a clutter of materials either, but rather a sufficient amount and variety to stimulate a child's curiosity.

We observed many teachers who carefully checked on the use of the materials. Puzzles that were not being used (or were being abused) were replaced by different puzzles. If no one paid any attention to the rabbit but several children complained of the animal's urine stench, the rabbit would be taken out of the center. This sensitivity to the presentation of materials is essential to a quality preschool program.

Another exciting observation was the way in which some programs combined materials from one or more learning areas to produce totally new experiences. This rather simple procedure opened up many new possibilities for the children and staff. Sand was used in paintings creating unusual designs, and play dough was painted and used with blocks. Sponge cloth and paint brushes were used simultaneously to create different mood and texture in paintings. Stories were read while children made block designs depicting parts of the story. Food coloring was added to water play for another type of aesthetic experience.

The adults' role in the use of materials is of a primary concern. Teachers must find time to assist children in discovering ways in which materials can be used. In centers where this was happening, we observed staff with children using the blocks to develop such diverse concepts as cooperation and symmetry. In other instances, we observed an adult assisting a child to deal with the perceptual confusion of their first jigsaw puzzle.

The preschool staff should not make the error of assuming that children are either capable or incapable of using developmental materials. Rather they should spend time observing the child's use of toys, games, and other instructional materials and record the ways in which they are being used. They should then use this information in helping the children develop and in discovering new ways of using the preschool to promote development.

Amount and Type of Adult-Child Interaction

During our visits to various preschool programs, we encountered a wide range of feelings concerning the importance of adult-child interaction. Some preschool personnel believed that they could best play their role by removing themselves from the child's activity. In other programs, the staff was convinced that close, regular and purposive contact with all children was a necessary part of promoting total development. The higher quality programs tended to embrace the second position and made the additional qualification that certain types of interaction are better than others. These adults were promoting real conversation with the children. They listened to the children and replied in ways that expanded their language and concepts. There was warmth in these staff-child relationships and a great deal of mutual respect.

We also found a direct link between the amount of adult-child interaction and the types of activities in which the children were engaged. In programs which had lots of interaction, children were alert, attentive, curious, and had a sense of humor. They cooperated with each other and exhibited confidence with adults. In programs with little adult-child interaction, the children seemed to be more inattentive and shied away from adults. Also, reduced adult-child interaction seemed to be related to much more acting out behavior and physical aggression.

There is support for our argument among child psychologists. One study[4] indicated the ways in which the nursery school children's personality and social adjustment vary with the atmosphere and teaching techniques of the school. The following statement sums up the results:

> In short, from the points of view of the pre-school child's social and emotional adjustment, active teacher guidance and participation are more beneficial than detachment. The favorable changes in children's behavior following nursery school training . . . may be attributable to the "high teacher guidance, active participation qualities" of the school they attended.

In those programs giving attention to the need for considerable adult-child interaction, we found adults engaged with one child or a small group of children. Few adults were separated from children for long periods of time, but rather they seemed to invite the participation of the children in all manner of activity ranging from cleaning up the breakfast dishes to mixing paint for the easel. These teachers, too, were somehow able to involve the children in moving rather large pieces of equipment, such as balance boards, indoor jungle gyms, and wagons up and down entry stairs. The most pervasive attitude seemed to be that child and adult

---

[4]P. H. Mussen, J. J. Conger, and J. Kagan, *Child Development and Personality* (New York: Harper & Row, 1963).

were together in the center for long periods of time each day and that the best way for both to be happy was to develop a sense of cooperative interaction.

The question may be asked, what are the staff doing if they are not interacting with the children? We found that for the most part they were organizing and tidying up the room or setting up activities for the children. The staff would arrange an activity, bring the children to it, supervise its beginning, and then move on to arrange for another.

When we questioned the staff in programs with much interaction, we found they usually arranged as much of the physical environment as possible before the children arrived and involved the children in cleaning up when an activity was over. They also encouraged independent use of materials so that children were not always dependent on adult direction.

It may appear that we are advocating that children seldom get a chance to be alone or with other children without the intrusion of an adult. This is not the case. What we are advocating is that the staff of each preschool not disengage themselves from much direct contact with children. On the contrary, they should be helping the child use the facilities that are available rather than performing a custodial function. Certainly it is true that quality preschools are also noted for the amount of freedom a child has to pursue his interests. Whether this becomes a growth producing activity or a counter-productive experience rests largely on those adult-child interaction factors we have outlined here.

We noticed a phenomena in some preschool programs which struck us as somewhat odd. The amount of time any staff member spent interacting with the children seemed to vary inversely with the amount of authority the staff member had. In day care, Head Start, and nursery schools, the teaching director or lead teacher, who is usually the most experienced and highly trained member of the staff, often spent the least amount of time with the children.

In general, we can say that the children's behavior appeared to reflect the behavior of the adults around them. When staff worked closely with children and behaved in ways suggesting that their interest was to be with the children, the children stayed at activities for long periods of time and were friendly and outgoing. When staff were constantly moving from one project to the next and seemed, at times, to be avoiding children, the children had a short attention span and avoided contact with adults.

Summary

Observations of preschool programs, ranging from day care to nursery school, have convinced us that the quality of each program is dependent upon three factors. The physical arrangement and utilization of space, the availablility and diversity of materials, and the amount and kind of adult-child interaction, alone and in concert, have a strong effect on the worth of any program.

The following chart is intended to show how these factors relate to the behavior of children in any program. The column on the left reflects some of the behavior we observed in children in preschools where space, materials, and the role of adults had been seriously integrated into the program. The right-hand column lists behavior all too frequently observed in programs which reflected a lack of sensitivity to these three factors.

Space, materials, and adult roles integrated	Space, materials, and adult roles not integrated
1. Many instances of adults and children working cooperatively.	1. Little long lasting adult-child contact.
2. Children have considerable autonomy within expanding limits.	2. Unnecessary constraints for each learning-play area established by adults well in advance of children's use. The children's behavior in each learning area prescribed by the staff.
3. Most materials available to children with their use of them in constructive, developmental ways.	3. Only a few, routine materials available. Most materials are not accessible to children; they are brought out and put away by staff.
4. Much child-adult and child-child communication on activities at hand.	4. Much child-to-child talk that is often transitory and uncommunicative.
5. Children's efforts seemed to be focused on completing play or work. Much attention to what is going on.	5. Children were inattentiven listless, and easily distracted. Great amounts of random, undirected movement.
6. Little acting out and aggression directed at other children.	6. Children using toys in very aggressive games. Aggression often aimed at other children.
7. Program directed by the staff but evolved with the participation of the children.	7. Not much of a program. The day seemed to be organized around one big, teacher directed activity, between long periods of adult inattention to children.

There is nothing startlingly new in our findings. It is probably true that good preschool teachers knew intuitively that these factors must be accounted for if a good program was to be developed. Our intention here, is to make it possible for us to move beyond our intuitions as we rush to provide expanded early care and educational experiences for young children. We believe that a consideration of the ideas developed in this paper would tend to increase the chances that preschool programs would be of even higher quality.

Larry M. Raskin, William J. Taylor, and Florence G. Kerckhoff

The Teacher as Observer for Assessment: A Guideline

Some teachers may be unsure of when to refer children for special help. Many have asked about what to report, how to report it clearly, and how to cut down the lag between referral and action.

Experience indicates that much critical information is lost when the teacher is not included as a member of an assessment team, not as a psychologist or diagnostician, but in the very special observant role as teacher. It is evident that teachers are aware of, and sensitive to, certain behavior patterns which have diagnostic significance. The problem is often one of organization and description, not a general lack of expertise. Sometimes teachers may hesitate to report behaviors which appear to indicate that a child is "just going through a phase," but many behaviors do not represent phases. Failure to report for whatever reason reduces the advantage of an early and crucial opportunity to help the child before repeated frustrations have been experienced.

As an aid to teachers in this task, the following questions are suggested as guides for organizing observations. This set of guideline questions does not represent the diagnostic function, nor does it aim to make diagnosticians out of the teachers. It is suggested, rather, as an aid to teachers in their efforts to organize observations to include material which will be particularly useful to the entire assessment team. We have found that such descriptions are useful to the teachers of young children. These are descriptions of directly observable behaviors, ones that can be seen by more than one person and which are objective rather than judgmental.

Communication is sharp and clear when the teacher reports and describes behaviors in terms of what she has seen instead of just applying a label. For example, reporting that a child got out of his seat an average of

28 times in several 10-minute periods communicates much more than does the more popular but perhaps inaccurate label of hyperactive.

The teacher notes the time of occurrence of the observed critical behavior and any other aspects of the event, such as what preceeded the behavior and what followed it, as well as any other important factors. For example, the teacher may note that during a cutting and pasting task, both B.J. and Maria had their eyes very close to the paper when they used scissors. At the first opportunity, the teacher would record the incident briefly, indicating these two children manifested that particular behavior under those circumstances. When the teacher has the opportunity to observe the children under similar circumstances or tasks, on at least five different days, and similar results occur, a referral would be appropriate. This procedure eliminates snap judgments and premature referrals, and gives the consultant objective information as a basis from which to begin work.

The following behaviors have been organized into categories which are critical for the analysis and prediction of academic, social, and psychological difficulties. The areas lend themselves to a variety of uses by different consultants; they are by no means all-inclusive.

Larry M. Raskin, Ph.D., is Chief Psychologist at the Child Evaluation Center in Louisville, Kentucky.

William J. Taylor, Ph.D., is a faculty member of the Department of Child Development and Family Life at Purdue University in West Lafayette, Indiana.

Florence G. Kerckhoff, M.S., was Director of the Child Development Laboratories at Purdue University and an advisor to Parent Cooperative Preschools International. She died on August 26, 1978.

Visual

1. Eye movements: Do the child's eyes seem to work as an integrated pair? Do they point in different directions or do they seem to move independently? Does the child have trouble converging his or her eyes on a close-in object, or have difficulty keeping both eyes on a fixed or moving target?

2. Winking: Do some children have difficulty closing their eyes when asked either both at once or one at a time? An inability to wink by five years of age should be noted.

3. Distance and position from work: Does the child continually hold dolls, puzzles, or pictures less than seven inches away from his or her eyes? Also, does s/he hold his or her head to one side when looking, or lean the whole upper trunk in one direction? Does the child avoid table work that requires looking and moving materials at less than an arm's length away, or is there a tendency to hold things far away from the body in an apparent attempt to see more clearly?

4. Signs of irritation: Have you noticed that the child rubs his or her eyes frequently, or the eyes are red-rimmed or runny? Does the child blink excessively when looking from the teacher to table top and back again, and soon stops looking at what is going on?

5. Visual-motor control: Does the child do puzzles only by feeling whether the pieces fit, or have trouble throwing a beanbag into a large opening, or never seem to be able to keep a flashlight on

229

target? These may be signs that more than poor vision is involved.

Motor Behavior

1. Strength: Is there a general lack of physical strength in comparison to others about the same age? This may show up in either small motor activities such as operating a wall light switch with the index finger or such large motor activities as hanging from a pull-up bar. Can the child sustain a leg lift for five seconds while lying on his or her back?

2. Agility: Does the child stumble and fall often or seem to avoid jumping, running, climbing, rhythm, or balancing tasks? Are both arms used as aids in balancing and running? Has the child failed to master the leg movements used in pumping while on a swing? Can the child jump with both feet off the floor simultaneously? Is an apparent lack of good judgment displayed when climbing or running? Stepping

off the top of a high place or other dangerous behaviors should be noted.

Use of Writing Instruments

1. Handling: Does the child still hold the crayon, paint brush, or pencil in his or her fist by about three and a half years of age, rather than between the thumb and forefinger or other fingers?

2. *Copying:* **Is the child able to imitate or copy simple lines, e.g., vertical or horizontal, without frequent overstroking or whorling, by three years of age? Is s/he able to reasonably reproduce such geometric shapes as a circle, cross, and square by five years of age? (Triangles and diamonds are more difficult and not usually accomplished until about age seven.)**

3. *Drawing:* **Are spontaneous pictures barren of details or composed of simple outline shapes? Do drawings of human figures include such major** parts as head, eyes, nose, mouth, a distinct body, and legs by five years of age?

Looking, Listening, Remembering, and Doing

1. *Remembering and doing:* **Can the child remember and follow three-part directions such as "After you have put away your blocks, you may wash your hands and come for juice"?**

2. *Shutting out distractions:* **Does the child shut his or her eyes in order to listen better, or cover the ears to watch better?**

231

3. Distractibility: Does the child remember and return to the task at hand following interruptions by five years of age?

Social-Emotional

1. Attitude: Does the child continually rely upon stubborn, negativistic, or extremely independent behavior when interacting with adults or other children?

2. Is the child destructively hostile? Are materials smashed, attacked without apparent cause, and the child's own productive work destroyed? Does the child cause physical or psychological harm to her or himself or others? Is s/he excessively aggressive with little or no provocation?

3. Cyclical behavior: Does the child have successions of good days and then bad days? This should be recorded over at least a three-week period.

4. Withdrawal: Does the child answer questions clearly and directly when asked? Does s/he avoid all contact with the teacher and classmates, possibly sitting alone in a corner?

5. Extreme attachment: Does the child have difficulty separating from the teacher or parents to start new activities or begin the day? Often a young child shows dependence through a predisposition to touch or hold the parent or teacher and takes every opportunity to be near them. During free play activities the child will follow the teacher or if engaged in an activity, will frequently ask for help in order to remain at the task.

All of the above are behaviors and characteristics which we have found important in recognizing inconsistent development. A particular behavior may occur in isolation and pass with little upset to the child or others, or it may be severely disturbing to the group. In either case, recognition and objective recording of such incidents are necessary.

Often, teachers with years of experience make rapid and successful judgments about children's behavior. Unfortunately, the items which contribute to their decisions may not be immediately apparent or easily communicated. Thus, teacher evaluation of this sort may lead to confusion or frustration in discussions with parents or consultants. We stress objective reporting because each child is different.

The keys to improved teacher observation and reporting are the use of reliable and nonjudgmental descriptions. One of the best opportunities for improving and broadening the validity or reality of child observations is in parent and staff conferences. Often when parents and teachers discuss behaviors at school, from their unique roles, similar patterns are found to appear in the home. Such information supports the teacher's observations and facilitates parent-teacher communication.

Whether the teacher is making a referral for further evaluation or working with a child individually, evaluation and re-evaluation based upon objective evidence will be beneficial. Without objective reporting, helping the child may be trial and error, and benefits may be hit or miss. It is important that the teacher use his or her special skills for assessing physical, cognitive, and social-emotional growth, not as a diagnostician nor a psychologist, but from the observational perspective of the child's teacher. ∇

Annotated Bibliography

Beery, K. E. *Developmental Test of Visual-Motor Integration.* Chicago: Follett, 1967. This is a geometric form copying test that may be administered to groups or individual children. The age range is from two to fifteen years. The test is easy to give, and the scoring is described clearly, illustrated with examples of passing and failing drawings. There is a good chapter in the *Manual* on the assessment and remediation of visual-motor difficulties.

Cratty, B. J. *Perceptual and Motor Development in Infants and Children.* New York: Macmillan, 1970. Cratty has written a clear and well-illustrated book describing the sequences of perceptual and motor development from infancy through childhood. Various activities that are age-appropriate are presented, as are critical reviews of several current perceptual-motor programs, e.g., Kephart, Delcato.

Feriden, W. E., and Van Handel, D. C. *Minimal Brain Dysfunction. Diagnosis, Management, and Remediation.* Linden, NJ: Remediation Associates, 1971. A brief definition and description of the characteristics of the hyperkinetic child. There is a section concerned with the psychoeducational evaluation of the hyperkinetic child. Of particular interest is the chapter on classroom management that contains suggestions useful to all teachers.

Harris, D. B. *Children's Drawings as Measures of Intellectual Maturity.* New York: Harcourt, Brace and World, 1963. A revision and extension of the Goodenough Draw-a-Man Test. There is a clear and objective tabulation of scorable items for both man and woman drawings, as well as developmental norms for ages three to fifteen years. Several chapters describe and document the rationale for the use of human figure drawings as indicators of developmental levels.

Johnson, D. G., and Myklebust, H. R. *Learning Disabilities.* New York: Grune and Stratton, 1967. An intermediate level treatment of the learning disabilities area with several illustrative cases and remediation techniques. Clear handling of problematic terminology and labels as well as an integration of theory and teaching adds to the book's value. Contains sections on verbal and nonverbal language as well as classroom and program planning for preschool and school age children.

Koppitz, E. M. *Psychological Evaluation of Children's Human Figure Drawings.* New York: Grune and Stratton, 1968. A more up-to-date book than that by Harris, with a detailed description of Koppitz's several years of research on this topic. An added plus is the inclusion of tables of component parts expected at ages five to twelve years as well as "exceptional" items. There are sufficient reproductions of the drawings made by "average" children as well as those experiencing difficulties.

Marwit, S. J., and Stenner, A. J. "Hyperkinesis: Delineation of Two Patterns." *Exceptional Children,* January 1972, pp. 401-406. An interesting paper which proposes that two distinct patterns of hyperkinesis exist. These are "hyperactive" in which there is an organic brain damage etiology, and "hyperreactive" in which there is rarely any evidence of maturational lags or organic involvement. Characteristics of both patterns are presented clearly.

Wolman, B. B. *Manual of Child Psychopathology.* New York: McGraw-Hill, 1972. This is an excellent reference book covering the wide area of psychopathology in children.

Articles Selected

All the articles appearing in this book have been selected from previous issues of *Young Children*, the journal of the National Association for the Education of Young Children.

Aggression and Hostility in Young Children, by Bettye M. Caldwell. From Vol. 32, no. 2 (January 1977): 4-13.

Awakening the Artist: Music for Young Children, by Dorothy McDonald and Jonny H. Ramsey. From Vol. 33, no. 2 (January 1978): 26-32.

Children's Art: A Vehicle for Learning, by Sylvia F. Burns. From Vol. 30, no. 3 (March 1975): 193-204.

Choice with Responsibility, by Davia M Veach. From Vol. 32, no. 4 (May 1977): 22-25.

Elements of a Better Preschool, by David E. Day and Robert Sheehan. From Vol. 30, no. 1 (November 1974): 15-23.

Encouraging Helping Behavior, by Robert F. Marcus and Marion Leiserson. From Vol. 33, no. 6 (September 1978): 24-34.

English as a Second Language, by Janet Gonzalez-Mena. From Vol. 32, no. 1 (November 1976): 14-19.

Focus on Movement: Practice and Theory, by Arline Kahn Julius. From Vol. 34, no. 1 (November 1978): 19-26.

From Curiosity to Concepts: From Concepts to Curiosity—Science Experiences in the Preschool, by Jean Durgin Harlan. From Vol. 30, no. 4 (May 1975): 249-255.

Helping Children Cope with Death, by Erna Furman. From Vol. 33, no. 4 (May 1978): 25-32.

"Is Today Tomorrow?" History for Young Children, by Carol Seefeldt. From Vol. 30, no. 2 (January 1975): 99-105.

Large Hollow Blocks: Relationship of Quantity to Block Building Behaviors, by Judith Bender. From Vol. 33, no. 6 (September 1978): 17-23.

Lobster on the Sidewalk: Understanding and Helping Children with Fears, by Marion Carey Hyson. From Vol. 34, no. 5 (July 1979): 54-60.

Mainstreaming in Early Childhood: Strategies and Resources, by James A. McLoughlin and Susan M. Kershman. From Vol. 34, no. 4 (May 1979): 54-66.

Old Games for Young Children: A Link to Our Heritage, by Ruth F. Bogdanoff and Elaine T. Dolch. From Vol. 34, no. 2 (January 1979): 37-45.

Parenting, Teaching, and Child Development, by Ira J. Gordon. From Vol. 31, no. 3 (March 1976): 173-183.

A Playground—Why Not Let the Children Create It? by Antoinette B. Suter. From Vol. 32, no. 3 (March 1977): 19-24.

Play Today? by Leila P. Fagg. From Vol. 30, no. 2 (January 1975): 93.

"Please Read That Story Again!" Exploring Relationships Between Story Reading and Learning to Read, by Judith A. Schickedanz. From Vol. 33, no. 5 (July 1978): 48-55.

Puppetry and Problem-Solving Skills, by Charles A. Smith. From Vol. 34, no. 3 (March 1979): 4-11.

Reading and Pre-First Grade: A Joint Statement of Concerns about Present Practices in Pre-First Grade Reading Instruction and Recommendations for Improvement. From Vol. 32, no. 6 (September 1977): 25-26.

Storytelling with Young Children, by John Lee Sherman. From Vol. 34, no. 2 (January 1979): 20-27.

SUCCESS: A Parent Effectiveness Approach for Developing Urban Children's Self-Concepts, by Kenneth R. Washington. From Vol. 32, no. 5 (July 1977): 5-10.

Table Toys: The Underdeveloped Resource, by Alice Whiren. From Vol. 30, no. 6 (September 1975): 413-419.

Take a New Look at Your Classroom with Piaget as a Guide, by Ann M. Bingham-Newman and Ruth A. Saunders. From Vol. 32, no. 4 (May 1977): 62-72.

The Teacher as Observer for Assessment: A Guideline, by Larry W. Raskin, William J. Taylor, and Florence G. Kerckhoff. From Vol. 30, no. 5 (July 1975): 339-344.

Teaching Children Non-Sense, by Charles A. Smith and Duane E. Davis. From Vol. 31, no. 6 (September 1976): 438-447.

Water Play for Preschoolers, by Patricia J. Eggleston and Mary Knox Weir. From Vol. 31, no. 1 (November 1975): 5-11.

What in the World Is Cooking in Class Today? Multiethnic Recipes for Young Children, by Val Kositsky. From Vol. 33, No. 1 (November 1977): 23-31.

Index

Selected NAEYC Publications

If this book was helpful to you:
1. The journal *Young Children* is available through NAEYC membership or by subscription. Write to NAEYC for further information.
2. Many of the ideas in this book are discussed at greater length in the books listed below. Order your copies today for even more ideas.
3. If you wish to adopt this or other NAEYC books as texts for classes or workshops, write to NAEYC for information about discounts on quantity orders.

Code #	Title	Price
214	Activities for School-Age Child Care	$3.85
315	Administration: Making Programs Work for Children and Families	$5.50
303	A Beginner's Bibliography	$ .55
132	The Block Book	$3.85
200	Careers with Young Children: Making Your Decision	$4.40
213	Caring: Supporting Children's Growth	$2.20
127	Cognitively Oriented Curriculum	$3.85
313	Cultural Awareness: A Resource Bibliography	$5.20
119	Curriculum Is What Happens	$2.20
121	Developmental Screening in Early Childhood: A Guide	$2.75
314	Directory of Educational Programs for Adults who Work with Children	$3.30
300	Early Childhood Education: An Introduction	$1.65
215	A Festival of Films	$2.00
212	A Good Beginning for Babies: Guidelines for Group Care	$4.95
302	A Guide to Discipline	$1.65
210	The Idea Box	$6.25
131	Language in Early Childhood Education	$3.30
101	Let's Play Outdoors	$1.10
312	Mother/Child, Father/Child Relationships	$5.20
308	Mud, Sand, and Water	$2.20
107	Music in Our Lives: The Early Years	$2.75
135	Parent Involvement in Early Childhood Education	$3.30
102	Piaget, Children, and Number	$2.20
115	Planning Environments for Young Children: Physical Space	$2.00
306	Play as a Learning Medium	$3.00
129	Play: The Child Strives Toward Self-Realization	$2.75
126	Promoting Cognitive Growth	$3.00
309	Science with Young Children	$3.55
128	The Significance of the Young Child's Motor Development	$2.45
402E	Some Ways of Distinguishing a Good Early Childhood Program	$ .30
310	Talks with Teachers	$3.30

Order from: NAEYC
1834 Connecticut Avenue, N.W.
Washington, DC 20009

All prices include postage and handling. Please enclose full payment for orders under $10.

For information about these and other NAEYC publications, write for a free publications brochure.